Burma

a travel survival kit

Burma – a travel survival kit
4th edition

Published by
Lonely Planet Publications
Head Office: PO Box 88, South Yarra, Victoria 3141, Australia
Branch Office: PO Box 2001A, Berkeley, CA 94702, USA

Printed by
Colorcraft, Hong Kong

Photographs by
Tony Wheeler, Peter Campbell, Michael Clarke

Cover Photograph
Tony Wheeler

First published
1979

This Edition
January 1988

National Library of Australia Cataloguing in Publication Data

Wheeler, Tony, 1946– .
Burma, a travel survival kit.

4th ed.
Includes index.
ISBN 0 86442 017 X.

1. Burma – Description and travel – 1981– -
Guide-books. I. Title.

915.91'045

The Authors

Tony Wheeler was born in England but spent most of his younger years overseas due to his father's occupation with British Airways. Those years included a lengthy spell in Pakistan, a shorter period in the West Indies and all his high school years in the US. He returned to England to do a university degree in engineering, worked for a short time as an automotive design engineer, returned to university again and did an MBA then dropped out on the Asian overland trail with his wife Maureen. They've been travelling, writing and publishing guidebooks ever since, having set up Lonely Planet Publications in the mid-70s. Travelling for Tony and Maureen is now considerably enlivened by their daughter Tashi and son Kieran.

Joe Cummings has been involved in South-East Asian studies for many years and was a Peace Corps volunteer in Thailand during the '70s. Since then he has been a translator/interpreter of Thai in San Francisco, a graduate student in Thai language and Asian art history (MA 1981) at the University of California at Berkeley, an East-West Center Scholar in Hawaii, a university lecturer in Malaysia, and most recently a bilingual consultant for public schools in Oakland, California. He is also the author of Lonely Planet's *Thailand – a travel survival kit* and *Thailand Phrasebook*.

Lonely Planet Credits

Editor	Elizabeth Kim
Design & Mapping	Peter Flavelle
Typesetter	Ann Jeffree

Thanks also to Hugh Finlay for final proofing and indexing.

This Edition

The first three editions were researched and written by Tony but this time Joe took over the duties and tripped in and out from Bangkok.

Thank You

Special thanks to my travel companion Michael Clark, and to the following people who assisted along the way: Ko Tun, Hla Maung, Yo Maung, Zin Myo Hlaing, Than Than Nwe, Katherine Wells, 'Tatts' Bishop and Julie Frankham. Thanks also to Naw Angelene and Thein Lwin, who introduced me to 'our Burma' in Hawaii.

Thanks to Eland Books for permission to quote a delightful description of a Burmese truck from *Golden Earth*. And to David Cooke for the photograph of the Father Lamont church in Mandalay. Thanks must also go to the many travellers who took the time to tell us of their Burmese adventures. Thank you:

Mark Addis, Allen Ayres (A), Brigid Ballard (A), Anthony Bateman (UK), Carsten Bondersholt (Dk), Adam Booth (UK), Carin Burchell (HK), Gregg Butensky (US), Jennifer Buzun (US), F de Vooys (NL), Gill Eastgate & David King (A), Bill Eldridge (UK), Pep & Pete Fisher (UK), A & J Forster, Barbara Friedel (US), Keith Gore (US), Mary Goulding (US), H & S Harders (Dk), Harriet Haritos (US), Peter Haynes (UK), Jo Heard-White (UK), D R Hood, Peter Hook & Willow Mead (UK), Andrew Inkpen (S), Andrew Karney (UK), Temba Lama, Leon McDonald, Jack Newkirk (US), Jeremy Palmer (UK), Clifford Pereira (UK), Yaron Katz (Isr), Tim, Mark & Betty Riedler (US), Joseph Rubin (US), Steve Shucart, Janet & Paul Sleath (UK), Barry Temple (A), Pamela Ward (A), Rolf Westlin (Sw), Jack Willson (A), Mary Wiseman (US), Hso-Khan-Pha Yawnghwe (C)

A - Australia, C - Canada, Dk - Denmark, HK - Hong Kong, Isr - Israel, NL - Netherlands, S - Singapore, Sw - Sweden, UK - UK, US - USA,

And the Next
Things change even in socialist Burma - prices go up (and sometimes down),
places go off and on the approved list. Interesting new travel possibilities appear, new hassles develop on the standard old ways. So if you find things better, worse, cheaper, more expensive or even simply different please write and tell us about them. The letters we get from 'our travellers' out there on the road are a constant delight. Keep them coming. As usual the best letters will be rewarded with a copy of the next edition, or another LP guide if you prefer.

And a Special Warning
One of the problems of writing about a country as zany as Burma is fear that you'll kill the golden goose. I don't think the whisky and cigarettes deals are going to disappear just because I write about them because they're comparatively minor and long established. I am pretty certain that some other deals, like the buying and selling of goods from the Diplomatic Stores, have been circumscribed because some travellers took excessive advantage of them. There are some little wrinkles about Burmese travel that I have felt it best to be quietly discreet about - don't think I didn't notice them, even try them; you'll just have to do a little research of your own, folks!

Contents

Introduction

To the west Burma is still a virtual unknown – a slightly exotic eastern country that has been on some sort of total seclusion plus mad socialism binge since WW II and has also been torn by continual internal strife involving a whole dictionary of anti-government rebels, guerrillas, insurgents and assorted malcontents. True, true, true and yet somehow all false.

Burma is exotic yet its exotic flavour is accessible, understandable and enjoyable. There are places in Burma, like the great ruined city of Pagan or the glittering Shwedagon Pagoda in Rangoon, with more 'magic' than almost anywhere on earth. Burma has been secluded – for many years no tourists were allowed and even today seven days is all you get – yet the Burmese people are incredibly outgoing, friendly and considerate.

Burma is still intent on implementing its unique, slightly madcap Burmese brand of socialism – it's so Burmese and at times works so badly that even to the Burmese it's something of a joke. And, yes, there is a whole assortment of rebel groups dedicated to the overthrow of the government – but even the mightiest kings of Pagan at its height never brought Burma's hill tribes to heel, so really things are no different today than they've ever been; within the regions you're allowed to visit you are most unlikely to face any problems.

Burma is far from the easiest or most comfortable country in Asia to visit. If you abide by the letter of the law it can even be rather expensive. But the rewards are worth the effort – it's a most unusual, culturally satisfying and highly enjoyable country for the visitor.

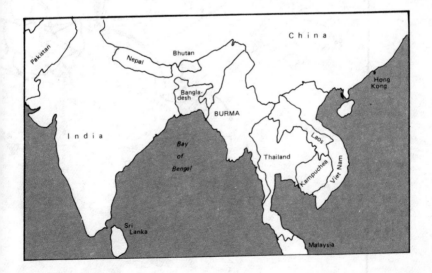

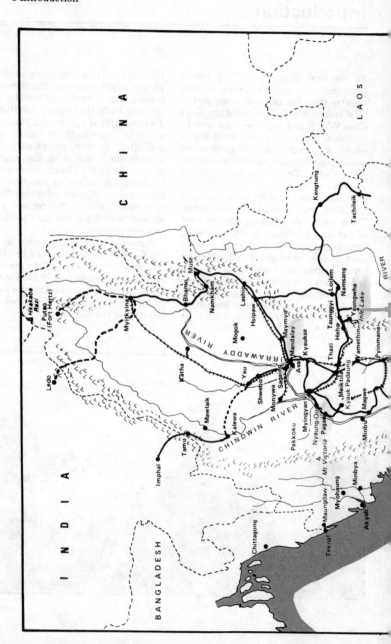

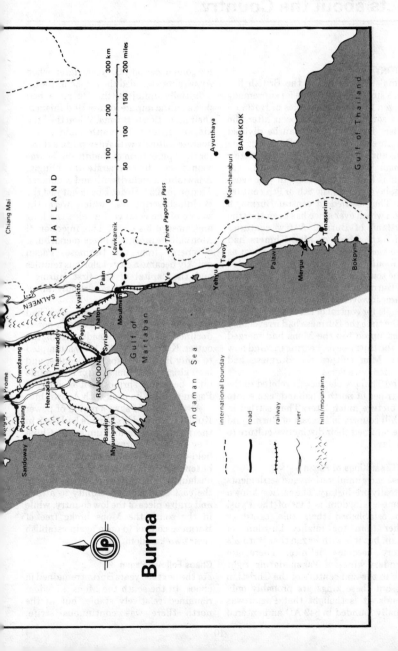

Burma

THAILAND

Chiang Mai

SALWEEN

Gulf of Martaban

Andaman Sea

Gulf of Thailand

BANGKOK

Ayutthaya

Kanchanaburi

Tenasserim

Tavoy

Yehyu

Palaw

Mergui

Bokpyin

Three Pagodas Pass

Kawkareik

Paan

Kyaikto

Moulmein

Thaton

Ye

Pegu

Syriam

RANGOON

Tharrawady

Henzada

Bassein

Myaungmya

Padaung

Shwedaung

Prome

Sandoway

international boundary
road
railway
river
hills/mountains

0   50   100   200   300 km

0   50   100   150   200 miles

Facts about the Country

HISTORY

Burma's history before the British has been a story of the struggle for supremacy between the various peoples of Burma – as in some ways it has been after the British. Basically these can be divided into three groups – the Burmese, the Mons and the Thais. The Burmese were a Mongol people who came south into Burma from somewhere in the east Himalaya around the 8th or 9th century AD. They settled in central Burma, a region which ever since has been the true heartland of Burma. A few centuries earlier the Mons or Mon-Khmers had come east from the area now known as Cambodia (or Kampuchea) and settled in the south of Burma. Almost as soon as the Burmese arrived these two groups became involved in a long and complicated struggle for control of the whole country. By the time the Burmese had irrevocably ended up on top the Mons had merged into the Burmese or, bearing in mind how much Mon culture the Burmese had absorbed, vice versa.

The Thai people, closely related to the hill tribes of north Thailand, came into the picture much later. They settled in the hill country in the east of Burma and have retained their distinctive culture to this day.

The Great Kings of Pagan

These early immigrations and settlements are really pre-history. The earliest known Burmese kingdom is that of the Pyus, who established their rule centuries earlier than the mighty kingdom of Pagan, but it is with Pagan that Burma's history becomes definite. There are legendary kings of Pagan dating right back to the 2nd century of the Christian era, but these kings are probably only legends. It is thought that Pagan was actually founded in 849 AD and entered its golden period 200 years later when Anawrahta ascended the throne in 1044.

Initially animists, the Burmese had picked up an impure form of Buddhism in their migration to Burma. When the Mon king of Thaton to the south would not co-operate willingly with Anawrahta's thirst for their purer form of Buddhism, he was soon forced to co-operate unwillingly. Anawrahta marched south and conquered Thaton in 1057. He took back not just the Buddhist scriptures, which were the source of the conflict, but also the king and most of his court. This injection of Mon culture inspired a phenomenal burst of energy from the Burmese. Pagan quickly became a city of glorious temples and the capital of the first Burmese kingdom to encompass virtually all of present-day Burma.

None of Anawrahta's successors had his vision or energy, and Pagan's power declined slowly but steadily from the outset. Kyanzittha (1084-1113) attempted to unify Burma's disparate peoples, and later kings like Alaungsithu or Htilominlo built beautiful shrines, but essentially Pagan reached its peak with Anawrahta.

At the end of Pagan's period of power Kublai Khan and his Tartars had risen in the north, and from Yunnan in China they invaded Burma in 1287. Pagan's hold over Burma immediately proved to be tenuous – it collapsed before the Tartar onslaught. Shan tribes from the hills to the east took the opportunity to attack and grab a piece of the low country, while in the south the Mons broke free of Burmese control to once again establish their own kingdom.

Chaos Follows Pagan

For the next 250 years Burma remained in chaos. In the south the Mons' kingdom remained relatively stable, but in the north there was continuous strife.

Between the two a weaker Burmese kingdom was established at Toungoo, east of Prome, and retained its independence by playing off one major power against the other.

At first the Mons established their new capital close to the present Thai border at Martaban near Moulmein, but after a series of skirmishes with the Siamese it was shifted to Pegu, near Rangoon, and the Mon country became known as the Kingdom of Pegu. In 1472 Dhammazedi came to the throne; he was the greatest of the Pegu kings. A major Buddhist revival took place and the first contact with Europeans was made. During this time the great Shwedagon Pagoda in Rangoon began to assume its present form.

In upper Burma, Ava, near present-day Mandalay, became the capital in 1364. Although not as unified as the Kingdom of Pegu, the area of upper Burma became known as the Kingdom of Ava. Surprisingly, neither Pegu nor Ava was the catalyst to reunify Burma, but tiny Toungoo. In the 1500s a series of Toungoo kings extended their power north nearly to Ava, then south, taking the Mon kingdom and shifting their own capital to Pegu. Their hold was initially fragile but in 1550 Bayinnaung came to the throne, reunified all of Burma and managed to defeat the neighbouring Siamese so convincingly that it was many years before the long-running friction between the Burmese and Siamese re-emerged.

With Bayinnaung's death in 1581 this new Burmese kingdom immediately went into decline; and when in 1635 the capital was shifted north from Pegu to Ava, the idea of a kingdom taking in all of Burma was effectively renounced. Ava was the heartland of Burma, but it was a long way from the sea and from communication with the outside world. This isolation eventually contributed to the conflict with the British.

The Final Kings of Mandalay

In the 1700s the decline became serious as hill tribes once more started to raid central Burma and the Mons again broke away and established their own kingdom in Pegu. In 1752 the Mons actually took Ava, but in the same year Alaungpaya came to power in Shwebo, 80 km north of Ava, and spent the next eight years rushing back and forth across Burma – conquering, defeating and destroying all who opposed him. He was the founder of the last Burmese dynasty and it was his near invincibility that later deluded the Burmese into thinking they could take on the British.

His son Hsinbyushin charged into Siam for good measure, and so thoroughly levelled the capital of Ayutthaya that the Siamese were forced to move south to their present capital of Bangkok. Bodawpaya, who came to power in 1782, was also a son of Alaungpaya and managed to bring Arakan back under Burmese control. This was to be the direct cause of the first Anglo-Burmese conflict.

Arakan, the east coast region of the Bay of Bengal, had long been a border region between Burma and India; its people, although basically Burmese, were also to some extent Indian. Refugees from Arakan fled into British India and from there planned to recapture their country. This so irritated the Burmese that they, in return, mounted raids across the border into British territory. This did not make the British officials of the Raj very happy.

At this time the British, Dutch and French were all vying for power in the east, and all had established at least some sort of contact with the Burmese. The Burmese proved a difficult nation to deal with commercially, which they had a perfect right to be if they wished, but their attitude over frontier incidents was, to the British, quite another matter. In 1819 Bagyidaw came to the throne in Burma and a situation developed in Assam, to the north of Burma, very similar to that in Arakan. When in 1824 the Burmese prepared an army to march into British India in pursuit of refugees from Assam, the British decided to draw the line.

To some extent it was Burma's self-enforced isolation that led them to this conflict – secure in central Ava, the Siamese convincingly defeated, the Mons reintegrated into the nation, Assam and Arakan regained – who were these feeble intruders, the British? The British hardly proved to be all-powerful; due to a series of bungles it took them two long years to defeat the Burmese, although Rangoon fell almost immediately. In 1826 Burma emerged stripped of Arakan, Assam and Tenasserim, the southern strip running beside Siam (Thailand). The Burmese were also obliged to accept a British 'Resident' at their capital who eventually smoothed out many problems and established reasonable relations with Bagyidaw.

Unfortunately Bagyidaw was followed by the much less reasonable Tharawaddy, and he in turn by his even crazier son Pagan Min. It had long been the custom for a new king to massacre all possible pretenders to this throne, but Pagan Min took this policy to new extremes. In the first two years of his reign 6000 people were executed. The British resident had been forced to withdraw during Tharawaddy's brief reign, and frontier incidents again began to flare up. An attempt by the Burmese to extort money from the British by arresting two ship's captains on false charges was the incident that sparked Anglo-Burmese war number two.

Minor skirmishes went overwhelmingly to the British, but when an ultimatum was presented to the Burmese they did not even bother to reply. In 1852 the British quickly took Rangoon, Martaban and Bassein, but still the Burmese government would not discuss terms. The British therefore marched north and took Prome, again with ease, and annexed all of lower Burma which, together with Arakan and Tenasserim, became a new province of British India.

Pagan Min, now extremely unpopular, was deposed and Mindon Min became king of Burma, or at least what remained of it, in 1853. Mindon proved to be a wise realist who eventually came to amicable terms with the British yet cleverly balanced their influence with that of other European (and American) powers. During this period the industrial revolution came to full flower in Europe, and lower Burma became an important and profitable part of the British Empire due to its enormous teak resources and vast potential for growing rice.

Unhappily for the Burmese, Mindon made one important mistake – he did not adequately provide for a successor. When he died in 1878 the new king, Thibaw, was propelled into power by his ruthless wife and scheming mother-in-law. Thibaw was so far down the list of possible successors that the 'massacre of kinsmen' reached unheard-of heights, and in this new age of the telegraph and steamship the news soon reached Europe in lurid detail. Thus European and British attitudes towards the new king were tarnished from the start.

Thibaw proved to be a totally ineffective ruler. Upper Burma soon became a sorry scene as armed gangs and ruthless officials vied with each other to extort more money from the hapless peasants. Enormous numbers of Burmese fled to the stability of British lower Burma, where there also happened to be a great demand for labour for the new rice trade. Finally in 1885 another Anglo-Burmese conflict flared up – the British resident had again withdrawn from Mandalay and a petty dispute over the exploits of the Bombay Burmah Trading Company was the excuse the British needed to send the gunboats north to Mandalay. In two weeks it was all over, the money Thibaw had thought was going into defence had actually gone into corrupt officials' pockets (or whatever a Burmese has in his longyi) and the British took Mandalay after only the most token resistance.

The British Period

So once again Burma was united, but this time with the British as masters. To the British, Burma was just another chunk of Asia that now had the good fortune to be part of the Raj. To the Burmese the situation was not nearly so pleasant – upper Burma may have been only part of the whole country, but it was the heartland of Burma; Thibaw might have been a bad king, but he was a Burmese king. Now Burma was just a part of British India – and what was worse, Indians, whom the Burmese had traditionally looked down on, came flooding in with the British. As the swampy delta-land of the south was turned into rice paddies, it was Indians who supplied the money to improve the land, and those same Indians who came to own it when the less commercially adept Burmese proved unable to make it pay or to pay for it. As Burma's national income grew, the country became increasingly dependent upon imports, and the profits from rice cultivation were whisked out of the country to pay for more and more imported goods.

Burmese nationalism grew somewhat as a shadow of the movement in India, but grow it did and in the 1920s and '30s the British were forced to make an increasing number of moves towards Burma's self-government. In 1937 Burma was separated from India, but internally the country was torn by a struggle between the opposing Burmese political parties. There had also been a peasants' uprising earlier in the '30s and sporadic outbursts of anti-Indian and anti-Chinese violence.

World War II

Japanese-Burmese contacts had been made well before Japan entered WW II. Indeed Bogyoke Aung San, who had first made his name through university-level political action and was later to become the 'father figure' for independent Burma, had fled to the Japanese in 1940. The Japanese army marched into Burma within weeks of Pearl Harbor and by mid-1942 had driven the retreating British-Indian forces, along with the Chinese Kuomintang forces which had come to their aid, out of most of Burma. Bogyoke Aung San and his '30 comrades' returned to Burma with the Japanese and set up the BNA or Burma National Army.

The Japanese attempted to enlist Burmese support politically, but at the same time managed to alienate the Burmese by harsh and arrogant conduct. The imaginative 'Chindit' anti-Japanese

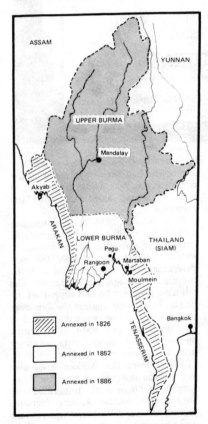

19th-century British expansion in Burma.

ASSAM

YUNNAN

UPPER BURMA

Mandalay

Akyab

ARAKAN

LOWER BURMA

Pegu

THAILAND
(SIAM)

Rangoon   Martaban

Moulmein

Bangkok

TENASSERIM

Annexed in 1826

Annexed in 1852

Annexed in 1886

operation, mounted by the Allies with air-supplied troops behind the Japanese lines, also emphasised anti-Japanese feelings. Soon an internal resistance movement sprang up and towards the end of the war the BNA hastily switched sides to the British.

Independence

That Burma was heading rapidly towards independence after the war was all too clear, but who should manage this progress was a different question. The British wanted a gradual transition with time to rebuild the shattered economy and political system before the handover. Aung San wanted independence now, because if given time, other political parties could gain ground on his strong position at the close of the war. Eventually his views were to win, but too late for his own position. In July 1947 Aung San, still aged only 32, and seven of his assistants were assassinated in a plot fomented by U Saw, a pre-war political leader who had been imprisoned by the British during WW II after attempting to make a secret agreement with the Japanese.

On 4 January 1948, at an auspicious middle-of-the-night hour, Burma became independent and left the British Commonwealth. Almost immediately the new government of U Nu was faced with the complete disintegration of Burma. The hill tribe people, who had supported the British and fought against the Japanese throughout the war, were distrustful of the Burmese and went into armed opposition. The communists withdrew from the government and attacked it. Muslims from the Arakan area also opposed the new government. The Mons, long thought to be totally integrated with the Burmese, revolted. Assorted factions, private armies, WW II resistance groups and plain mutineers further confused the picture.

In early 1949 almost the entire country was in the hands of one rebel group or another, and even Rangoon suffered fighting right in its suburbs. At its worst stage the government was almost on the point of surrendering to the communist forces, but gradually, and with particularly valuable assistance from loyal hill tribe contingents, the government fought back and through 1950 and '51 regained much of the country.

Although much of Burma was now at least tenuously under government control, a new problem sprang up for the battered Burmese. With the collapse of Chiang Kai-Shek's Chinese KMT forces before Mao Zedong, the tattered remnants of his army withdrew into Burma and mounted raids from north Burma into Yunnan, the bordering Chinese province. Unable to counter the Chinese communists, the KMT decided to carve their own little fiefdom out of Burmese territory. The Burmese government now found itself fighting not only a mixed bag of rebels, communists and out-and-out gangs of brigands and dacoits, but also a US-supported anti-communist Chinese army. Amazing as it may seem, while operating an embassy in Rangoon and espousing friendly relations with the new Burmese government, the US was also flying in supplies to the Chinese forces encamped within Burma's borders. Forces whose main source of income was the cultivation of opium poppies for the production of heroin!

The Burmese Road to Socialism

In the mid-1950s, although the central government strengthened its hold on the country, the economic situation went from bad to worse. A number of grandiose development projects succeeded only in making foreign 'advisers' rather wealthy, and in 1953 the Burmese bravely announced that aid or assistance from the US was no longer welcome while US-supplied Chinese nationalist forces were at large within Burma. Despite the sickly economy U Nu managed to remain in power until 1958 when, with political turmoil about to become armed chaos yet again, and the KMT problem still unresolved, he voluntarily handed the reins over to a military government under General Ne Win. Freed from the 'democratic' responsibilities inherent in a civilian government, Ne Win was able to make some excellent progress in the 15 months his military government operated. A degree of law and order was regained, rebel activity was reduced and Rangoon was given a massive and much-needed clean up.

In early 1960, elections were held and U Nu came back to power with a much improved majority, but once again political turmoil developed, his party threatened to break up into opposing groups and in early 1962 Ne Win took power again. This time U Nu did not hand over power voluntarily, and along with his main ministers was bundled into prison, where he remained until 1966. He later ineffectively opposed the Ne Win government from abroad. In 1980, U Nu returned from exile under an amnesty program for political offenders and is now involved in translating Buddhist scriptures.

Soon after coming to power in 1962 Ne Win announced the new path which Burma would henceforward follow – 'The Burmese Way to Socialism'. Some say it has been a steadily downhill path. Nationalisation policies were extended right down to retail shop level when in 1966 it was announced that a long list of items would only be available from 'Peoples' Shops'. The net result was frightening – many everyday commodities immediately became available only on the black market, and vast numbers of people were thrown out of work by the closure of retail outlets. Despite a subsequent rethink on this policy, Burma's flourishing black market has now become the only source for many everyday items.

An ingenious 'sock the rich' measure de-monetised the largest banknotes (K50 and K100 – about US$7.30 and US$14.70 respectively at the present 'realistic' exchange rates). Anybody so unfortunate as to have those notes found them to be worthless. Many of the retail traders who became unemployed following the nationalisation of retail trade were Indians, who were hustled out of the country with draconian thoroughness. No compensation was paid for their expropriated businesses, and each adult was allowed to depart with only K75 to his or her name plus K250 in gold – even a woman's jewellery in excess of that amount was to be confiscated. As many as a quarter of a million people of Indian descent left Burma during the '60s.

Burma's staunchly Marxist approach may have visibly harmed the economy, but far more pervasive has been the growth of a second shadow-economy. If you can't get something through government outlets or government-approved dealers, it will always be available, at a price, through the black market. Yet despite murmurings of discontent and talk of government spies round every corner, opposition to the government – apart from the ever-present rebels – seems very low key. As a foreigner you'll be assumed 'safe' to talk to and will have plenty of opportunity to hear of what's wrong with Burma.

In late 1974 there were serious student disturbances over the burial of former UN Secretary General U Thant, a long time Ne Win political foe, yet overall the government appears firmly in control and determined to continue its strange progress towards a Burmese utopia. In late '81 Ne Win retired as president of the Republic (retaining his position as chair of the Burma Socialist Programme Party, the country's only legal political party), but his successor was more or less a hand-picked man and the government is still very much guided by Ne Win's political will. Many Burmese say they expect major political changes to occur when Ne Win dies.

In the early '80s Burma seemed to show signs of real progress in the economy. Improved agricultural methods resulted in spectacular increases in the size of cotton, maize, wheat and, most important, rice crops. The government was also moving towards better relations with the outside world and had a number of major foreign-aided projects underway, including its first-ever joint ventures with foreign-owned companies. During the latter part of the decade, however, the overall economy and quality of life have taken an obvious plunge. In 1985 the government closed the offices of all Japanese businesses in Burma (which were the only joint private ventures allowed entrance into Ne Win's Burma), in spite of the fact that Japan provides about two-thirds of the country's aid and loans.

Burma currently carries a foreign debt of close to US$3 billion, and hard currency reserves have fallen to between US$35 million and US$55 million – roughly one month's revenue from imports. Annual per capita income has stayed below US$200 (the average civil servant has not had a wage hike in 12 years) while prices have soared. In spite of all the economic indicators which place Burma on the 'Ten Poorest Countries in the World' list, many overseas observers feel the Burmese approach to life isn't so bad after all – Burma may have missed out on a lot of 20th-century progress, but it has also managed to avoid a good collection of 20th-century problems.

Insurgency

The Union of Burma has been plagued by non-union-like rebellion since its 1948 inception. By 1983, outside observers estimated there were as many as 28 insurgent groups operating inside Burma, including national/ethnic liberation parties, 'warlord organisations' and Nationalist Chinese Army (KMT) remnants. The estimated numbers within these individual groups range from 50 (Tai National Army, Palaung State Liberation Organization,

Kayah New Land Revolution Council) to the tens of thousands (Burmese Communist Party). Most have formed loose affiliations amongst themselves (eg the KNLRC and the BCP), while some are splinter groups or factions vying for local supremacy (Ma Ha San faction of the Wa National Army; Karenni People's United Liberation Front vs the Karenni Liberation Army) and some are tactical arms for political parties (Karen National Liberation Army for the Karen National Union).

The naming can be quite confusing; one group may have more than one title, as in the case of the United Pa-O Organization and the Pa-O Shan State Independence Party, while different, unaffiliated groups may have similar names, as in the Shan State Army (ethnic Shans, member of the National Democratic Front), Shan United Revolutionary Army (ethnic Shans, ally of the Third Chinese Irregular Forces - a remnant of the 93rd Nationalist Chinese Army) and the Shan United Army (a 'warlord' group made up of ethnic Shans, Chinese and other minorities, under the leadership of the infamous Khun Sa, aka Chang Chi-fu aka Sao Mong Khawn). These groups operate primarily in the various states of outer Burma, where Burmans are in the minority, as opposed to 'Burma proper', where Burma's military has control, although they do occasionally cause mischief outside their own territory: the Karens attacked Burmese strongholds in Pegu, Tavoy and Kyaikto in 1983, and were responsible for a mistimed train bombing in the primarily Karen suburb of Insein in Rangoon in 1984.

Among these groups, probably the most significant government opponent is the National Democratic Front (NDF), an alliance of nine non-communist insurgent groups formed in 1976. The avowed purpose of the NDF is to provide military assistance to members under government attack and to work towards common political ends on a national level while retaining local independence. As of late 1984, the nine member groups and their estimated strengths were: Arakan Liberation Party (150-200); Kachin Independence Organization (6000-8000); Karenni National Revolutionary Council (500); Karen National Union (5000-8000); New Mon State Party (100); Pa-O National Organization (not known); Palaung State Liberation Organization (50); Shan State Progress Party (Shan State

Army, 2000-4000); Wa National Organization (450).

The NDF has been seeking to enter into negotiations with the Burmese government in order to come to a peaceful resolution of the age-old majority-minority conflict. At this point meetings arranged and conducted by the Burmese have proved unsuccessful and the NDF refuses to talk again until representatives of both parties can meet outside Burma under a neutral chairmanship. If the NDF military coalition continues to foil Burmese attempts to crush insurgency, they may eventually be able to force the government into a bilateral settlement.

The most conspicuous non-member, the Burmese Communist Party, is a seasoned group numbering 12,000 to 15,000 which has become isolated due to changes in attitude in China since 1979, when Beijing began distancing itself from the heavily Maoist BCP. In contrast, Chinese relations with the Burmese government have improved greatly since the end of the Chinese Cultural Revolution - Ne Win finally paid a visit to Beijing in 1985, just one month after China stopped broadcasting the Voice of the People of Burma from across the border. Outside observers believe, furthermore, that the Chinese supply of arms to Burmese Communists has diminished to a trickle in the last seven years. Despite this apparent isolation, however, BCP tactical units continue to operate in north-east and north-west Burma, and in Arakan and Tenasserim, with personnel drawn from Shan, Chinese, Kachin, Wa, Lahu, Akha, Lisu and other minority groups.

The military leadership in Rangoon uses the widespread insurgency as an explanation for their hard-line policies with regard to human rights and as an excuse for draining public funds (30% of the total) into military confrontations with rebel forces. Most recently they have escalated offensives in upper Burma, especially against the BCP and the KNU, their two most powerful adversaries. In January 1987 alone there were 750 deaths as a result of fighting between Burmese regulars and the Burmese Communists in the Kachin State. Until recently the Burmese policy was one of containment, but that now seems to have changed to 'exterminate them once and for all', with political support from China. Burmese regular forces number around 163,000 but are known to be remarkably ill-equipped in both weaponry and military logistics.

The issues are compounded by the fact that insurgency in the Golden Triangle area is firmly linked to the thriving opium trade there. Some western opponents of the trade, which is largely controlled by the BCP and the SUA, have expressed unqualified support of Burmese efforts to eradicate insurgency in the north-east. Interestingly enough, there has been heated conflict among insurgents over opium smuggling, and the argument is not over trade routes, as was common in the '60s and '70s. In fact, in 1985 an NDF force composed of Was, Karens and Shans took military action against smugglers in the southern Shan State, perhaps because the NDF is trying to discourage associations between rebellion and Golden Triangle opium.

It's all very complicated but one thing seems certain: as long as Rangoon ignores demands for self-determination, equality and democracy from groups representing 32% of the population, the insurgency will most likely continue.

PEOPLE

The Burmese are not a homogeneous people – a fact of life which has caused the country many problems over the years. For years Burma was torn by the struggle for supremacy between the Burmese and the Mons, a struggle which eventually ended with the Burmese in control only to be overwhelmed by the British and the long arm of the Raj. Since independence the internal instabilities of Burma have shown themselves again, and today large tracts of the country are only nominally under government control – or not at all. The main opposition comes from the hill tribe people, many of them ethnically related to the hill tribes of Thailand and Laos. These groups were long distrustful of the lowland Burmese, and with their British 'protection' gone their distrust grew into armed resistance which the central government has taken many years to mollify or overcome.

The people can be basically divided into three groups – Tibeto-Burmans, Mon-Khmers and Thai-Chinese. The Tibeto-Burman group includes the main Burmese people and over 30 smaller tribal groups. The other two groups are less sub-divided, but still include many diverse peoples. Under the British many other nationalities also came into Burma – particularly Indians and Chinese. Prior to independence Rangoon was much more an Indian city than a Burmese one, for the hard-working Indians were generally preferred by British employers. A large proportion of the Indian population has been expelled since independence, although there are still many people of Indian descent in Burma. The Chinese have got equally short shrift from time to time – particularly during the Cultural Revolution in China, when many Chinese found themselves very unpopular in Burma. There are still plenty of Chinese restaurants though – thank goodness.

It's always dangerous to try to pin national characteristics on a people, but throughout Burma you seem to meet people of quite amazing friendliness. It could be this is just a result of the small flow of foreign visitors to Burma, but I think it is much more likely that the Burmese are simply a very friendly and outgoing people. It's certainly the impression most visitors come away with. The Burmese economy may still not be in first-class shape, but poverty is something that hardly exists here – they may not be able to export so much rice anymore, but nobody goes hungry. Beggars (monks apart, of course) are virtually non-existent. Rip-offs are also rare events – people are honest and straightforward; they're one of the best memories brought back from a visit to Burma.

POPULATION

Since the government does not control the entire country, a complete census has not been possible since the British days. A census in '73 was extrapolated to 28.8 million. The population is now estimated to be about 36.4 million with an annual growth rate of around 2%. Populations of the major cities at the time of the '73 census were:

Rangoon	3,200,000
Mandalay	420,000
Moulmein	200,000
Bassein	335,000
Akyab	145,000
Taunggyi	150,000

The ethnic breakdown is roughly as follows: Burman 68%, Shan 9%, Karen 7%, Rakhine (Arakanese) 4%, Chinese 3%, Indian 2%; Chin, Kachin, Mon, Assamese and other minorities comprise less than 1% each. The Chinese and Indians are found primarily in urban areas.

The Burmese have a national literacy rate of 66%, an infant mortality rate of 96 per 1000, and an average life expectancy of 57 years.

ECONOMY

Burma's value to the British during the colonial era was summed up in one word – rice. The 19th century was a time of major upheaval in world economies – with industrialisation, a world market for agricultural products suddenly came into being as some countries found it more profitable to produce industrial goods and import food with the proceeds rather than grow their own food. Burma proved ideally suited for supplying a large proportion of the world's rice demand.

Prior to WW II Burma exported as much as 3.5 million tons of rice a year, but much of the profit from this enterprise went to British or other foreign parties. As in a number of other colonial countries, it was a frequent complaint that foreign rule had turned Burma into a one-product country with all the dangers this entailed. Burma's rice-growing potential was devastated just as much as all its other assets during WW II, but the path of development since the war has not been a happy one.

The Burmese governments have proved totally incapable of making the country less dependent upon one product. In fact Burma has become steadily more dependent upon rice as a major source of foreign earnings while at the same time its efficiency as a rice producer has steadily declined. It took nearly 20 years after the war for the area under rice production to regain its pre-war levels, but during that same time the actual productivity declined. Despite all the worldwide advances in agriculture – miracle rice, fertilisers and everything else – the Burmese managed to produce less per hectare. So in the mid-60s, with the area of rice growing slightly above pre-war levels, the actual output was still slightly lower. Yet the population had increased by over 50% compared to the pre-war figures and by now is probably reaching a figure 100% higher. The end result can easily be imagined – the pre-war export figures had tumbled to less than two million tons by the early '60s and by '67-68 had dropped to 350,000 tons. Yet no other export had dramatically increased.

Basically this means in the end that the average Burmese is worse off now than his or her pre-war counterpart, and without dramatic changes will probably stay that way. Burma is potentially one of the richest countries in South-East Asia; in practice it is one of the poorest. Its enormous potential as a rice producer and exporter is squandered. Its vast mineral resources are barely exploited. Of course it does have the advantage in our oil-short world of being self-sufficient in petroleum products.

Many of Burma's economic difficulties are a result of history both past and present. Burma suffered major damage from WW II – far more than most of its neighbours: Malaysia and Indonesia were quickly overrun and thus suffered little damage; Thailand collaborated and thus also escaped damage; the war never physically reached India. Yet in Burma the conflict raged right to the end and caused enormous loss. Furthermore,

Burma quickly threw off the colonial yoke after the war and never enjoyed the benefits of huge overseas aid for reconstruction and replacement of ruined assets. The internal difficulties since independence have further complicated the situation and prevented efficient restoration.

Despite this the Burmese governments must also bear some of the blame for the unhappy economic story. Burmese socialism almost looks like an advertisement for capitalism – 'market forces' may be a nice capitalist expression, but 'out of the market' is an equally descriptive Burmese one. When government-set prices for rice and other agricultural products are actually less than the cost of production, it's not surprising that you read items like this in the *Working People's Daily*:

Although private traders are offering between K5 and K5.50 for a viss of wa-gyi, the cotton growers are dutifully and enthusiastically selling their produce to the State at K4.50 a viss . . . .

I bet they are!

Bearing these 'out of the market' possibilities in mind, it's quite probable that government figures are a long way from reality. How do you know how much is produced in the areas not under government control? How do you know how much is produced and disposed of 'out of the market'? How do you know how much government figures are improved to look as if things have really got better since the days of 'colonial oppression'?

Apart from agricultural output, which is primarily rice, Burma's main products are timber and a variety of minerals, but despite a strengthening teak market and improved mining there is no single product that provides more than 5% of total exports apart from rice. For the forseeable future Burma's economy will be built on rice, with teak as a second main industry and, some say, smuggling as a third. When the World Bank led a

rescue operation for the Burmese economy in the early '70s, a condition of the loan was that Burma temper its idealistic policies with a little realism. This condition seemed to pay off, for in the mid-80s the Burmese markets were bursting with produce, and many of the agricultural sectors, including rice, were supposedly setting new production records. Even consumer products were becoming much more readily available. Perhaps, in its own peculiar fashion, the Burmese way to socialism really does work, thought many critics. But the reality of stagnant wages and increasing inflation has led Burma experts to pronounce Burma's current economic state as its worst in years, with a trade deficit of about US$150 million (37% greater than import revenues) for fiscal year 1984-85.

GEOGRAPHY

Burma occupies a total area of 671,000 square km (261,000 square miles). It is sandwiched between India and Bangladesh on one side and China, Laos and Thailand on the other, while to the south are the Andaman Sea and the Bay of Bengal. Burma has several important river systems, including the Irrawaddy which runs virtually the entire length of the country (except for the southern strip beside Thailand) and enters the sea in a vast delta region south-west of Rangoon. Rangoon, incidentally, stands on the Rangoon River, not the Irrawaddy.

Other major rivers are the Chindwin which joins the Irrawaddy between Mandalay and Pagan; the Sittang which flows through Toungoo and meets the sea between Pegu and Moulmein; and the Salween which has its headwaters in China and for some distance forms the border between Burma and Thailand before eventually reaching the sea at Moulmein. The Mekong River forms the border between Burma and Laos.

The Himalaya rise in the north of Burma, and Hkakabo Razi, right on the border between Burma and Tibet, is the highest mountain in South-East Asia at 5881 metres (19,297 feet). Gamlang Razi is only slightly lower at 5835 metres. West of Pagan towards Arakan, Mt Victoria rises to 3053 metres (10,018 feet). A wide expanse of comparatively dry plain stretches north of Rangoon, but hill ranges running north-south separate the central plain from Burma's neighbours.

For administrative purposes, Burma is divided into seven divisions where Burmans are in the majority (Rangoon, Irrawaddy, Pegu, Tenasserim, Magwe, Mandalay, Sagaing); and into seven states where non-Burmans are in the majority (Shan, Kachin, Chin, Rakhine, Kayah, Karen, Mon).

RELIGION

Over 80% of the Burmese are Buddhist, although it is not the official state religion and since the Ne Win government takeover it has actually enjoyed a less central place in Burmese life – officially at least. In the Arakan region towards Bangladesh there are many Muslims, and some of the hill tribes are still staunch animists. Indeed the Burmese temper their belief in the Buddha with a healthy respect for the powers of *nats* or spirits. The Burmese, it is said, 'love the Buddha, but they fear the *nats*'. Christian missionaries have been active in Burma for over 150 years. The American Baptists were first on the scene, but apart from certain hill tribes they have had little success with the Burmese. Nevertheless the Church of Burma has about 30,000 members and a large cathedral in Rangoon.

Buddhism

Strictly speaking, Buddhism is not a religion since it is not centred in a god, but in a system of philosophy and a code of morality. Buddhism covers a wide range of interpretations of the basic beliefs which all start from the enlightenment of the Buddha in northern India 2500 years

ago. Siddhartha Gautama, born a prince, was not the first Buddha nor is he expected to be the last. Gautama is said to be the fourth Buddha or 'enlightened one'. Since Buddhists believe that the achievement of enlightenment is the goal of every being, eventually we will all reach Buddhahood.

The Buddha never wrote his *Dharma* (teachings) down, and a schism later developed so that today there are two major schools of Buddhism. The *Theravada, Hinayana* 'doctrine of the

elders' or 'small vehicle' holds that to achieve *nirvana*, the eventual aim of every Buddhist, you must 'work out your own salvation with diligence'. In other words it is up to every individual to work towards *nirvana*. The *Mahayana* or 'large vehicle' school holds that our belief is enough to eventually encompass all of humankind and bear us to salvation.

The *Mahayana* school have not rejected the other school, but claim they have extended it; the *Theravada* see it as a corruption of the Buddha's teachings. It is true that the *Mahayana* offers the 'soft option', have faith and all will be well, while the *Theravada* is more austere and ascetic, harder to practise. In the Buddhist world today *Theravada* Buddhism is practised in Sri Lanka, Thailand and Burma. *Mahayana* Buddhism is followed in Vietnam and Japan and amongst the Chinese Buddhists.

The 'large' and 'small' vehicle terms were coined by the *Mahayana* school, who saw their belief as more encompassing. There are other more esoteric divisions of Buddhism such as the Hindu-Tantric Buddhism of Tibet, also practised in Nepal, or the Zen Buddhism of Japan.

The Buddha taught that life is suffering and that although there may be happiness in life this is mainly an illusion. To be born is to suffer, to live and toil is to suffer, to die is to suffer. The cycle of life is one of suffering, but human suffering is caused by ignorance which makes one crave things which one feels could alleviate the pain. This is a mistake, for only by reaching a state of desiring nothing can one attain true happiness. To do this one must turn inward, master one's own mind and find the peace within.

Buddha preached the four noble truths:

1. all life is suffering
2. this suffering comes from selfish desire
3. when one forsakes selfish desire suffering will be extinguished
4. the 'middle path' is the way to eliminate desire

The middle path to the elimination of desire and the extinction of suffering is also known as the 'eight-fold path' which is divided into three stages: *Sila* – the precept, *Samadhi* – equanimity of mind, *Panna* – wisdom and insight. The eight 'right' actions are:

1. right speech
2. right action
3. right thought
4. right exertion
5. right attentiveness
6. right concentration
7. right aspiration
8. right understanding

This is an evolutionary process through many states of spiritual development until the ultimate goal is reached – death, no further rebirths, entry to *nirvana*. To the western mind this often seems a little strange – for us death is the end, not something to be looked forward to, but something to be feared.

The idea of rebirth, of moving through a cycle of lives towards eventual *nirvana*, has been corrupted over the years. If you're good, some say, 'women can be reborn as men, poor men as rich men, non-Burmese as Burmese, it's all very logical'. Actually Buddha taught that all things are part of the whole, that there is no part of man which is called the soul. 'In the beginning is the One and only the One is. All things are one and have no life apart from it; the One is all things and incomplete without the least of them. Yet the parts are parts within the whole, not merged in it'.

Supreme enlightenment is the only reality in a world of unreality, the teachings continue. All else is illusion and there is no unchanging soul which is reborn life after life, but a consciousness which develops and evolves spiritually until it reaches the goal of *nirvana* or oneness with the all. *Karma* is central to the doctrine of rebirth, but this is not 'fate' as it is sometimes described. *Karma* is the law of causation; each rebirth results from the actions one has committed in the previous life. Thus in Buddhism each person is alone responsible for his or her life, and since each being is part of the whole, all actions of each part affect the whole. The Buddha did not claim that his way was the only way, since in the end all beings will find a path because the goal is the same for all.

Ashoka, the great Indian emperor who was a devout Buddhist, sent missions to all the known world including Suvannabhumi – the 'Golden Land' – which is taken to be Burma. This is the first official record of the establishment of Buddhism in Burma. Initially the Buddhism that developed in central Burma was a blend of *Mahayana, Hinayana* and *nat* worship, but when King Anawrahta of Pagan conquered the southern kingdom of Thaton *Theravada* Buddhism became the dominant school.

Buddhism emphasises love, compassion, gentleness and tolerance. Its tolerance has often resulted in its assimilation into other religions, as eventually happened with Hinduism, or in its absorption of already extant beliefs, as happened with the Burmese *nats*. The personal experience one has of Buddhism remains the same from country to country despite local adaptations, changes, amalgamations and inclusions – it's an overriding impression of warmth and gentleness; a religion practised by friendly people who are always eager to explain their beliefs.

Books

Buddhism by Christmas Humphreys (Pelican, London, 1949)
The Manuals of Buddhism (Mahatters Ledi Sayadaw) and *What Buddhism Is* (Department of Religious Affairs, Rangoon), both available from the bookshops at the Shwedagon entranceway. *Living Buddhist Masters* by Jack Kornfield (Shambhala, Boulder, Colorado, 1984).

CULTURE

Burmese culture, at the court level, has not had an easy time since the collapse of the last kingdom – architecture and art were both royal activities which without royal support have floundered and faded. On the other hand, at the street level, Burmese culture is vibrant and thriving, as you'll see at the first *pwe* you visit.

Drama, Dance & Music

Drama, the key to modern Burmese culture, is accessible and enjoyable for visitors. The *pwe* ('show') is the everyday Burmese theatre – a religious festival, wedding, funeral, celebration, fair, sporting event – almost anything can be a good reason for a *pwe*. Once under way a *pwe* can, and generally does, go on all night, which is no strain – if the audience gets bored at some point during the performance they simply fall asleep and wake up when something more to their taste is on.

There are various forms of *pwe*. A *zat pwe* is a live performance which may be a re-creation of an ancient legend or Buddhist epic. In *anyein pwe* the emphasis in on comedy, slapstick and dancing but the borderline to the more serious theatre is often crossed, and indeed in an all-night performance there is plenty of time for both. *Pwes* are great fun; you immediately sense that the audience is really enjoying itself and the surprising thing is that you can enjoy it too. Particularly during the comedy segments it is very easy to understand what is happening – slapstick comedy hardly needs to be translated. In one *pwe* we saw in Rangoon a prolonged skit involved an obviously hen-pecked and accident-prone husband who, at every opportunity, showed his nervousness by untying, hitching up and then retying his *longyi*. An equivalent gesture in our culture might be compulsively straightening a necktie or fiddling with a ballpoint pen. It soon had the audience, and us, falling around with laughter. That's a comic *pwe*, but you'll also see more serious dance, drama and music. Tourist Burma, if asked, can give you directions for finding the cheap *pwes* that are often held in Rangoon.

Yein pwe is singing and dancing performed by a chorus or ensemble; there are no soloists. Since Burmese dancing emphasises pose rather than movement it can soon become a little boring for western tastes. The *yokethe pwe* is a Burmese puppet show using puppets up to a metre high. It is thought of as a forerunner to the live *zat pwe*, and the Burmese have great respect for an expert puppeteer; indeed a *yokethe pwe* is thought of as a more skilled and artistic performance than a live *zat pwe*.

Burmese music, which of course features strongly in any *pwe*, can be rather hard for western ears to enjoy. As with other Asian music it is very short on the harmony so important in western music and tends to sound 'harsh, tinkly and repetitive'. The perceived harshness is probably due to the fact that Burmese scales are not 'tempered' as western scales have been since the Bach era. As in western music, the Burmese diatonic scale has seven tones, but they are arranged equidistantly within the octave, without the 'accidentals' or tempering of the 4th and 7th intervals in, say, the western 'major' scale.

Traditional Burmese music is primarily two-dimensional in the sense that rhythm and melody provide much of the musical structure, while repetition is a key element in developing this structure; subtle shifts in rhythm and tonality provide the modulation usually supplied by the harmonic dimension in western music. These techniques are currently being 'rediscovered' in western musical trends like the minimalism of Steve Reich, Philip Glass and Brian Eno. The original inspiration for much of traditional Burmese music came from Siam during the reign of King Hsinbyushin, particularly after the second conquest of Siam in 1767 when Siamese court musicians, dancers and entertainers from Ayuthaya were brought to Burma by the hundreds in order to effect 'cultural augmentation'. Burma's kings were very good at 'capturing' culture – the same was done with Mon culture from Thaton.

Musical instruments are predominantly percussive, but even the circle of tuned drums, the *putt waing*, may carry the melody in Burmese music. Other instruments in the traditional Burmese ensemble (*saing*) include the *saung kauk*, a boat-shaped harp with 13 strings; the *kyee waing* or circle of gongs; the *pattala*, a sort of xylophone; the *hne*, an oboe-type instrument; the *palwe*, a bamboo flute; the *puttma*, a bass drum; and the *yagwin* (small cymbals) and *wa-let-khoke* (bamboo clappers), which are purely rhythmic in nature and often played by Burmese vocalists. It is also not uncommon to see a violin or two in a *saing*, and I once saw someone playing a dobro (an American acoustic slide guitar played on the lap) in an otherwise very traditional ensemble. At the National Museum in Rangoon you can view an exhibit of Burmese musical instruments, including old Mon violins whose use may predate that of violins in Europe. A good place to see traditional Burmese music and dance performed is the Karaweik Restaurant on the Royal Lake in Rangoon.

These days a lot of western influence is creeping into Burmese music – the pervasive power of rock music can even penetrate the Burmese Way to Socialism. Modern Burmese pop actually borrows from many sources – Burmese folk melodies and old Scottish reels, as well as modern tunes taken directly from hit records by Madonna, Dire Straits, Bruce Springsteen, etc.

Art & Literature

Early Burmese art was always a part of architecture – paintings were something you did on the walls of temples. Since the decline of temple building the old painting skills have considerably deteriorated. Modern Burmese paintings in western style reflect only a pale shadow of the former skill. Unfortunately, wood-carving and sculpture have had a similarly sad decline with the loss of a religious or royal purpose. Burmese wood-carving was mainly reserved for royal palaces, which were always made of timber and were showpieces for the skillful wood-carver. When royal palaces ceased to be built, the wood-carving skills rapidly declined. Similarly, sculpture today is simply a process of churning out dull look-alike Buddha images.

Printing came late to Burma and much of the writing effort has been channelled into writing *pwes*. The Burmese are great readers, as you'll realise from the piles of books in the street at every night market. Burma also has a busy cinema business with many films being produced for local consumption (30 to 40 a year) as well as great interest in Hollywood movies. TV has, however, recently arrived in Burma.

Architecture

It is in architecture that one sees the strongest evidence of Burma's artistic skill and craftsmanship. Burma is a country of pagodas; the Burmese seem unable to see a hilltop without wanting to put a pagoda on top of it. Wherever you are – boating down the river, driving through the hills, even flying above the plains – there always seems to be a pagoda in view. It is in Pagan that you see the most dramatic results of this national enthusiasm for religious monuments; for over two centuries a massive construction programme here resulted in thousands of temples, pagodas, monasteries and other religious buildings.

Burmese Buddhist buildings take two basic forms – pagodas and temples. Traditionally only these have been made of permanent materials; monasteries and all secular buildings were, until quite recently, constructed of wood and thus there are few non-religious buildings of any age to be seen. A pagoda is basically a focus for meditation or contemplation, and often particularly important ones will house a relic from the Buddha – the great Shwedagon in Rangoon enshrines eight of his hairs. A pagoda is generally a solid structure – people do not congregate inside it as they do in a church or a mosque. If there is a need for some sheltered gathering place or a place to house images or other paraphernalia, then this will usually be an ancillary to the pagoda. There may be small temples,

pavilions, covered walkways or other such places all around a major pagoda.

Pagodas go under different names in other Buddhist countries – they may be called *dagobas* in Sri Lanka, *chedis* or *jedis* in Thailand, *stupas* or *chaityas* in India, but basically they are all the same thing. Although at first glance all pagodas may look alike, you'll soon realise there have been many, often subtle, design changes over the years. Early pagodas were often hemispherical (see the Kaunghmudaw at Sagaing near Mandalay) or bulbous (the Bupaya in Pagan), while the more modern style is much more graceful, a curvaceous lower bell merging into a soaring spire as in the Shwedagon in Rangoon. Style is not always a good indicator of a pagoda's original age since Burma is earthquake prone and many pagodas have been rebuilt over and over, gradually changing their design through the centuries.

One thing many pagodas seem to have in quantity is an air of tranquillity. Even when it's noisy around a pagoda, when some sort of festival or ceremony is going on, the atmosphere is still charged with that tranquil magic that seems to pervade everything around them. High above you can hear the wind bells tinkling from the *hti*, the decorative metal 'umbrella' that tops a pagoda. Around the base people are meditating, or strolling around, or simply chatting. Pagodas have a warmth, a feeling of easy-going friendliness, that is quite unmatched by any other religious building.

Temples are constructed mainly to house images of the Buddha. Again you will see most in Pagan, where temple building reached its peak so many centuries ago. There are a variety of other religious structures still to be seen, but in general these are exceptions to the rule that brick and masonry were reserved for pagodas and temples. Even the great palaces were all made of wood, and with the destruction of Mandalay Palace during WW II there is no remaining

Burmese wooden palace. The only reminder of these beautifully carved buildings is the Shwenandaw monastery in Mandalay, made from a palace building that was removed from the compound about a century ago. Even this is deteriorating today due to lack of protection.

Although so little remains of the old wooden architectural skills, there are still many excellent wooden buildings to be seen. The Burmese continue to use teak with great skill, and a fine country home can be a very pleasant structure indeed. Unhappily the Burmese have proved far less adept with more modern materials, and Burma boasts some appalling corrugated-iron-roofed buildings and concrete monstrosities. Even with the finer, older buildings the emphasis has always been more on quantity than quality – Burma boasts no great buildings of meticulous craftsmanship like India's Taj Mahal. But when it comes to location – balancing a delicate pagoda on a towering hilltop or perching one on the side of a sheer precipice – the Burmese have no match.

FESTIVALS & HOLIDAYS

Traditionally Burma goes by the 12-month lunar calendar, so the old holidays and festivals will vary in date from year to year. Burma also has a number of more recently originated holidays whose dates are fixed by our calendar. The Burmese months are:

Tagu	March/April
Kason	April/May
Nayon	May/June
Waso	June/July
Wagaung	July/August
Tawthalin	August/September
Thadingyut	September/October
Tazaungmon	October/November
Nadaw	November/December
Pyatho	December/January
Tabodwe	January/February
Taboung	February/March

Festivals are drawn-out, enjoyable affairs in Burma. They generally take place or culminate on full-moon days, but the buildup can continue for days. There's often a country fair atmosphere about these festivals – at some convenient grounds there will be innumerable stalls and activities which go on all night. *Pwes*, music, boxing bouts will all be part of the colourful scene. The normally calm Burmese can get really worked up during these festivals – at a full-moon festival on one of my visits to Rangoon the supporters of the defeated favourite in a boxing bout were so enraged they wrecked the arena.

January Independence Day on 4 January is a major public holiday marked by a seven-day fair at the Royal Lake in Rangoon. There are fairs all over the country at this time; one traveller reported hand-propelled ferris wheels at Maymyo. The Myin Khin Thabin Pwe, which used to be held in the month of Pyatho and featured horse races, has now largely died out.

February Union Day on 12 February celebrates Bogyoke Aung San's short-lived achievement of unifying Burma's disparate racial groups. For two weeks preceding Union Day, the national flag is paraded from town to town, and wherever the flag rests there must be a festival. The month of Tabodwe culminates in a rice-harvesting festival on the new-moon day. *Htamane* is a special food offering made and eaten at this time – it consists of glutinous rice mixed with sesame, peanuts, shredded ginger and coconut.

March Two holidays fall during our month of March: 2 March is Peasants' Day, while 27 March is Resistance or Armed Forces Day, celebrated with parades and fireworks. The full-moon day in Taboung is an auspicious occasion for the construction of new pagodas, and local pagoda festivals are held.

April Around the middle of April the three-day Thingyan or 'water festival' starts the Burmese new year. This is the height of the dry and hot season and, as in Thailand, it is celebrated in a most sensible manner – by throwing buckets of cold water at anyone who dares to venture into the streets. Foreigners are not exempt! Buddha images are ceremonially washed on the morning of New Year's Day, and *phongyis* (monks) are offered particularly appetising *soon* (alms).

Although the true meaning of the festival is still kept alive by ceremonies such as the one in which young people wash their elders' hair, these days it's mainly a festival of fun. In between getting soaked there will be dancing, singing and theatre. In the latter the emphasis is on satire – particularly making fun of government red tape, the latest female fashions and any other items of everyday interest. The word 'Thingyan' translates more or less as 'change over' – it's a transition from one year to the next.

. . . we arrived at the start of the water festival in April, quite unknowingly, and because celebrations start a day earlier in the south than in the north we got not three days of it but four! After a day spent soaked in Rangoon, we took the train to Mandalay which was interspersed with water bombs (balloons full of water) flying through the window and even at only 10 mph these can make quite an impact when they greet you in the face. As I discovered prior to my reflexes hotting up sufficiently to let the wooden shutters down on approaching any huts.

In Mandalay not so much as a big toe could venture outside of the hotel door without being swamped, not with just a sprinkling of water but either a bucket or, more often, a fire hydrant hose sweeping you off your feet! Even on the top of Mandalay Hill, where surely no fool would go to the extreme of carrying water up all those stairs, we were greeted with a bucket of water over our heads. Our camera equipment as a consequence took quite a bashing and having spent *every* meal we ate soaked to the skin, the loss of latent heat ultimately resulted in my going down with the first cold I'd had since leaving England two years prior! I would like to go back but sometime other than that one week in the year.

Linda Fairbairn

May The full-moon day of Kason is celebrated as the Buddha's birthday, the day of his enlightenment and the day he entered Nirvana. Thus it is known as the 'thrice blessed day'. The holiday is celebrated by ceremonially watering Bo trees, the sacred banyan tree under which Buddha attained enlightenment. Being a true socialist country, Burma also celebrates 1 May, May Day, as the Workers' Day.

June During Nayon monks take their exams.

July The full moon of Waso is the beginning of the three-month Buddhist 'Lent'. This first day commemorates Buddha's first sermon 2500 years ago. During the 'Lent' period monks are restricted to their monasteries for a prolonged period of spiritual retreat. Ordinary people are also expected to be rather more religious during this time – marriages do not take place and it is inauspicious to move house. This is a good time for young men to temporarily enter the monasteries.

The 19th of July is Martyr's Day, commemorating the assassination of Bogyoke Aung San and his comrades on that day in 1947. Wreaths are laid at his mausoleum north of the Shwedagon.

August At the festival in Wagaung lots are drawn to see who will have to provide monks with their alms. If you're in Mandalay try to get to Taungbyone, about 30 km north, where there is a noisy, seven-day festival to keep the *nats* happy.

September This is the height of the wet season so what better time to hold boat races? They're held in rivers, lakes and even ponds all over Burma, but the best place to be is Inle Lake where the Buddha images at the Phaungdaw Pagoda are ceremonially toured around the lake in the huge royal barge, the *Karaweik*.

October In Thadingyut, the Buddhist 'Lent' comes to an end and all those couples who had been putting off marriage now rush into each other's arms. The Festival of Light takes place during Thadingyut to celebrate Buddha's return from heaven, his way lit by angels who lined the route of his descent. For the three days of the festival all Burma is lit by oil lamps, fire balloons, candles and even mundane electric lamps. Every house has a paper lantern hanging outside and it's a happy, joyful time all over Burma – particularly after the solemnity of the previous three months.

November The full-moon night of Tazaungmon is again an occasion for a festival of lights. It's particularly actively celebrated in the Shan States – in Taunggyi there are fire balloon competitions. There are also speed-weaving competitions during the night – young Burmese women show their prowess at weaving by attempting to produce robes for Buddha images between dusk and dawn. The results, finished or not, are donated to the monks. Burma's national day falls in late November or early December.

December During Nadaw 'Nat Pwes' or spirit festivals are held. Despite Burma's predominantly Buddhist background, Christmas Day is a public holiday.

LANGUAGE
Burmese is the predominant language although substantial tribal minorities speak Karen, Chin, Shan and various Kachin dialects. English is also quite widely spoken although, as in other Asian countries, it's easy to be deceived in the cities into believing that English is more widespread than it actually is. It doesn't take a long bus ride into the country to raise a few communication problems. If you do find difficulty in making yourself understood, a simple rule of thumb is to look for somebody older. There are more likely to be English speakers amongst the older generation.

Burma has its own alphabet and script – it looks rather like a lot of mating bubbles and circles, very distinctive and quite indecipherable! It's descended

from South Indian models which emphasised curves rather than straight lines because early writing was done on palm leaves – if you used straight lines you ended up with torn leaves. You're hardly going to have time in Burma to pick up the alphabet, but it is worth making the effort to learn the numerals, if only so you can read bus numbers. The fervent de-anglicisation of Burma resulted in many English signs being taken down and nothing being substituted. It can be very difficult to determine how far you've come while on a Burmese train, as railway station signs are very rare. On the other hand that agreeable Burmese vagueness also comes into play – in Rangoon they've actually gone so far as to put up new English-language signs showing the changed street names, while at the same time the old signs are still there.

Since Burmese has its own alphabet there can be a variety of interpretations of Burmese words into our script. Further confusion is added by the practice of sometimes running words together, sometimes separating. The Shwe Maw Daw and the Shwemawdaw are exactly the same pagoda in Pegu, for example.

Some useful words and phrases:

	number	numerical	money	time
1	*tit*	၁	*ta chat*	*ta nar ye*
2	*nit*	၂	*na chat*	*na nar ye*
3	*thone*	၃	*thone chat*	*thone nar ye*
4	*lay*	၄	*lay chat*	*lay nar ye*
5	*ngar*	၅	*ngar chat*	*ngar nar ye*
6	*chak*	၆	*chak chat*	*chak nar ye*
7	*kun nit*	၇	*kun na chat*	*kun nar ye*
8	*shit*	၈	*shit chat*	*shit nar ye*
9	*co*	၉	*co chat*	*co nar ye*
10	*ta sair*	၁၀	*chat ta sair*	*sair na ye*
11	*sair tit*	၁၁	*sair ta chat*	*sair ta nar ye*
12	*sair nit*	၁၂	*sair na chat*	*sair na nar ye*
20	*na sair*	၂၀	*chat na sair*	
25	*na sair ngar*	၂၅	*chat na sair ngar*	
30	*thone sair*	၃၀	*chat thone sair*	
50	*ngar sair*	၅၀	*chat ngar sair*	
100	*ta yar*	၁၀၀	*chat ta yar*	
200	*na yar*	၂၀၀	*chat na yar*	
500	*ngar yar*	၅၀၀	*chat ngar yar*	

yes
: *hoke ket*

no
: *ma hoke boo*

how are you?
: *maa yeh laa*

I'm well
: *maa bah day*

good day
: *min ga la baa*

please
: *chay-zoo pyu-baa*

thank you
: *chay-zoo tin-baa day*

goodbye (I'm off)
: *pyan dor may*

excuse me
: *kwin pyu-baa*

do you understand?
: *kin byar nar lai tha laa*

I do not understand
: *chun note nar ma lai boo*

come
: *lah pah*

go
: *thwah pah*

I
: *chun note*

you
: *kin byar*

he/she
: *thu*

places:

airport	*huhlay yin p'yan kwin*
bus stop	*bus car hmat tine*
railway station	*bu dar yon*
police station	*yeh sa khan*
market	*zay*
hospital	*say yon*

purchases:

carving	*pa bu*
ivory	*sin zwe*
jade	*chou seine*
lacquerware	*yung hte*
painting	*pa-gee*
parasol	*bassein hti*
silk	*poh*
Burmese face make-up	*tha-na-kha*
where is . . . ?	*. . . beh mah lay?*
what is available?	*baa ya ma lay?*
how much?	*bah lout lay?*
too much	*myar day*
very good	*ah lung kaung pa da*
good	*kah-oong day*
no good	*mah kah-oong boo*

Forms of Address

The Burmese have a greater variety of forms of address than our basic Mr, Mrs, Miss and Ms, but it is not possible to tell a person's marital status from the prefix to their name.

U (or Oo as it is pronounced) literally means 'uncle' and is a respectful form of address for any adult male.

Ko literally means 'elder brother' – it's a familiar term usually used among males of similar age.

Maung is used to address a younger male or a small boy, but it is also used by some men as a sign of modesty.

Bo is a 'leader', usually a military officer.

Ma means 'sister', and can be used for any woman from a little girl to an older lady, but should always be used for young girls.

Daw means 'aunt' and is a respectful form of address for an adult woman of any age, married or single.

The Burmese have no 'family names'. A person's name consists solely of his or her given name, whether one, two, or three syllables, normally preceded by one of the customary forms of address mentioned above. In other words, you cannot discern the blood relationship between people by their names; even the terms 'brother' or 'sister' are of no help since these can be used among friends.

Likewise, Burmese women do not sacrifice their own names when they marry. Thus, when U Hla Tun and Daw Than Mya are married, the wife does not become Mrs Hla Tun or Than Mya Tun; her name remains exactly the same as before marriage.

A final thing to remember about Burmese names is that two or three-syllable given names cannot be shortened by omitting one or more of the syllables. Thein Lwin is always called Thein Lwin, never Thein or Lwin. While travelling in Europe, he might call him self 'Mr Thein Lwin' instead of 'U Thein Lwin' to avoid confusion, but not Mr Lwin. It helps to remember that a Burmese name is a complete semantic unit, eg Ne Win means 'bright sun', while Aung Sein is 'victorious diamond'. Would you call Mr Hopkins 'Mr Hop' or 'Mr Kins'?

Note

For a more complete guide to the Burmese language, keep an eye out for the Lonely Planet *Burma Phrasebook*.

Facts for the Visitor

VISAS

Probably the biggest single problem about visiting Burma is the visa situation – visas are readily available (so long as you're not a journalist or some such questionable person) but seven days is all you get. For quite a period in the '60s the doors into Burma were firmly shut, then slowly reopened. First of all 24-hour stays were permitted, then along came the seven-day visa, but despite rumours for quite a few years about the 15-day visa it seems no nearer reality. The rumours of its impending arrival surface regularly. It's probable that when the 15-day visa does eventually become available it will be in neighbouring Thailand first of all.

Despite this short stay period visas are issued quickly and efficiently and you can, if you really want to see more of Burma, re-apply for another visa as soon as you depart. This, suggested one traveller, is not as profligate as it might sound. If, for example, you were visiting Burma on your way from Australia to Nepal you could quite easily re-visit Burma on your way back again. With two weeks in the country you could follow a more leisurely pace and get to see more out-of-the-way places. Most Burmese embassies seem totally unconcerned if you apply for visas over and over again, though the one in Bangkok sometimes claims that visitors must wait a month between visas. We were able to get around this supposed requirement in 1987 only by appealing to the consul in person.

And just what does happen if you overstay your seven-day, non-extendable visa? Well, not necessarily all that much if you've got a valid reason. I've met lots of travellers who have overstayed, including two people on my last trip who found their Royal Nepal flight had been changed to two days later between booking the flight and arriving in Rangoon. Similarly, two other visitors who couldn't get on their flight due to some booking problem and had to spend an extra day reported that it took just an hour at the immigration office to extend their visas for one day. The cost was K35. Bangladesh Biman seem to cancel their weekly flight with some regularity; in that case you get a whole extra week in Burma! There also appears to be a one-day 'grace period' in that immigration doesn't seem to mind if you fly out on the eighth day rather than the seventh – for example, if you arrive the evening of the 23rd and leave the afternoon of the 31st.

Although a 24-hour transit visa is still available, only the seven-day visa is worth considering. This visa generally costs around US$5 – in Bangkok B110. Two copies of the application form and three passport-sized photographs are required. Although they may claim it takes quite a time to issue visas, the Burmese embassies generally seem to be able to produce them within a day or two. If you go to Burma via Bangkok the embassy there is an excellent place to collect your visa, as they process them in 24 hours – although you must have your application in by noon if you want it back the next day. You will have to show your tickets in and out as well.

Addresses of some relevant embassies and consulates include:

Australia
    85 Mugga Way, Red Hill, Canberra ACT 2600 (tel 95 0045)
Bangladesh
    Plot 38, Road No 11, Bamani Model Town, Dacca (tel 30 1915/1461)
Canada
    116 Albert St, Ottawa (tel 236-9613/4)
China
    No 6 Tung Chih Men Wai St, Chao-yang District, Beijing (tel 52 1448/1425)

Germany
    Schumannstrasse 112, 53 Bonn (tel 0228-21-091)
Hong Kong
    AIA Building, Suite 106, 1 Stubbs Rd, Hong Kong (tel 572 9241)
India
    No 3/50F Shantipath, Chanakyapuri, New Delhi (tel 70251/2)
    (note that the Calcutta consulate has been closed for years)
Japan
    No 8-26, 4-chome, Kita Shinagawa, Shinagawa Ku, Tokyo (tel 441 9291)
Malaysia
    Jalan Taman U Thant 7, Kuala Lumpur (tel 25798)
Nepal
    Thapathali, Kathmandu (tel 13146/14083)
Singapore
    15 St Martin's Drive, Singapore 10 (tel 235 8763)
Sri Lanka
    53 Rosmead Place, Colombo 7 (tel 91964)
Thailand
    132 North Sathorn Rd, Bangkok (tel 233 2237/234 0278)
UK
    19A Charles St, London W1 (tel 01 629 9531/4486/6966/499 8841)
USA
    2300 'S' St NW, Washington, DC 20008 (tel 202 332 9044/5/6)

MONEY & COSTS

Burmese currency is the kyat (say 'chat') (K) which is divided into 100 pyas with a confusing collection of coins. During the British days it used to be the rupee. Coins available are illustrated below, but recently circular copper 5, 10 and 25-pya coins have been introduced to further confuse the picture. Learn your numbers!

In paper currency, K1, K5, K10, K25 and K75 bills are common – larger bills are hard to change. Do not accept any K50 or K100 bills, which are now worthless.

You have to continually think of things in two ways when it comes to money in Burma – official and real. The official exchange rates, as set out by the People's Bank and at which you are required to exchange any money, are:

travellers' cheques   *cash*

US$1 = 6.6 kyats	US$1 = 6.4 kyats
£1 = 10.9 kyats	£1 = 10.7 kyats
A$1 = 4.7 kyats	A$1 = 4.5 kyats

The real exchange rate to the US dollar would actually be something like K30 to

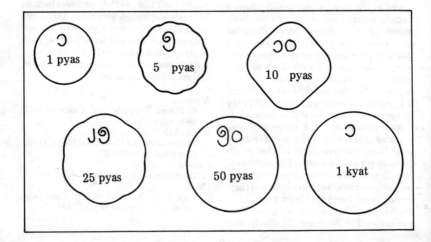

Top: Village life near Mt Popa (TW)
Left: Cosmetics stall (PC)
Right: Earthquake repairs (TW)

Top: Sandamuni Pagoda, Mandalay Hill (TW)
Left: Joining the monastery (TW)
Right: Shwedagon (TW)

K35 (for $20 or larger-denomination US dollar bills), a very considerable difference which, naturally, leads to a rather active black market. The Burmese government attempts to enforce their pipedream exchange rate by several methods. First of all it is illegal to bring kyats into the country. Second, it is illegal to exchange money except at the official banking outlets. Neither of these makes much difference – if you want to smuggle money in, you will, and every second person on the street would love to exchange money for you. The rate is, however, best in Rangoon.

The third method is to get you to fill in a lengthy currency declaration form listing all the cash and travellers' cheques you have, then entering every exchange transaction so that at the end of your trip the amount of money you have left should all be neatly explained. Of course there is nothing to stop you entering the wrong amount to start with and, of course, there is no physical way they can check everybody's forms on departure. After half a dozen transactions, in any case, your form is probably in too much of a mess to decipher! Don't alter the form though; they could always compare it with the carbon copy original. Try to avoid having to change money back at the end of your travels too; the re-exchange rate is rather worse than the original exchange rate.

Their fourth control method is to require that hotel bills and long-distance travel costs (air, rail and to some extent bus travel) be entered on your currency form. If you spend K200 on an air ticket your form must also indicate that you have changed hard currency into at least K200. This clearly is a more effective insurance that you do change your money officially. But equally clearly, hotels and long-distance travel are not the only things you spend money on, and if you don't have to spend expensive (K6.8 to the dollar) money, why bother?

First you should ask if Burma is expensive. Well, yes and no. Air fares are not really expensive in official kyats. In unofficial kyats to fly Mandalay-Pagan would be about US$5 – clearly ridiculously cheap. On the other hand the taxi fare between Rangoon airport and the city is supposed to be K60 – US$8.80 at the official exchange rate and no bargain by Asian standards. At the unofficial exchange rate the fare would be US$2 or less, much more like reality. So perhaps it would be fair to say that paying for the things you have to pay for in official kyats is OK, but it would be nice to have some unofficial kyats for other things.

Typically there is a straightforward Burmese solution to this little problem. One that does not involve messing around with the nasty black market or sneaking illegal currency past the watchful currency-control eyes. It's called the whisky-and-cigarette solution. From Bangkok it goes like this: At the duty-free counter in Bangkok airport buy a carton of 555 cigarettes and a bottle of Johnny Walker Red Label whisky. Total cost US$15.

At Rangoon airport the customs officer may even make some joke about that being enough whisky and cigarettes to last for seven days. Because he knows that the first words you are going to hear from a non-government Burmese are, 'Want to sell your whisky and cigarettes?' You will hear this actually inside the airport terminal, you will hear it as you step outside, you will hear it from your taxi driver, you will hear it from people around your hotel. You will very soon know what the going price is and will have disposed of both – all seemingly quite legal.

Prices do seem to vary, perhaps with the number of people coming through. Over the 12 years we've been visiting Burma it's varied from not much over K200 to as high as K650 for the two, and it sometimes gets up towards K700. On our last trip it worked out to an exchange rate of about K43 to the dollar. Other brands are also acceptable, but 555 cigarettes (Dunhill too say some people) and Johnny Walker Red Label are in the greatest demand. If you can't get that brand of whisky, move down-market rather than up, though Black Label now sells for a higher price than Red Label (costs more, too).

Flying from Nepal, you can get duty-frees at the airport at prices similar to Bangkok's, but from Calcutta you might find cigarettes are cheaper on board the Thai International flight than at the duty-free counter. Experts say you actually get more for 'British' 555s bought in Kathmandu or Calcutta than 'Singapore' 555s bought in Bangkok, but then no one ever looks at the cigarettes or booze anyway – you just hand over the duty-free bag. Some people report that you can also buy duty-frees at Rangoon airport on arrival. It's certainly worth repeating this exercise on departure from Rangoon if you're flying to Calcutta – where whisky and cigarettes are also in demand. Some people say you get a better rate in Mandalay than in Rangoon, but I think it is hardly worth carting your goodies all the way there.

Nor does this semi-official dealing end with whisky and cigs. The Burmese are starved for all sorts of western items of everyday use – ballpoint pens for example. You can have a little enterprise in small-scale importing. All over the country, and most especially in Rangoon and Pagan, you'll hear the following phrases over and over: 'Any business?' 'Change money, sell something?' 'I want to buy something.' Or there is the Diplomatic Store method. Typically, as in other peoples' states where some people are more equal than others, Burma has a diplomatic store where foreigners, and those in favour with the government, can buy things the common population cannot obtain. There are lots of people who would be only too happy to have you go in and do the obtaining for them. Again a blind eye is turned to this

activity and it is widely held that the 'favoured' Burmese use their diplomatic store privilege to make a little extra money on the side too. Burmese Duya export cigarettes are the main 'buy' from the Diplomatic Store. You're no longer allowed to buy unlimited quantities but the local market will happily absorb whatever you can purchase there, and several Tourist Burma outlets offer products and prices similar to those in the Diplomatic Store. This is also the only place in Burma where you can get cash dollars as change back from a large travellers' cheque – you'll appreciate how useful this is when you find yourself forced to change money to settle a small hotel bill officially and only have a $50 cheque. Cash is street money, too.

In brief, the various exchange possibilities are: 1 – you can legally change money at around K6.8 to the US dollar – either at the airport or at Tourist Burma. 2 – you can legally bring in whisky and cigarettes and get around K35 to K45 to the dollar. 3 – you can legally buy and sell from the Diplomatic Store and make a little less to the dollar. 4 – you can illegally bring in kyats with you from abroad. 5 – you can illegally change currency on the black market, in which case Rangoon (where the rate is somewhat higher than the rates at Mandalay or Pagan) is the best place to change money. The bigger the note the better the rate on the black market; US$50 and US$100 notes are very valuable.

American Express is the only international credit card accepted in Burma, and if you want to use your Amex card you must declare it upon arrival and have it entered on your currency exchange card! Likewise, any cash that you want to change legally must be entered on the form at arrival. On departure you can re-exchange a quarter of the official exchange transactions you have made, but if you change travellers' cheques then you are only allowed to change back a quarter of the amount of the final cheque

you change. Over the last few years inflation in Burma, officially at least, has been remarkably low. Many costs have not increased for several years, although air fares have gone up fairly dramatically since the previous edition. The official policy on having transactions noted on your form seems to have weakened; a number of people have commented that hotels are much more ready to allow you to pay them directly and forget about going through Tourist Burma, though this varies from time to time. In Pagan, for example, it was quite easy to get accommodation without getting your form stamped during late 1986; then in early '87 there was a clampdown and every place was asking for stamps.

A more significant control has been in effect since May '87: all visitors are required to exchange a minimum of US$100 into kyats at the official rate upon arrival. Since you can supposedly only change a quarter of that back when you depart Burma, this means a minimum US$75 outlay for your eight days. Before the government instituted this ruling, a traveller typically changed US$20 to US$30 on arrival in Rangoon. Along with the sale of whisky and

cigarettes, this gave most people enough Burmese money for a week's travel, if they didn't do any flying, and satisfied the authorities' official curiosity about currency forms. The week could be done on less if you were wily and played all the angles. Now you're stuck with a pocketful of expensive kyats at the very beginning. You still will need to count on further exchanges, legal or illegal, as K510 (US$75 at the current official rate) won't get most people through the week. K800 seems to be about the minimum. On the street, an extra K300 would only cost US$7.50 to US$10.

Burma can be a most frustrating country to visit and the frustrations are mainly due to the government. First of all there's the seven-day visa. This absurdly short time allowance results in your either haring round the country like the very image of a mad tourist or, alternatively, only doing a small fraction of what you'd like to do.

The seven-day frustrations are compounded by Burma Airways. When you've only got 168 hours you obviously may have second thoughts about 14-hour train or 24-hour boat trips, yet flying Burma Airways can be a completely random process. Schedules appear to be fixed day-by-day on many routes so you can plan only a little in advance. Furthermore, even what schedules exist are approximate only. When every hour counts you'll be forced to turn up at the airport at, say, 2 pm for a flight that, if it goes at all, will possibly go sometime between 2 and 5 pm, but just possibly could have operated as early as 11 am. This said, it must be conceded that in '87, at the height of the tourist season (December-February) domestic BAC flights were running mostly according to schedule, with delays, when they occurred, of only an hour or less.

Even more of your limited hours are wasted by Tourist Burma. In Mandalay, for example, in the cheaper hotels you don't pay your bill at the hotel – oh no, you have to drag clear across town to the Tourist Burma office, at least two km away. Similarly, but even further, you have to buy tickets for the Mandalay-Pagan riverboat not on the boat, but at the tourist office and that's over three km from the riverbank. Far too much time and energy is wasted getting to a central office to pay for something that could far more conveniently be paid for on the spot. It's difficult at times to think of Tourist Burma as anything but the traveller's nemesis. They would really rather deal with package tour groups than 'Foreign Individual Tourists' – FITs. Could stand for 'FIT to be tied'.

Finally there's the frustration of the double exchange rate although I've got to admit that, like so many things uniquely and nuttily Burmese, the two-tiered price structure seems to work OK. The increased value of black market dollars in Burma in recent times has also taken the edge off the price levels. Despite all the problems travelling in Burma can throw at you, it's a place the overwhelming majority of travellers seem to fall in love with.

*

'Everyday items from Thailand, luxury goods from sailors through Rangoon' was how one person summed up Burmese smuggling to me. So the cans and packages of food and medicines come by the overland route, the new watches and pocket calculators by sea. Whisky and cigarettes by air of course! The Burmese are very brand conscious – that's why 555 cigarettes fetch such a premium over other brands. No man could expect to maintain face at a wedding or other special occasion without a packet of 555 to offer around. Similarly a can

of Coke or 7-Up, brought in from Thailand, will fetch K13 in Mandalay Market – that's US$2 at the official exchange rate! Despite the import restrictions those enterprising smugglers manage to provide the Burmese consumer with a quite amazing choice – I even saw Australian beer for sale in one market stall.

CLIMATE

Burma has three quite distinctive seasons although the effects of the monsoon vary in different parts of the country. The best time to visit is the cool 'winter' season from November to February. During this time the weather is very pleasant – not too hot during the day, not too cool at night in Rangoon and Mandalay. In the hill country or Pagan the temperature can get rather chilly in the evening.

In February the temperatures start to rise, and during March, April and May it can be unpleasantly hot. In Rangoon the temperatures will often top 40°C (100°F) and in Pagan it will get even hotter. The annual water festival when people douse each other with cold water takes place in April at the height of the hot season.

In May the rains start as the monsoon sweeps northward from the Indian Ocean. The rain tends to fall mainly in the afternoons and evenings. Although it takes the edge off the intense heat of the dry, hot season, it does tend to make things unpleasantly humid. In October the rain tapers off and you're back to the cool, dry winter season.

The geography of Burma considerably affects the monsoon rains. The delta region around Rangoon gets about 250 cm (100 inches) a year, but the rainfall rapidly diminishes as the monsoon continues north; the central area of Burma (which includes Pagan) is a large dry zone with 60 to 110 cm (25 to 45 inches) of rain a year. Then north of Mandalay the hill ranges force the winds higher and the rain again gets heavier, reaching a drenching annual total of around 500 cm (200 inches). The Arakan coastal area near Bangladesh and the

Tenasserim coastal strip beside southern Thailand are also affected by their mountain ranges and get very heavy rainfall.

BOOKS & BOOKSHOPS

Finding books in Burma is not that easy. There is nothing much in the way of bookshops selling new or used English-language books on Burma. The best selection of out-of-print Burma books can be found at the Pagan Bookshop at 100 37th St, Rangoon. There is quite a large selection, although you may have to bargain a bit. The most expensive books are not, curiously, necessarily the rarest. Often the high prices are simply due to the books being currently out of favour – such as all books on Mahayana Buddhism! Another bookshop in Rangoon which has been recommended is the Theingi Maw Book Stall at 355 Maung Taulay St, opposite the Scott Market, where there is a huge selection of cheap English paperbacks and some rare old Burmese books.

Along Bogyoke Aung San St, across from the Bogyoke Market, there are a number of bookstalls, and some in the streets which run back from the main road. Several of these stalls have quite a selection of Burmese books if you ask for them. The odd book can also be found in the bookstalls on the main approach to the Shwedagon Pagoda, which is a good place to look for books on the Buddhist religion too. In addition, there are some interesting bookstalls around the Pagan Bookshop on 37th St. There you may spot oddities like the Raj-era 'Civil List' (read *Burmese Days* to understand its all-consuming importance in the colonial era). The Diplomatic Store has a number of books available, including the *Pictorial Guide to Pagan* – rather cheaper than its kyat price on the street or in bookstalls in Rangoon or Pagan.

Away from Rangoon you may spot some rare books in the pavement stalls at night or in the night market in Mandalay.

Guidebooks

I hope you'll find this the ~~tor 37~~ available on Burma but the~~.~~ it or not, some other books ~~.~~ Keep your eyes open for the ~~.~~ produced *Travellers' Guide to B~~u~~* Kanbawza Win, published by the ~~YMC~~ in Rangoon in 1977. It's quite a good little book but unfortunately was banned; you'll be very lucky to find a copy anywhere in Burma.

In contrast, the readily available government production *Rangoon Guide Book* and *Handbook to Burma* are not worth looking at – just a handful of statistics and drab pictures. *Burma – Facts & Figures & a Tourist Guide* is a similar compilation of statistics but is, at least, cheap if you want a list of embassy addresses, school populations, state capitals and so on. Out of print, and unfortunately very difficult to find, is *Welcome to Burma*, published by the American Women's Association in Rangoon – it has much rather out-of-the-way information about Rangoon, Mandalay and around Mandalay.

Apa Productions of Singapore include *Insight Burma* in their collection of coffee-table guidebooks. Written by Wilhelm Klein with photographs by Gunter Pfannmuller, it has a superb selection of modern photographs complemented by some equally interesting old black-and-whites from the colonial era.

Histories

There have been few recent studies of developments in Burma, so although there are many studies of pre-British history and the British conquest and subsequent colonialisation, and of the path to independence and the rocky path post-WW II, they mostly fade out at the end of the U Nu years and there is very little readily available about the changes in Burma since Ne Win came to power way back in 1962. Furthermore, many publications are out of print.

Burma by F S V Donnison (Ernest

London, 1970) gives a concise and readable history of Burma from its earliest development through the British period and into the troublesome '60s. There are also chapters on the country's economy and culture. *The Union of Burma* by Hugh Tinker (Oxford University Press, London, 1961) is a scholarly study of the path to independence in Burma and the difficult U Nu period. Frank N Trager's *Burma: From Kingdom to Independence* (Praeger, New York, 1966) is an equally scholarly account of this same period and its particular significance in Asia.

There are other recent accounts of earlier Burmese history, such as *The Pagoda Wars* by A T Q Stewart (Faber, New York, 1972) which covers the British takeover of Burma. A number of books concern the dramatic events in Burma during WW II, particularly the behind-enemy-lines actions of Wingate's 'Chindit' forces. Find a complete description of their activities in *The Chindits* by Michael Calvert (Pan-Ballantine paper-back), or read Bernard Fergusson's more personal accounts in *The Wild Green Earth* or *Beyond the Chindwin*. Some interesting articles can be found in back issues of the *Asia Magazine* – particularly 'The Land Where Time Has Stopped' and 'Burma's Road to Ruin'.

Two books by Burma expert David I Steinberg provide what is probably the most complete socio-political look at modern Burma. *Burma: A Socialist Nation of Southeast Asia* (Westview, Boulder, Colorado, 1982) is an overview of Burmese history, geography, ethnicity, politics and economics, while *Burma's Road Toward Development: Growth & Ideology Under Military Rule* (Westview, Boulder, Colorado, 1981) is a history of Burma since 1962, when Ne Win took power.

Temples, Palaces & Ruins

A book every visitor to Pagan must have is the *Pictorial Guide to Pagan* (Ministry of Culture, Rangoon, 1979), which contains illustrated descriptions of many of the important Pagan buildings plus a map inside the back cover. It's the one useful book you'll find fairly easily in Burma. *Pagodas of Pagan* (Buddha Sasana Council Press) is also fairly readily available, but not so detailed or interesting.

Historical Sites in Burma by Aung Thaw (Ministry of Union Culture, 1972) is an excellent illustrated description of the major buildings at Pagan, Pegu, Rangoon, Amarapura, Ava, Sagaing, Mingun and Mandalay plus a number of other sites that are currently 'off limits'. It has recently been reprinted and can be found at the Pagan Bookshop or in Pagan. *Mandalay & Environs*, which is long out of print, can be very hard to find. It is very difficult to find any material on places other than the straightforward Rangoon-Mandalay-Pagan triangle, but *Historic Sites & Monuments of Mandalay & Environs* by U Lu Pe Win (Buddha Sasana Council Press) is fairly easy to come across and describes the ancient cities around Mandalay – Ava, Sagaing, Amarapura and Mingun.

Finally, if you'd like to know a lot more about the Shwedagon then get a copy of *Shwedagon* by Win Pe (Printing & Publishing Corporation, Rangoon, 1972). You might find it in the Diplomatic Store or in the Rangoon airport departure lounge.

Other Books

Golden Earth by Norman Lewis (Eland Books, London) is a recently re-issued edition of a book originally written in 1952. It's a delightful tale of a ramble around Burma at a time when it was both more open and less open than it is today. At that time the varied rebellions were in full swing, but Burma had not yet entered its totally reclusive period. Much of the book sounds remarkably like Burma today, and his descriptions of Burma's elderly trucks have the real ring of truth –

no photograph could do a better job of summing up these miracles of mechanical endurance.

The Kodansha International 'This Beautiful World' series includes *Burma – Unknown Paradise* by Ulrich Zagorski (Tokyo, 1972) – the usual collection of evocative photographs. *National Geographic* have done a number of features about Burma. The February 1963 issue covered Burma as a whole, March 1971 was about Pagan, June 1974 had an article on the Inle Lake leg rowers, while in the June 1979 issue there was an article about the long-necked Padaung women – revealing that they're actually not long-necked at all. The heavy rings they wear around their necks actually push their shoulder blades and collar bones down, rather than extend their necks. Burma featured once again in June 1984, in a general article where it emerges that even National Geographic writers can't necessarily wangle more than a seven-day visa.

Paul Theroux's amusing and cynical bestseller, *The Great Railway Bazaar*, includes chapters on the train from Rangoon to Mandalay, from Mandalay to Maymyo – with a perfect description of Candacraig, and his amusing visit to 'forbidden' Gokteik.

Quite a few writers set novels in Burma, most famous being George Orwell's *Burmese Days*, of course. It's available in a Penguin paperback and makes an interesting, if depressing, read on up-country Burma in the British days. Maurice Collis (*Siamese White, Last & First in Burma*) also wrote about Burma.

The Soul of a People by H Fielding was an 1898 attempt to understand the Burmese. *Thibaw's Queen*, by the same author in 1899, is a romanticised story of the collapse of the final Burmese kingdom before British imperial might. It has been recently republished in Burma by the Buddha Sasana Council and is easily found. Towards the end of the war Longmans published a series of booklets about Burma known as 'Burma Pamphlets'. You may see some of these long, long out-of-print books in Burma; they make interesting reading. *The Burman* by Shway Yoe (alias Sir James Scott) is a long, detailed and fascinating book based on a series of articles by this British civil servant. In his many years in Burma he acquired an extraordinary knowledge about every aspect of the country.

For gourmets and cooking enthusiasts, the recently published *Cook & Entertain the Burmese Way* (Myawaddy Press, date & provenance unknown) by Mi Mi Khaing makes interesting reading. This volume contains a wealth of information on preparing, serving and eating Burmese food in the correct style and includes instructions on how to mix Burmese salads by hand, recipes for 'salivators and tongue titillators', and a very useful appendix that lists fruits, vegetables, spices and fish with their Burmese and English names. It's available at Tourist Burma in Rangoon and at tourist hotels throughout the country.

Finally, one of my favourite Burmese books is *Burmese Timber Elephant* by U Toke Gale (Trade Corporation 9, Rangoon, 1974). I was given a copy by a printer in Singapore and to my amazement found the whole book completely fascinating. It could be subtitled 'selection, care and use of your pet elephant' for it tells you everything you need to know and many things you don't need to know about timber elephants. Even what to do with your elephant when he's in *musth*. There's a chart showing the 90 nerve centres to which a mahout applies pressure to control his elephant or to get it to do things. But don't press 13, 25, 60, 61 or 63 for 'the animal will be infuriated'!

MEDIA

There are two English-language papers in Burma – the *Guardian* and the marginally higher-circulation *Working People's Daily*. Since they are both published by the People's Printing & Publishing Works the news inside tends to be identical, although the *Guardian* appears to have a little more content. In the Strand Hotel, perhaps in deference to western capitalistic attitudes, it's the *Guardian*, not the *Working People's Daily* which gets left by your door every morning. Not only does the government have a monopoly on publishing the newspapers, it has a monopoly on selling them. Only the government can sell them at the cover price and goodness knows where they do that. Newspaper vendors buy them from the government at the full cover price and mark them up accordingly!

The Burma Broadcasting Service has 2½ hours of English programmes a day, including three news bulletins at 8.30 am (42.14 and 314 metres), 1.30 pm (30.85 and 314 metres) and 9.15 pm (59.52 and 314 metres).

TV has also recently arrived in Burma, so far in Rangoon only. It broadcasts in colour from 7.30 to 9 pm with the odd, morally uplifting programme on Burma's economic progress interspersed with elderly American cast-offs. A typical evening's programming is shown below.

On the corner of Merchant St and Pansodan St there's a place that seems to be the *Time* and *Newsweek* agency for Burma, but they won't sell you one. All the copies go to Burmese who hand in what looks like a ration card – the issue date is noted on the card, entered in a ledger and then they're handed their copy. Second-hand copies of these and many other western magazines are readily available at bookstalls around Rangoon.

At the American Center, 508 Merchant St (a few doors east of the American Embassy), the ABC World News is shown on a large video screen from 5 to 6 pm Fridays. On occasions when the news is delayed (perhaps censored?) other programs will be shown. This can be an interesting place to meet outward-looking Burmese, not all of whom are necessarily pro-American.

Cinema is very popular in Burma and many

TV PROGRAMME

7.30 pm
1. Opening Song
2. Singing Stars

7.48 pm
3. Snagglepuss: "Lions Share Sheriff" (Cartoon)

7.55 pm
4. Gulp (Cartoon)

8.00 pm
5. News and Weather Report

8.20 pm
6. Zoos of the World

8.34 pm
7. The Three Stooges: "Cash and Carry"

8.52 pm
8. The Outcasts: "The Night Riders"

9.43 pm
9. Close down

quite recent western films are shown, often rather heavily censored. The cinemas are all government owned but videos, and smuggled-in videotapes, are also beginning to appear!

FILM & PHOTOGRAPHY

Apart from some colour print film in the Diplomatic Store there is little officially

THE GUARDIAN

THE WORKING PEOPLE'S DAILY

available film in Burma. Most film you might see on sale will be from visitors who have sold it while in Burma – with no guarantee on age or quality. Burma is a very photogenic place so bring lots of film with you. The usual tropical rules apply to taking photographs here. Allow for the intensity of the sun after the early morning and before the late evening. Try to keep your film as cool as possible, particularly after it has been exposed. Beware of dust, particularly at the height of the dry season when central Burma becomes very dusty indeed. And don't drop your camera in the Irrawaddy!

A benefit of Burma's low tourist flow is that the Burmese are not over-exposed to camera-clicking visitors and are not at all unhappy about being photographed. Even monks like to be photographed although, of course, it's rude to ask them to pose for you and it's always polite to ask anybody's permission before taking photographs.

HEALTH
There are currently no immunisation requirements for entry into Burma except for yellow fever if you come from an infected zone. The 'health check' at the airport means only a cursory look at your passport to see if you've come to Burma by way of Africa, in which case they may ask to see your immunisation certificate. Burma is in the malarial region and you should take anti-malarial tablets as prescribed by your doctor. Most hotels in

Burma now have mosquito nets, but in those that don't the mosquitoes can be a positive menace. A pack of mosquito coils is a worthwhile investment, although they are not always readily available in Burma. Bring some with you – for those who don't know, mosquito coils are incense spirals which you set up on a little stand, light at one end and let burn all night to keep mosquitoes away. Their ingredients are likely to include nasty substances like DDT, but I think I'd prefer a bit of that to malaria.

Do not drink unboiled water anywhere in Burma. Some travellers wrote that the water sellers in Rangoon are OK, but I'd be suspicious – even though I've taken the risk from time to time and got away with it. Soft drinks are generally pretty awful and so is Burmese tea, but most restaurants either supply weak Chinese tea in unlimited quantities as a matter of course or will provide it if asked.

POST
The GPO in Rangoon is on Strand Rd, just down from the Strand Hotel, on the corner of Sparks St. Mail out of Burma seems to get to its destination quite efficiently – surprisingly? Or at least I thought so; a number of subsequent writers either agreed that everything they sent got through OK (even from Mandalay) or totally disagreed saying that nothing at all ever arrived. Certainly embassies in Rangoon recommend that if you are sending any important correspondence to

Burma you should send it by air freight rather than trust the mail.

ELECTRICITY
When it's working it will be 230 volts, 50 cycle.

TIME
Burmese time is 6½ hours ahead of Greenwich Mean Time. Coming from Thailand you turn your watch back a half hour, from India you turn it forward an hour. When it is 12 noon in Rangoon it's 3.30 pm in Sydney or Melbourne, 5.30 am in London, 12.30 am in New York and 9.30 pm the previous day in San Francisco.

INFORMATION
Tourist Burma, officially known as the Hotel & Tourist Corporation, handles all the tourist information duties in Burma. Their main office is at 77-79 Sule Pagoda Rd in Rangoon, beside the Sule Pagoda. Tourist Burma have very little in the way of brochures or leaflets, unlike most other South-East Asian tourist offices. They are, however, very helpful if you visit them at their offices. Apart from the main Rangoon office there are also Tourist Burma desks in Mandalay, Pagan, Yaunghwe (Inle Lake) and Taunggyi.

Do not, however, approach Tourist Burma about visiting places not on their officially approved list. If you want to go to places which, while you are not totally banned from visiting you will certainly not be encouraged to visit, you will find Tourist Burma very lukewarm about your chances of getting there. In such cases it's better to simply ignore them and go!

ACCOMMODATION
Since the Burmese government centralised tourist operations you are only officially allowed to stay in a selected list of hotels in Rangoon, Taunggyi, Yaunghwe, Kalaw, Pindaya, Mandalay, Pagan and Maymyo. Other places are officially 'off limits'. Worse, apart from the Tourist Burma-run places – generally the most expensive

hotels in each location – and a select list of other hotels (including the YMCA and the Dagon in Rangoon, and the Mya Mandalar and Aung Thi Yi Guest House in Mandalay) all accommodation is supposed to be paid for with vouchers from Tourist Burma offices. This can entail a lot of wasted time in scooting back and forth between the tourist offices and your hotel.

Fortunately this system is far from watertight. For a start there are lots of hotels in places where Tourist Burma's tentacles either don't reach or at least don't reach too efficiently. Plus some hotel operators are only too happy to conveniently forget about the voucher system if they feel Tourist Burma aren't watching. A few smaller hotels and guest houses will stamp your currency form on the premises.

At the cheapies you should come equipped with your own toilet paper and be prepared to wage war with the mosquitoes – should there be no mosquito nets. Fortunately nets seem to have become more common in Burma over the last few years. Don't count on great comfort in the cheaper hotels – straw mattresses are still gradually being phased out, Asian-style squat toilets are the low-price norm and in Pagan the cheap places generally feature rural-style, bottom-of-the-yard outhouses.

What the cheap hotels lack in creature comforts they often make up for in friendliness and atmosphere. They always seem glad to see you and go out of their way to make you feel at home. In Pagan in particular, if there should be a crowd of you at your rest house you'll find meal times a pleasant communal affair – everybody sitting around a big table talking over what they've seen during the day. In most guest houses throughout Burma hot Chinese tea is usually available in the lounge area and a fresh pot may be put before you whenever you wander in from a day's exploring.

Burma's cheaper hotels are generally

reasonable enough value, particularly at the unofficial exchange rates, but many of them are definitely rather spartan and basic. Few travellers complain about Burmese shoestring accommodation, though.

Burma's better class of hotels are fairly utilitarian by 'international' hotel standards. Things don't always work too well and the usual lack of upkeep seems to show through. A glance through the guest books in these Tourist Burma-run places often indicates a steady flow of disgruntled guests, but Burma is most definitely not a place you should visit simply for high-class hotels – there's far more to this country than air-conditioning and 24-hour room service.

FOOD

Burma is another of those countries where you can eat very well and at reasonable cost, but where it is difficult to find local food. If you want to try Burmese food the best way is to befriend a Burmese

and get invited home for dinner – there are few Burmese restaurants. In Rangoon you could try the relatively expensive *Bamboo House* which does a few Burmese dishes in addition to their regular menu of Chinese Muslim and Indian food; or try the rather touristy Burmese buffet at the *Karaweik* 'floating restaurant' on the Royal Lake.

In Mandalay the *Mann* and *Too Too* restaurant will do some Burmese dishes, but these places apart, only street and market stalls provide the local flavours, and in these you must be a little wary of cleanliness. Burma has many excellent and reasonably priced restaurants, but in the main they specialise in Chinese or Indian food – Burman cuisine is primarily a home and festival-centred activity. When the Burmese dine out, it is generally either at Chinese restaurants or at the myriad tea shops found in every town and city. In the larger hotels there will also be western or, more correctly, English food.

Ice cream advertisement in Rangoon

The Burmese do not have one of the world's great cuisines, although skilfully prepared it can be quite interesting. Rice, of course, is the core of any Burmese meal. To this is added a large assortment of curry dishes from which you can pick and choose. There will almost inevitably be one or more fish curries, plus chicken or prawns, fresh cooked vegetables, and a spicy salad made with raw vegetables. Almost everything is flavoured with *ngapi*, which is concocted from dried and fermented fish or shrimp paste and can be very much an acquired taste. Popular dishes include *oh-no khauk swe*, rice noodles with pieces of chicken in a spiced sauce made with coconut milk; *lethok son*, a spicy vegetarian rice salad; and *mohinga*, a fish soup with rice noodles. Most families dine around a low, round table about 30 cm in height, sitting on reed mats. The entire meal is served at once rather than in courses.

Although you may not have much opportunity to try these delicacies, you almost certainly will not go hungry in Burma. There are many Chinese restaurants, including quite a few of the regional specialties which are a world (well half of China anyway) distant from the hum-drum Cantonese dishes we think of as Chinese food in the west. In a run-of-the-mill Chinese restaurant a meal will cost around K10, often less. In true Chinese fashion you almost invariably get soup with your meal and free Chinese tea.

Indian restaurants are also common although much more so in Rangoon than in other towns. Excellent chicken biriyani is easy to find in the capital. For western food the best places to look are the big hotels, the Strand in Rangoon in particular.

In Mandalay and around Inle Lake (Kalaw, Pindaya, Yaunghwe and Taunggyi) it is also fairly easy to find Shan food, which is very similar to northern Thai cuisine. Popular dishes are *khausen* - Shan-style wide rice noodles with curry - and various fish and meat salads.

Like most Asians, the Burmese are great snackers, and in the evening many street stalls sell tasty little snacks. I recommend that you avoid the crunchy grasshopper kebabs I've seen for sale on the trains! At all times of day you'll see Burmese sitting in tea shops where the tea flows freely and the assorted pastries are very inexpensive.

Burma has a wide variety of tropical fruits, and in season you can get delicious strawberries in Maymyo and Mandalay (even in Rangoon). Don't miss the avocados if you're in the Inle Lake area. In Rangoon and Mandalay snack bars have excellent, and seemingly healthy, ice cream but you should avoid the street sellers of ice cream unless you have a very strong stomach.

food words:

restaurant	*sar thow syne*
where can I eat?	*bear mhar sar ya mhar le?*
may I have the bill?	*sayin logindee*
hot	*ah poo*
bread	*pow moh*
toast	*pow moh kin*
butter	*taw but*
cakes	*cake moh*
egg (boiled)	*chet ou byoke*
egg (fried)	*chet ou chor*
omelette	*chot ou chet thon chor*
noodles	*kau swe*
rice	*san*
rice (cooked)	*ta min*
soup	*hin jo*
beef	*tha jar*
chicken	*chet thar*
fish	*ngar*
pork	*wet thar*
prawns	*pa zoon*
tangerine	*lain maw thee*
banana	*ngaw pyaw thee*
pineapple	*na nut thee*
avocado	*dopati*

Drinks

Only drink water when you know it has been thoroughly boiled – which in most reputable restaurants it should be. One should be suspicious of ice although I've had lots of ice drinks in Burma without suffering any ill effects. Burma is a thirsty country and not a good one for slaking that thirst safely, pleasantly and at reasonable cost.

Burmese tea is cheap, but absolutely dreadful to most western palates. Like the Indians, the Burmese specialise in brewing up tea that's over-strong, over-sweet and over-milked. Plus it will dye your tongue an alarming shade of orange! Surprisingly many restaurants, the Chinese ones in particular, will provide as much weak Chinese tea as you can handle – for free. It's a good, safe thirst quencher and, to my taste, far better than regular Burmese tea. You can always buy some little snack if you'd like a drink but not a meal. Tea shops are a good place to drink safely boiled tea and munch on inexpensive snacks like nam-bya (Burmese chappatis) or Chinese pastries.

Soft drinks are very expensive, if you're thinking at the official exchange rate. A bottle from the People's Soft Drink & Ice Factory will cost you K2.50 to K7, usually K3 or K4. Some soft drinks are really terrible, but they can also come in quite pleasant flavours – particularly if they're well diluted with ice. One of the better ones is Lemon Barley, but only the kind made in Rangoon – its Mandalay counterpart is not so good. Half-and-half soft drink and soda water is another recommendation.

After the first edition one traveller wrote that I was far too kind to Burmese soft drinks, which he found to be universally terrible with 'the honourable exception of a brand called Vimto, a strange relic of British rule now found only in remote parts of north England'. This prompted several other travellers to write that Vimto was worse than other drinks. On my last trip to Burma I found and tried a bottle of Vimto. The verdict? I'm amazed it's still hanging on in even the remotest corner of north England; it's foul!

Beer is also a little expensive, although not too bad by Asian standards. A large bottle of Mandalay Beer costs from K17, if bought in a government shop or hotel. In a private restaurant or shop it may cost as much as K40. It's very similar to Indian or Sri Lankan beer – rather watery but quite pleasant on those hot and dusty occasions when only a beer will do. 'Bucket beer' is also available here and there, served warm in a bowl and quite cheap.

Very popular in the Shan State is an orange brandy called shwe le maw which varies in price from K14 to K25 per bottle, depending on how close to the source you buy it – much of it is distilled in the mountains between Kalaw and Taunggyi. It's a pleasant-tasting liqueur, sort of a poor man's Grand Marnier, and packs quite a kick. The wine-fancying rector of the North-Eastern Goldfields parish of Western Australia wrote that a bottle of 'Lychees Wine' which he found in Rangoon's main market for K15 had a subtle flavour hinting at muscat and was quite a fine tipple! There is also a variety of stronger liquors, including ayet piu or 'white liquor', which varies in strength from brandy-like to almost pure ethyl; and taw ayet or 'jungle liquor', a cruder form of ayet piu. Sugar-cane juice is a very popular streetside drink – cheap, thirst quenching and (from my stomach's experience at least) relatively healthy.

drinks:

cold drinks shop	ah aye syne
tea shop	la bet yea syne
cold (with ice)	ah aye (yea geh)
drinking water	thow yea
tea	la bet yea
coffee	caw pee
sugar	tha jar
lime juice	than ba yar yea.
orange juice	lain maw yea

THINGS TO BUY

Burma isn't the place it used to be for things to buy, although you can still pick up some nice items. Of course one shouldn't 'buy' too much; at the official exchange rate many straightforward items are very expensive – far better to do a little bartering because anything has a value in Burma. The Bogyoke Market in Rangoon and the Zegyo Market in Mandalay are good places to look for handicrafts. In fact one traveller wrote that everything he bought around the country he later found just as cheap right there in Rangoon. The big hotel shops and the shop in the departure lounge at Rangoon airport are extremely expensive. Note my warning below on precious stone rip-offs, but beware of other more mundane rip-offs. A couple of travellers wrote of being persuaded to buy betel nut to resell in Bangladesh!

Lacquerware

Probably the most popular purchase in Burma is lacquerware – you'll find it on sale in the market in Rangoon and Mandalay, in the Mahamuni Pagoda entrance walks in Mandalay, and most particularly in Pagan – where most of the lacquerware is made. Burmese lacquerware is fairly similar to that made in the north of Thailand, and although connoisseurs of Japanese lacquerware say that in comparison the Burmese items are inferior, I find them rather pleasant.

To the Burmese, lacquerware is *Yung Hte*, literally 'the wares of Yunnan' which is the Chinese province to the east of Burma; this is where the art is said to have come from. To make a lacquerware object, first of all a bamboo frame is made. If the item is first quality only the frame is bamboo; horse or donkey hairs will be wound round the frame. In lower-quality lacquerware the whole object is made from bamboo. The lacquer, which is an oil from the kusum tree, is then coated over the framework and allowed to dry. After several days it is sanded down

with ash from rice husks, and another coating of lacquer is applied. A high-quality item may have seven layers of lacquer altogether.

The lacquerware is engraved and painted, then polished to remove the paint from everywhere except in the engravings. Multicoloured lacquerware is produced by repeated engraving, painting and polishing. From start to finish it can take five or six months to produce a high-quality piece of lacquerware which may have as many as five colours. Flexibility is one characteristic of good lacquerware. A first-quality bowl can have its rim squeezed together until it meets without suffering damage. The quality and precision of the engraving is another thing to look for.

Lacquerware is made into bowls, trays, plates, boxes, containers, cups, vases and many other everyday items. The octagonal-topped folding tables are another popular lacquerware item – I bought one of these on my first trip to Burma several years ago and it is still one of the nicest things I've bought while travelling. A table costs around K100 to K150 now.

Umbrellas

The graceful and beautifully painted little parasols you see around Burma are a product of the port of Bassein – in fact they're known in Burma as 'Bassein *hti*'. Everyday umbrellas have wooden handles, the more ceremonial ones have handles of silver. You can pick up a nice small umbrella for less than K10. The Bogyoke Market is a good place to look in Rangoon.

Shan Shoulder Bags

Brightly coloured cotton shoulder bags from the Shan states can be found all over Burma, but most particularly at Inle Lake. Fancy models have a zip pocket in the front.

Precious Stones & Jewellery

Burma still has a considerable income

Opium Weights

from the mining of precious stones, but the main mining area at Mogok, north of Mandalay, is off-limits for visitors. Be very wary of people who come to you with stories of large profits from taking Burmese gemstones to sell in the west. There are a lot of red glass rubies waiting for the unwary. Also, precious stones are very much a government monopoly and they are very unhappy about visitors buying stones privately. If any stones are found when your baggage is checked on departure, they will be confiscated.

Having said all this, I should add that on my last trip to Burma I bought a 'ruby' from someone I ran into one day. I know nothing about precious stones so he could have sold me anything, but it turned out to be a fairly good real ruby. A traveller who seemed to know rather more about stones wrote that the finer imperial jade or pigeon-blood rubies can only be purchased at a special dealer's session (the 'Jade & Pearl Emporium') in February; but that he bought good gem stones quite openly at a stall in the Scott Market. From official sources stones are almost always only sold in uninteresting jewellery and they are really no bargain at all. If you buy loose stones, cut or uncut, take them with you to a place like Kathmandu or Bali where you can get

them made into jewellery very cheaply.

Wood & Ivory Carving
You can still find some pleasantly carved Buddha figures and other items from workshops in Mandalay, but in general you will not see too much wood-carving on sale. Ivory, in my opinion, is best left on elephants.

Tapestries
One of the better bargains in Burma, along with lacquerware. Called *kalaga* in western countries, they consist of pieces of coloured cloth of various sizes heavily embroidered with silver or gold-coloured thread, metal sequins and glass beads, and feature mythological Burmese figures in padded relief. The greatest variety is found in Mandalay, where most tapestries are produced, but mark-up can be high there because of a tout system (horsecart drivers who hook customers may receive as much as 50% commission). However, if you locate the shops on your own and bargain well, you can get fair prices. Shopping for tapestries is easier in Pagan because all the shops are lined up along the tourist strip with the goods in full street view and the selection is good. You can also purchase tapestries in Rangoon at craft shops in the Bogyoke Market –

prices are similar to those in Upper Burma but the selection not as great.

Good-quality merchandise is tightly woven and doesn't skimp on sequins, which may be sewn in overlapping lines rather than spaced side by side as a sign of embroidery skill. Metals used should shine, even in older pieces; tarnishing means lower-quality materials. Age is not necessarily a factor in value except when related to better-quality work. Prices vary according to size and quality, from smaller squares (say 30 cm by 30 cm) for K50 to K150, to the larger (say 1.5 metre by 1.2 metre) for K3000 or US$65. You can often get better deals by paying in cash US dollars.

Antiques
They're not all as ancient as made out, but you can see some interesting items – particularly opium weights, the little animal shapes in descending sizes that are traditionally used to weigh out opium. The older system of weighing opium used a series of nine weights; a set of these should cost about K60. The newer system uses six weights and these go for around K50. Folding opium scales in carved wooden boxes start at K60 for the smaller ones. Check prices in shops in Bangkok before blithely looking for bargains in Burma, though.

WHAT TO BRING
Even at the height of the cool season you'll rarely need anything more than a sweater while on the plains – and that probably only for the nights in Pagan, where it can get a little chilly. It can get rather cold up in the hill country, so if you're going to Maymyo or Inle Lake bring a warm sweater or light jacket. A sleeping bag might also be useful in the Inle Lake area, especially in Kalaw and Taunggyi where the one or two blankets per person supplied by guest houses is not always enough during the cool season.

Otherwise it's normal tropical gear – lightweight clothes, but 'decent'. Burma is a prim, conservative country – shorts (especially on women) or short skirts do not go down well. When touristing in Burma I strongly advise that you wear sandals or thongs rather than shoes – simply because you take them off and put them on so often when visiting temples and pagodas. Remember that the sunlight is intense in Burma – protect your head in open places like Pagan, or when out on the Inle Lake. Mosquitoes can be a major irritant, so bring protection in the form of insect repellent, mosquito coils or even a mosquito net. Cheap hotels rarely have top sheets, so a sleeping bag or even just a sarong will provide some added protection against the little buggers.

Bring any items you feel may not be available in Burma – mosquito repellent or coils, film, batteries, medicines are obvious examples. Simple toiletries like soap, toothpaste or toilet paper are readily available; in fact toilet paper is much easier to find and cheaper than in India. Remember that anything western which is difficult to find in Burma will have an absurdly high value. Western clothes (interesting T-shirts), electronic gadgets, disposable lighters, ballpoint pens, lipstick and make-up – they're all items every Burmese would love to have. They have to be name brands though, something from the US or Europe, not any old Asian product! You can always barter for handicrafts or simply give them away and make people happy.

CONDUCT
The usual Asian rules of conduct apply in Burma, plus a few specially Burmese/Buddhist ones. As elsewhere in Asia it is unseemly to show too much emotion – losing your temper over problems and delays gets you nowhere, it just amazes people. Stay calm and collected at all times. The Burmese frown on such displays of anger just as much as they frown on too open displays of affection. As in other Buddhist countries the head is the highest part of the body – spiritually

Top: Ascending Mt Popa (TW)
Left: Maymo (TW)
Right: Family transport on Inle Lake (TW)

Top: En route to Taunggyi (TW)
Bottom: Rangoon river traffic (TW)

as well as literally. You should never deliberately touch somebody else on the head or pat a child on the head. Equally, the feet are the lowest part of the body – don't point your feet at somebody.

Most important of all in Burma, remember to take your shoes (and socks) off at every opportunity. Even at the most dilapidated, run-down, ruined pagoda in Pagan the 'no footwearing' rule still applies. You must go barefoot virtually everywhere. In the middle of the day barefooting it can get a little painful as the paved area around a pagoda often becomes very hot. At major pagodas there will often be a mat walkway around the platform.

At one time this restriction caused quite a little stir between the Burmese and the British. As part of the growing surge of nationalism between the wars, and a neat way to put the British in their place, the Burmese decided to rigidly enforce the no-footwear rules, from which the Europeans had previously been exempted. Signs also suddenly appeared announcing that there was to be 'no umbrellaring' – in case you've never seen anyone do this, it means using an umbrella to point things out!

SAFETY

Tales of insurgents, terrorists, forbidden areas and so on make Burma sound as if it is a rather unsafe country to visit – the truth is actually very different. Burma's insurgency problem is a tricky one; the insurgents and guerrillas do not have enough support, equipment or energy to be more than a major irritation. They certainly have no hope of unseating the government. On the other hand the government is also sadly short of support and enthusiasm, so they have little hope of totally overcoming their armed opponents. The result is a long-running stalemate.

So long as you do not venture into those no-go areas (a possibility which the Burmese government is firmly determined not to allow to occur), you're very unlikely to run into any difficulty. Apart from occasionally blowing up the Rangoon-Mandalay railway line the insurgents seem happy enough to stick to their own territory and leave the government's territory to the government.

Added to this, one has the overwhelming impression that the Burmese would simply be too polite and well mannered to think of inconveniencing a foreigner! Of course in the government-controlled areas, the places where you are permitted to go, the possibility of being mugged, robbed, held up or otherwise enjoying any of those other unpleasant, everyday western events is similarly remote although there has been one isolated case of a woman getting robbed in Pagan. Basically Burma is a very friendly and safe country, despite which I recommend that you keep a close eye on your valuables, particularly on overnight train trips. The severe shortage of consumer goods can make your possessions just a little bit too tempting at times.

Getting There

There's little choice in getting to Burma – you are simply not allowed to enter by land, and people who arrive by sea must be few and far between. That only leaves arriving by air, and even there the choice is fairly restricted since few airlines fly into Rangoon. A number of European airlines used to fly to Burma but in recent years they have all switched their Asian routes to wide-body equipment (DC-10s, 747s), and Mingaladon, the Rangoon airport, is still unable to take anything larger than a DC-8 or a 707. One by one they have all deleted Rangoon from their ports of call, not without a sigh of relief one suspects.

Most visitors to Burma will arrive there by one of three means. First, and most commonly, they may out-and-back from Bangkok in Thailand. The second possibility is to slot Burma in between Thailand and Bangladesh, India or Nepal – many people travelling from South-East Asia to the sub-continent manage a week in Burma in between. The third alternative is to out-and-back from Calcutta.

Other less likely possibilities are to arrive in Burma from China or from Vietnam and Laos. The most important factor to consider when booking your flight in and out of Burma is to make sure you get your full week. There are, for example, far more flights Bangkok-Rangoon and vice-versa than Calcutta-Rangoon and vice-versa. If you are heading through to the sub-continent from Bangkok, you don't want to choose a flight in unless there is a flight out exactly seven days later.

Bangkok is a good place to look for tickets to Burma. Some travel agents will not only sell you tickets at knock-down prices, but will fix up your visa too. Typical costs are Bangkok-Rangoon-Bangkok for around US$140, Bangkok-Rangoon-Calcutta for a similar figure, Bangkok-Rangoon-Kathmandu for around US$180. The airlines that fly into Rangoon are:

Thai International Thai currently fly Bangkok-Rangoon-Bangkok several times each week. They use DC-8s and the flight takes about 50 minutes.

Bangladesh Biman Biman fly Bangkok-Rangoon-Dacca once a week. They are usually the cheapest operator although not always that reliable. In fact many people fly Biman simply because of their unreliability. There's always the chance of getting stuck in Burma for a bit longer than your seven-day visa would normally allow, due to the Biman flight not turning up!

If you're flying through to Calcutta with Biman you (sometimes) get a free night's stop-over in Dacca. Note that if you plan to stop in Bangladesh it's still worth getting a ticket to Calcutta since the price is the same and you may, therefore, start your Bangladesh travels with free airport transport and a free night's accommodation.

A traveller's warning to people arriving late on days when there are more than the usual number of flights:

If you arrive in Rangoon on the Monday-night Biman flight from Bangkok, all accommodation may be full when you get into town as there are four international flights that day and the hotels simply cannot handle all the tourists. There are three solutions: 1) Get a traveller on an earlier flight or earlier in the week to make a reservation for you. 2) Go to the police and get permission to use a 'locals only' hotel. This involves a lot of hassle late at night, but can be done. 3) The YMCA will let you sleep on the stage or a table on the balcony for one night. Before you leave Rangoon reserve your accommodation for the following week, when the situation will be the same.

Burma Airways Corporation BAC fly Bangkok-Rangoon and vice versa daily. On Tuesdays, Thursdays and Saturdays they fly Rangoon-Calcutta-Kathmandu and vice versa. Twice a week they fly between Singapore and Rangoon. They use F-28s for these flights. Some travellers reckon that it's worth flying BAC because the fewer passengers on their smaller aircraft means you suffer fewer delays getting through the airport formalities.

A nervous flight report from one traveller:

Soon after leaving Rangoon and half way through handing out breakfasts they grabbed them all back and announced a return to Rangoon due to 'minor problems'. We cruised around for an hour, low over paddy fields. I couldn't find a safety card in the seat pocket. The staff looked tense and since the flight deck door was open I could see in from my front row seat. Out came big red manuals and they began tearing up the carpet and attacking floor panels with a screwdriver. Then I saw the red lights on the undercarriage display which they finally cranked down by hand, the stewardess shouting out with delight to everyone. We finally landed back in Rangoon; a group of Japanese package tourists hadn't understood the original announcement and thought it was Bangkok!

A comment from another:

Flying BAC shortens your seven days in Burma to almost five. You won't get in to Rangoon airport earlier than noon on Day 1, and you have to check in at 7 am on Day 7. Thai is better.

Royal Nepal Airlines Corporation RNAC fly between Rangoon and Kathmandu.

Aeroflot The Russian national airline fly into Rangoon once a week from Moscow via Ho Chi Minh City (Saigon) and Vientiane. If you managed to get a visa to Vietnam and Laos this would be an interesting route into Burma.

Civil Aviation Administration of China CAAC fly between Kunming (Yunnan) and Rangoon once a week. As more and more independent travellers visit China, this is likely to become an increasingly popular route, although few visitors use it at present. If you are travelling around China and then continuing to South-East Asia it can actually be economical, since from western China you would not have to backtrack all the way east to Hong Kong, then fly all the way west to Bangkok. The flight costs Y390 plus Y10 airport tax, about US$200. You have to plan ahead for visas and you may experience difficulty if you don't get the CAAC ticket until you get to China. A Swiss couple I met in Burma who used this route reported that CAAC had to refer to Beijing for reservations, but the flight had a total passenger load of five – two businessmen and three travellers!

ARRIVAL IN RANGOON

On your flight to Burma you will be handed a currency control form to fill in – see the 'Money' section for all the details. On arrival you will probably find there is a bit of a race on to get into the terminal building. Your first taste of Burmese bureaucracy is likely to be a lengthy one, and the early arrivals will save quite a bit of time. The process is first to squeeze past the health-control counter where your passport and/or vaccination certificate is checked to see if yellow fever immunisation is required. Then across to the immigration counter where your visa and immigration form is inspected.

Then it is on to the customs counter, where you will have to fill in a form if you have a camera, calculator, typewriter or any other marvel of western technology. This form states number of items, brand name and value – undervalue them since if they are stolen or lost it's better to have a lower cost to argue about. This must be carefully kept aside until departure – it is as important as your currency control form.

A bit of a bottleneck now builds up until you can be escorted by a customs officer personally to your baggage and have it inspected. Arriving on a full Thai International flight, you may find the immigration/customs procedures take a full hour to complete, which is all the more exasperating since it will be the only incoming flight on the airport runway. Then it's through the arrival area exit, where you will most likely meet your first 'black market' dealer, eager to purchase your duty-free whisky and cigarettes. This brazen entry right into the heart of Burmese officialdom doesn't seem to worry the Burmese entrepreneurs at all, nor the officials. In fact on my last visit 'whisky, cigarettes?' was first whispered to me actually inside the customs hall! It's not unusual to see travellers selling duty-free across the Tourist Burma counter at the airport – but it's best to hang on till you get into town, where it will fetch a higher price than anywhere at the airport.

Next, it is out to the Peoples' Bank counter where you can change your first money into kyats and have the first entry made on your currency form. From there you must go to the Tourist Burma counter directly across from the exchange window and book a taxi into town – you are not allowed to hire a taxi on your own outside the terminal. The standardised rate for taxis to Rangoon is K60, but one taxi will take up to four people and at the Tourist Burma counter they will divide the endorsement across four currency forms (eg K15 each) upon request. There is an up-to-date list of authorised Rangoon accommodation here as well, with the number of vacancies chalked alongside.

Outside the terminal you will find what looks like a collection of old cars escaped from the scrapyard. This is the Rangoon taxi fleet. Your driver will have been assigned to you by TB and he will lead you to his machine/museum piece and toss your bags in the back. It is then simply a matter of rattling and shaking your way

into town, although your taxi may very well stop along the way to pick up a 'businessman' who will try very hard to purchase your whiskey and cigs and change money. If the price is right (K650 to K700 in early '87 for duty-frees; K35 to the cash dollar), why not?

It is possibly indicative of Burma's attitude toward tourists that BAC provides a bus to convey you from town to airport for your departure, but not from airport to town on arrival, except for domestic flights. If you're determined to save the kyats, get out to the main road from the terminal (about two km) and you can get a bus No 9 into town for a kyat or so.

Reconfirming

If you are counting on flying out of Rangoon on your scheduled date of departure, then you must reconfirm your outbound flight at the appropriate ticket counter *before* leaving the airport the day of your arrival. This applies regardless of whether your flight is officially 'confirmed' on the ticket or not. You may notice a sign in the airport waiting lounge which reminds you of this rather recent requirement. If you do not reconfirm, the airlines (this goes for any of the airlines flying in and out of Rangoon) cannot guarantee your outbound seat. Especially during the height of the tourist season (November-February), most flights out of Rangoon seem to be intentionally overbooked. On the other hand, if you're looking for a few extra days in Burma, just give it a miss and you're quite likely to get bumped – particularly if you neglect to arrive for check-in until an hour or less before departure.

If you do get bumped, make sure you visit immigration to extend your visa sometime before your rescheduled departure. Otherwise, the airlines may refuse to give you a seat when you arrive for check-in and you will have to deal with the airport immigration office. This process has been known to delay check-in until the very last minute, in which case you may find yourself bumped a second time.

DEPARTING RANGOON

Departing from Burma is just about as complicated as arriving, particularly if you have an early morning flight out and have to crawl out of bed in your 'exhausted-after-seven-days-in-Burma' state. BAC make it less pleasant by sending round their bus to collect you at an unnecessarily early hour. The bus costs K5 and starting from the Strand Hotel criss-crosses all over town on its way to Mingaladon. If there are four of you, a shared K60 taxi to the airport will only cost K15 each and will give you an extra hour (almost) in bed. If you happen to be flying out of Rangoon on Union Day, 12 February, you need to get out to the airport before noon because the road to the airport is closed to non-parade traffic after that time.

At the check-in counter you are handed a green departure form, and K15 airport tax is extracted from you. At the Peoples' Bank counter you can change back any surplus kyats and then follow your baggage into the departure hall. Here you are supposed to hand over for inspection your:

    passport
    ticket with airport tax stamp
    green departure form
    boarding pass
    pink visitor's form
    currency form
    customs form

Your currency form continues to be an exercise in futility since there is obviously no hope whatsoever of checking that each individual in a planeload of passengers has the right amount of money on departure. Your baggage is now cursorily inspected to make sure you are not exporting any precious stones or Buddha images – and that you are exporting any

valuables you brought in with you. And that is goodbye to Burmese bureaucracy.

In the departure lounge you can buy any handicrafts you forgot on your way round or purchase whisky and cigarettes at the duty-free counter – quite possibly exactly the same ones you brought in with you. As by now will seem normal, there is no departure announcement and everyone just seems to spontaneously start heading to the aircraft. Still, there is very little chance of missing a flight out of bustling

Mingaladon, even though your boarding pass reminds you: *Don't miss your flight.*

If you have time on your hands between check-in and boarding, there is a restaurant/bar/lounge on the 2nd floor of the airport, where the food's not bad.

OVERLAND THROUGH BURMA

With the current difficulties in Iran and Afghanistan, 'overlanding' through Asia is nowhere near as popular an activity as it was a few years back. Nevertheless the idea of a route through Burma has long been a dream for overlanders. If you could only drive through Burma it would then be possible to travel by car all the way from London to Singapore, and Asia overland would be much more of a reality than it has been in the past.

Prior to WW II that route would not even have been a dream – there simply were no roads through Burma. After the war there were three new roads and a railway across the Burmese borders – but these fascinating routes had a short civilian life. The railway was built by the Japanese across the infamous 'Bridge on the River Kwai' and up to the Burmese border at the Three Pagodas Pass, from where it ran to Moulmein. After the war most of the railway was torn up, leaving only a stretch from Kanchanaburi in Thailand which runs into the jungle for less than half way to the border. Forget that one.

Road number one was the famous 'Burma Road' and runs into China's Yunnan province to the city of Kunming. It was built to supply the forces of Chiang Kai-Shek in his struggle against the Japanese. It may yet be in good condition and the roads to the Burmese side of the border are still usable, but the border is well beyond Lashio, far into Burma's 'forbidden' region.

Roads two and three were built by the Allies as they advanced against the Japanese. The Indians and the British built a road from Imphal in India to Tamu on the Burmese border while further north the Americans, under General 'Vinegar Joe' Stillwell, built a 430-km road running from Ledo in the remote Indian North-East Frontier Agency to Myitkyina in the north-east of Burma. At a cost in 1944 of US$137 million it must rank as one of the most expensive roads in the world, because after a few months' use in 1944 it has hardly been used since. Both these roads have now probably returned to the jungle.

You can read a quite fascinating description of driving through Burma, using the Stillwell road, in *First Overland* by Tim Slessor. It tells of a 1956 trip from London to Singapore by two Oxford and Cambridge University crewed Land-Rovers. They may well have been not only the first but also the last overland, for a 1962 edition of *The Motor Roads of Burma* (published by the Burma Oil Company) states that only the first 190 km from Myitkyina to Tanai is 'motorable during all weathers'. The rest of the way to Ledo required four-wheel-drive plus 'preparation, patience, perseverance and luck'. The road from Mandalay to Myitkyina via Maymyo, Lashio and Bhamo was 780 km long and generally trafficable according to that same road guide. Turn-offs lead to the Chinese border from just beyond Mongyu and Bhamo.

The British-Indian road sounds an equally forbidding operation. Mandalay-Tamu was 490 km via Amarapura, Sagaing, Shwebo, Yeu and Kalewa. After Shwebo, 93 km out, the road rapidly deteriorated (according to this 1962 report), with many unbridged *chaungs* (canals) to cross. In wet weather this would be an impossible proposition, although the booklet also noted that it was sometimes possible to ship vehicles from Monywa to Kalewa by riverboat – thus avoiding the worst part of the route. Once at Tamu the road on the Indian side of the border was quite good.

The usual route from Burma into Thailand is more likely to be in usable condition, although this runs through the opium poppy harvesting area of the 'Golden Triangle' and is, therefore, also most definitely off-limits. The route runs directly east through Taunggyi to Kengtung, then turns south to the Thai and Laotian borders. It is 450 km to Kengtung from Taunggyi and another 163 km on to the border at Tachilek. The road is often in rather poor condition and you've also got the danger of meeting unfriendly opium dealers!

Although you're unlikely to be able to see this area from the Burmese side of the border, you can go right up to it on the Thai side. There's even a popular little hotel perched on the corner of the Golden Triangle where Burma, Laos and Thailand meet - it's appropriately called the *Golden Lodge*. Visitors can hop across the river for a short visit to Burma.

Further south there is a route from Moulmein to Kawkareik and Myawaddy on the actual Thai border, although my road booklet notes: 'This road is not at present open right through to civilian traffic and none of the car ferries beyond Kawkareik is operating'. As in the Golden Triangle area to the north it is possible to go right to the border on the Thai side; it's about six km beyond the town of Mae Sot - during the dry season you can wade across the river that forms the border. There is also a road from Mergui, right in the south of Burma, across the border to Prachuap Khiri Khan.

Border Crossings

Although land entry into Burma is illegal and 99% of official visitors arrive through Rangoon airport, there are plenty of highly unofficial visitors who cross the border to or from Thailand smuggling consumer goods in and bringing opium out. The central government has little control over the border regions. A report on the main border crossings from south to north:

Prachuap Khiri Khan Not only is there a road over the Mawdaung Pass between Ban Huei Yang and Tenasserim, there is a major business smuggling timber in from Burma. The 'toll gate' is controlled by Karen guerrillas from the Karen National Union/Karen National Liberation Army, who collect a 5% tax on smuggled goods crossing the border in either direction. If you can find a local who knows the area well, it's possible to visit the border crossing point.

Three Pagodas Pass This is one of the most interesting and accessible of the border crossing points. Although the railway is long gone, the Japanese-built road is still there; trucks full of contraband go up to the pass

every day and transfer the goods to caravans of bullock carts which carry it down to the train station at Ye. It's quite a spectacle early in the morning as endless lines of bullock carts carry refrigerators, radios, sewing machines, medicines, bicycles, cloth and everything else imaginable.

From Kanchanaburi (the site of the 'Bridge on the River Kwai') you can get a Land-Rover or minibus or can rent a motorcycle and drive the 150 km along dusty, winding jungle roads to Sangkhlaburi. The trip takes six to eight hours and costs around 140 baht. The road is OK as far as Thong Pha Phum, but deteriorates after that little town. Sangkhlaburi is a tiny outpost in the middle of nowhere, a pretty little town where towns are usually very ugly. A fantastic wooden bridge crosses the River Kwai here, and there is a small Baptist mission for the Karens, with a school and hospital. There is also a cheap hotel.

It can be difficult finding transport from here to the Three Pagodas Pass, and you will probably have to think up an excuse to get by the Thai border checkpoint. A doctor, or the hospital, don't speak Thai - they all help! The pass itself is unreal, three little pagodas standing on a crest in the jungle - a sort of South-East Asian Khyber Pass, but more remote and difficult to get to. This has been a route for invading armies for many centuries and now is a major smuggling route. Right on the Burmese side of the border is the small village of Hko Ther Pler, inhabited by enterprising Indian and Chinese businesspeople from Bangkok and Rangoon, plus guerillas from the KNU/KNLA and the Mon State Army/New Mon State Party, another insurgent group. Both these organisations have 'customs offices' where they collect taxes. To visit this village you need a letter of introduction from the Karen or Mon representatives in Bangkok.

Mae Sot-Myawaddy There's nothing very interesting here, just a bridge, and on the Burmese side a Buddhist temple, a village school and thatched-roof compounds. There are regular buses from Tak to Mae Sot. If you could cross the river here, you could proceed on to Moulmein by road. Myawaddy is one of the few towns along Burma's border with Thailand actually controlled by the Burmese government, who have kept the Myawaddy-Moulmein route open to black marketeers - in order to avoid civil unrest in Rangoon due to consumer shortages and rising prices. Just north of

Myawaddy is the Karen-controlled Wangkha, and a bit south is Phalu (Thai side Waley), also a smuggling post. Between Mae Sot and Tha Song Yang, south of Mae Sariang on the Thai side, are several Karen refugee camps (at last report seven camps with a total of about 13,000 refugees) populated by civilians who have fled Burmese-Karen armed conflicts. The fighting was particularly bad in 1983 and 1984 and this area continues to be hot.

Mae Sariang-Mae Hong Son To visit this point you must have an invitation from the Karen, Karenni and Shan guerrillas. Some hill trek operators on the Thai side can arrange visits.

Chiang Dao A dirt track turns left 10 km north of Chiang Dao and leads through the small town of Muang Ngai to Na Ok at the border.

This was the most popular opium route from Burma 20 years ago, but is no longer used to the same extent. The main trading items now are water buffaloes and lac (for lacquerware). It's wise to be very careful in this area though.

Mae Sai-Tachilek The infamous bridge was Lo Hsing-han's former 'Golden Triangle' passageway for opium and heroin. You can see it from the Thai side, but you're only allowed half way out on the bridge. Thais and Burmese are allowed to cross in either direction during the day – many Burmese come over from Tachilek to work at day jobs in Mae Sai. Further to the south, in Mae Chan district, it is possible to cross the border almost everywhere – with a local and reliable guide. This is opium country and Sunday strollers are not welcome.

Getting Around

AIR

Until a few years ago Burma Airways Corporation was known as Union of Burma Airways. The change from UBA to BAC appears to have been just another of those confusing change-for-the-sake-of-change operations that Burma specialises in. Since the flights are still prefixed UB and at least half of the references you'll see will indicate UBA, it makes very little sense.

BAC operate a small fleet of F-28 jets for international and major internal connections, a number of F-27s for other domestic routes and Twin Otters for the routes into smaller airstrips. All the aircraft are in decidedly tatty condition and the whole operation seems to be a little on the haphazard side, which does not do wonders for one's nerves when flying BAC. However, flights do seem to have improved a bit in the last couple of years.

There are a number of points to watch when flying in Burma. First of all, it is hardly worthwhile buying your BAC tickets outside Burma. In Bangkok the BAC office will simply not ticket you for internal connections. Elsewhere, if you buy a ticket for BAC flights you will find that reservations cannot be made until you arrive in Burma. And since BAC is not IATA and does not conform to the IATA exchange rates, whatever you paid abroad will probably be less than what they will charge within Burma. BAC or Tourist Burma will simply take your ticket, credit you for what you have already paid, charge you the difference with their own local price and write you a new ticket.

Even ticket in hand things may not go strictly to plan; schedules don't mean all that much – if the passengers turn up early the flight may go early. If insufficient passengers show up the flight

may not go at all. If too many passengers want to fly, another flight may be slotted in. Even having a confirmed reservation and being first in line may not get you there because Burmese VIPs can jump the line with ease and package-tour people also get preference over the independent travellers. On the other hand, if you show up at the last minute and buy a ticket, you will get on board ahead of any expatriate residents in Burma and, of course, the poor Burmese, who are right at the bottom of the pecking order when it comes to clambering aboard the people's airline. Recently they've actually been laying on tourist-only flights during the main season, and flights during these months seem to run regularly and on time – one plus for travelling during high season. The most annoying aspect of flying BAC is that you inevitably waste a lot of time at the airports. Flights often go late, but given the difficulty of getting seats you daren't risk showing up late yourself. Besides, if you take the Tourist Burma bus to the airport, you have no choice of when to go. In places like Taunggyi, the TB bus is about the only reasonable way of getting to the airport in Heho – ordinary bus transport is too shaky timewise.

At the airport you will find there is unlikely to be any announcement of impending departures. Simply keep an eye on everybody else, and when people start to move towards the plane, move too. I think it is wisest in Burma to travel as lightly as possible and carry your own baggage out to the aircraft rather than trust that it will find its own way there. In Heho, everyone except package-tour groups carry their own luggage on anyway, regardless of quantity. You will save time (a valuable commodity in Burma) if you also carry it off at the other end. Except for international flights you are unlikely to be served anything apart from a cup of Burmese tea or a glass of fruit juice on BAC.

The diagram below details the only flights visitors are allowed to take. Flights between Rangoon and Mandalay may go via Magwe or Heho or they may go direct. If you cancel your booking within 24 hours of departure there is a 25% cancellation charge; within six hours it jumps to 50%. Transport to and from the airport is provided for all foreigners, including flights to Rangoon from Upper Burma. On my last trip I (Joe) was the only foreigner on a packed Heho-Rangoon flight, and after arrival at Mingaladon Airport, I was chauffeured to the Strand in a Tourist Burma bus that was empty except for myself and the driver!

Domestic Flights & Fares

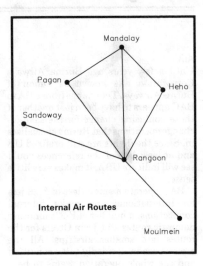

Internal Air Routes

route	dep	arr	fare
Rangoon-Pagan	6.45 am	8.15 am	K445
Pagan-Mandalay	8.35 am	9.05 am	K152
Mandalay-Heho	9.35 am	10.05 am	K152
Heho-Rangoon	10.20 am	11.45 am	K357
Rangoon-Mandalay	6.45 am	9.05 am	K461
	1.00 pm	3.10 pm	
Mandalay-Rangoon	9.35 am	11.45 am	K461
	3.40 pm	6.00 pm	
Rangoon-Heho	1.00 pm	2.25 pm	357
Heho-Mandalay	2.40 pm	3.10 pm	152
Mandalay-Pagan	3.40 pm	4.10 pm	152
Pagan-Rangoon	4.30 pm	6.00 pm	445

There are no scheduled flights to Sandoway or Moulmein.

Do not buy tickets for BAC domestic flights before you arrive in Burma. I met two people who made this mistake and it caused them quite a little hassle. BAC is not an IATA member and will not accept IATA tickets written for their internal flights – although these are quite acceptable for international flights into or out of Burma. The first person I met had a ticket purchased in Europe for Rangoon-Mandalay-Pagan-Rangoon. Although she could not use it, Tourist Burma refunded the initial cost of her ticket, then wrote her a new ticket (on BAC's delightfully amateurishly printed domestic tickets) and charged her a small amount extra.

The second person had a ticket bought in New Zealand for flights all the way from there to London with many stopovers and the Burma loop included. Because there was no separately stated cost for those internal Burmese flights, they would not refund that part and she had to lay out for the BAC flights again, then claim a refund from the agent who originally wrote the ticket when she got back to the west. Answer: buy BAC internal tickets inside Burma, not before you arrive.

RAIL

Burma has 4270 km (2670 miles) of metre gauge railway line – not much of which is open to foreign tourists. The 716-km (430-mile) trip from Rangoon to Mandalay is the only train trip most visitors consider – there are daily and nightly special reserved cars on express trains on this route where you can be sure of getting a seat. There are three classes of passage: ordinary, 1st class and upper class (which under the old British system would have been 3rd, 2nd and 1st class). The main difference between upper and 1st is that the seats recline in upper class, while ordinary is unreserved. These express trains are far superior to the general run of

Burmese trains. In fact I'd recommend putting a lot of effort into avoiding most other Burmese trains for any long trip – one 12-hour train trip that ends up running 15 hours late is enough for most people. Especially when everything in the farm except old MacDonald himself is also aboard the train.

Apart from the straightforward Rangoon-Pegu-Thazi-Mandalay line which is open to tourists, you can also take the branch line from Pyinmana to Kyauk Padaung (about 50 km from Pagan) or the branch from Thazi to Shwenyaung (about 11 km from Inle Lake). At Mandalay there are three branches – one running slightly north-west across the Ava Bridge and up to Yeu, one directly north to Myitkyina in the Kachin State, and one north-east through Maymyo to Lashio in the North Shan State. The Mandalay-Maymyo section of that latter route is the only part open to visitors. From Rangoon lines also run north-west to Prome, with a branch off to Bassein, while from Pegu there is a branch off south-east to Moulmein.

All train tickets must be bought through Tourist Burma, which causes the usual problems of dealing with this centralised bureaucracy. For example, from Mandalay the tourist office has a quota of eight seats in upper class and either 10 or 20 (depending on the season) in 1st class. These can be bought by tourists from the office in the Mandalay Hotel between 8 am and 8 pm. A day's notice is usually enough for booking a seat. After 8 pm any unsold tickets are available to all comers from the station – but you, a foreigner, aren't allowed to buy tickets from the station, so even if seats were available after 8 pm, you couldn't get one. You used to be able to buy ordinary (non-tourist) tickets at Thazi for any train – even when there were no seats left – but now a Tourist Burma official appears at the station around the time each Mandalay-Rangoon express train stops there. He makes sure every foreigner has the proper ticket, or he'll

sell you one. On the night train between Rangoon and Mandalay there are upper-class sleeping berths, but these are not sold to foreigners. The friendly Tourist Burma chap at the Thazi station, who retired from Burma Railways after 30-odd years of service, claims this is because the sleeping cars are in such bad condition. Thazi-Rangoon tickets purchased in Mandalay cost the same as Mandalay-Rangoon tickets.

It's worth going straight to the Tourist Burma office in Rangoon (remember it closes at 8 pm) from the airport to book train tickets to upper Burma on arrival in Rangoon – you might save yourself some time or even depart Rangoon the night you arrive, if you want to. Take special note, in the relevant section, of the suggested routine for getting back to Rangoon from Pagan or Inle Lake via Thazi by train.

I've had some widely varying experiences on trains in Burma. Coming back from Pagan on one occasion Maureen and I took the train from Kyauk Padaung, which we earnestly suggest visitors should not take. It goes down as one of

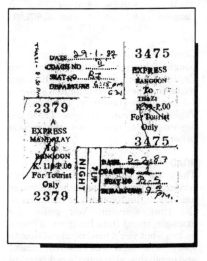

the most miserable train rides I've ever taken. On another trip I took the train down from Thazi to Pegu. By hanging around the station master's office until just before departure time I managed to get a 1st-class berth from the 'VIP Quota' and travelled south in some style and comfort. The only catch came at the southern end where, it turned out, the train did not stop in Pegu. It did, however, slow down to a mere crawl and, like a number of Burmese intent on a visit to Pegu, I simply hopped off the moving train and my compartment companions tossed my bag off after me!

Train Schedules & Fares

route	dep	arr	fare (Ord/ 1st/Upper)
Rangoon-Mandalay	6.00 am	8.00 pm	
	6.15 pm	8.30 am	K44/88/110
	9.00 pm	11.30 am	
Mandalay-Rangoon	6.00 am	8.00 pm	
	6.15 pm	8.30 am	K44/88/110
	9.00 pm	11.30 am	
Rangoon-Thazi	6.00 am	5.00 pm	
	6.15 pm	5.30 am	K36/72/99
	9.00 pm	8.30 am	
Thazi-Rangoon	9.00 am	8.00 pm	
	9.15 pm	8.30 am	K36/72/99
	12.00 mid	11.30 am	

Combined bus-train tickets may be bought through Tourist Burma for Pagan-Rangoon and Taunggyi-Rangoon routes in either direction for K55 added to 1st and upper-class fares. The 'buses' to Pagan and Taunggyi from Thazi are Japanese pick-ups – see the section below.

ROAD

There are a surprising number of bus services around Burma, although you're unlikely to use too many of them due to the time element. You could, for example, travel from Rangoon to Pagan by bus – but you'd need plenty of time to spare. Buses tend to be crowded, ancient and unreliable, although there do seem to

be more modern Japanese pick-up trucks installed with bench seats (rather like an Indonesian *bemo* or Thai *songthaew*) coming into use in the country. In the last few years the government has been making an effort to legitimise some unofficial imports. Sailors, who have always been a major source of imports, are now allowed to legally import cars and motorcycles and sell them in Burma. The result has been a considerable upgrading of Burma's once incredibly ancient vehicle population. These modern Japanese pick-ups provide reliable transport all over the country both locally and longer distances. In fact, don't say I told you so, but it's possible to persuade people to take these trucks a very long way indeed.

Jeeps of WW II vintage also ply some routes, particularly in the hill country. Places where you might consider taking to the road include Mandalay, from where you can take a jeep up to Maymyo, or Pagan, to which there's a relatively efficient bus service now supplemented by Japanese pick-up trucks. There are also a few jeeps for rent out of Kalaw. The standard Japanese pick-ups run from Mandalay to Taunggyi, although that is a rather long trip by road. Departing from the Inle Lake area or from Pagan, you might consider getting to Thazi by road; it's definitely faster than trying to get there by rail. Up-country roads in central Burma are generally in reasonable condition on the main routes but they're always narrow. When oncoming vehicles meet or when one has to overtake another, both vehicles have to pull partly off the road.

Burma is no longer quite self-sufficient in oil, and petrol is rationed and can usually only be purchased in the area where the vehicle is registered. Officially petrol costs just K3.50 a gallon and the ration is four gallons a day. On the black market it can cost K35 a gallon and up. When a Burmese vehicle owner makes an up-country 'road trip' he either has to buy fuel on the black market or carry numerous jerry cans of petrol with him.

Burmese Cars

Although the recent easing of import regulations – or is it a case of turning a blind eye to would-be importers? – has upgraded the vehicle population, most of the cars that ply the roads of Burma are unlike those almost anywhere else in the world. They are positively ancient and in the totally run-down condition that seems to epitomise Burma as a whole. Apart from a few diplomats' cars and cars which one suspects have been handed on by diplomats, a car newer than the mid-50s is a pretty rare sight. Up-country, 'car' usually means 'jeep' and the jeeps were generally left behind by the Americans from WW II. The chassis and engines are largely original, though spare parts of varying quality are manufactured in Burma to meet the high demand. New bodies for everything from Hino trucks to Land-Rovers and vintage Willys Jeeps are hammered out of old petrol drums and other scrap metal in factories near Mandalay – they say one jeep body takes about a month to manufacture. That explains the occasional sleek Willys you'll see in the middle of nowhere that looks like it just rolled off a 1940s assembly line.

Coming down from Maymyo, Maureen and I had to be back in Mandalay very early in order to share a ride out to see Sagaing. We arranged for a jeep to pick us up at 5.30 am, about an hour before dawn. In order to save precious light bulbs few Burmese drive at night with their lights on for longer than absolutely necessary. But our driver didn't switch his lights on even after we left the dimly lit town and proceeded to negotiate the downhill bends, sneak around the unlit oxen carts and broken-down vehicles and miss the upcoming trucks, all totally without the aid of lights. He simply did not have any. Fortunately nothing much else worked either, and by the time we had broken down four times in the first couple of km dawn was already coming up 'like thunder on the road to Mandalay'.

Arriving back at Rangoon airport from Mandalay, four of us agreed to share a taxi into town. We got in, the car was started and then a series of horrible graunching noises followed as the driver tried to get into gear without the aid of his clutch. His elderly Humber had as much clutch left as our Maymyo jeep had headlights. With the aid of half a dozen other drivers we got

moving, but what was going to happen when we arrived at the first red light in town? Clutchless changes on the move are one thing, while stationary they're quite another. Sure enough, at the first traffic light we stopped and could not restart. Passing Burmese then had the amusing sight of four tourists pushing their defunct taxi to the roadside and abandoning it. Presumably our driver thought that Buddha would be on his side and ensure a stopless trip all the way from the airport to our hotel.

In his delightful book on a trip round Burma in 1951, *Golden Earth* (Eland Books, London), Norman Lewis describes a vehicle, close relations of which can still be seen all over Burma:

The post-wagon was undoubtedly the most decrepit, the most exhausted vehicle in which I had ever travelled. It was a phantom from a breaker's yard, something which had been unearthed from a bombed building. The treads of all four tyres displayed a rippling pattern of canvas. There was no spare. Before the steering wheel could influence the car's direction, it had to be spun through half a turn. Gaping sockets showed where all the instruments had been wrenched out of the dashboard. The floor-boards above the engine had been removed, releasing a furnace heat and the rattling vibration of a million nails being shaken in a metal box. Above this pit sat the driver, stabbing like a frantic organist at the control pedals, which in some way had lost their normal independence of each other, since the application of the brake slightly opened the throttle, and the engine had to be switched off, or the accelerator held back, whenever this was necessary. Whenever he wanted to blow the horn, the driver, reaching out as if to catch a butterfly, seized two dangling wires and held them together. The body was insecurely fixed to the chassis, but settled down on a straight road to a steady see-sawing motion to which one soon became accustomed, although the sudden opening of the doors as we took corners continued to surprise.

It's not always so humorous – on a recent road trip one of us made by rented jeep (a Willys) between Pindaya and Yaunghwe, the vehicle almost turned over near Heho when one wheel sheared completely off the axle, probably due to metal fatigue. The Australian woman clinging to the top had quite a fright!

BOAT

There are still many riverboat possibilities in Burma, although the trips you are able to make are severely limited both by the government's outright bans on foreigners travelling in some areas and by the length of time required to make most trips by riverboat. You would probably get away with travelling all the way from Mandalay to Rangoon via Pagan and Prome, for example. But you'd use up your seven-day visa on just that one trip!

Today the Inland Water Transport Corporation (headquarters at 26th Rd in Mandalay) has 600 boats totalling 1.36 million tons and they annually carry 14 million passengers. That is just a pale shadow of the former glory of the Glasgow-owned Irrawaddy Flotilla Company which ceased operations in 1948. Their Siam Class steamers carried 4200 deck passengers plus 40 more in staterooms; they were 100 metres long and travelled faster up-river than the present-day boats can manage down! The captains of these mighty riverboats were so important that a Mandalay shop once had a sign announcing they were 'Silk Mercers to the Kings and Queens of Burma and the Captains of the Steamers'. The Flotilla Company was struck a disastrous blow by WW II, and the wrecks of 96 of their boats are still at Mandalay, scuttled in the river.

There are 8000 km of navigable river in Burma, most important being the Irrawaddy, of course. Even in the dry season boats can travel from the delta all the way north to Bhamo, and in the wet they can reach Myitkyina. Other important rivers include the Twante Canal, which links the Irrawaddy to Rangoon, and the Chindwin, which joins the Irrawaddy a little above Pagan. The Salween River in the east is only navigable for about 200 km from its mouth at Moulmein.

Today the red-and-black boats of the nationalised water transport corporation are rather run down and ramshackle, but it still takes great expertise to navigate Burma's waterways. Rapidly changing sandbanks and shallow water during the dry season mean the captains and pilots have to keep in constant touch with the changing pattern of the rivers' flow. Seven pilots are used on the stretch from Mandalay to Prome, for example. Each is an expert on his own particular segment of the river.

Because of the travel restrictions and shortage of time only a few boat trips are regularly used by visitors. Best known is the Mandalay-Pagan service which departs Mandalay early morning twice weekly and arrives at Nyaung-Oo, just north of Pagan, 12 to 14 hours later. So long as you don't get stuck on a sandbank along the way, that is. There is a quite amazing amount of transport shuttling up and down this riverine 'road to Mandalay' and it's a trip which, despite the mosquitoes and discomforts, most people seem to enjoy. Other shorter trips you can make quite easily include the trip up-river from Mandalay to Mingun and the short haul across the Rangoon River to Syriam from Rangoon. You can also make short day excursions by rented boat out of Pagan.

There are other, less well-known, river trips the adventurous traveller can also consider. Twante, for example, is only a few hours from Rangoon, but you could continue all the way to Bassein, 18 hours away. You could even do Bassein as a long day-trip – an overnight trip from Rangoon, the day in Bassein, and back again overnight. From Pagan it's a further two days' travel down the river to Prome, from where you can change boats and have another couple days' travel before reaching Rangoon. Alternatively, you could take the train back to Rangoon before Prome but you will still use up a lot of your visa time on board a boat.

LOCAL TRANSPORT

Around towns in Burma there are grossly overcrowded buses, bicycle rickshaws, vintage taxis, jeeps, more modern little three-wheelers somewhat akin to auto-rickshaws, and modern Japanese pick-up trucks used like Indonesian *bemos* or Thai *songthaews*. In Pagan and Maymyo you can rent bicycles, but don't plan to bring your own bicycle to Burma with you and pedal around in seven days. The one bike rider I heard of had his wheels impounded at Rangoon airport and returned to him seven days later!

BURMA IN 7 DAYS

Seeing Burma in the seven days you are allowed can be a pretty frantic business. In fact, no matter how hard you try, it will really prove impossible to even just touch on all the main sights. For shoestring travellers unable to afford the costs of the flights, the Rangoon-Mandalay-Pagan-Rangoon loop is quite enough to manage. However you plan it, the vagaries of Burmese travel are likely to trip you up, but the following is one possible day-plan for those travelling on the cheap:

Day 1
    Arrive, book Mandalay train tickets, see Rangoon
Day 2
    Train all day to Mandalay
Day 3
    See Mandalay
Day 4
    Bus or boat to Pagan; bus may not be quite so interesting but it does give you an extra afternoon in Pagan
Day 5
    See Pagan
Day 6
    Morning in Pagan, then travel back to Rangoon by pick-up and train; takes most of the day and all night
Day 7
    Arrive Rangoon, after stop-off in Pegu if desired, see Rangoon some more
Day 8
    Depart

That is just one very straightforward way of making the most of your seven days. It would be easy to spend the whole week around Mandalay, visiting the various deserted cities and making an excursion to Maymyo. On my last trip to Burma I met one independently minded individual who spent his whole week in Rangoon and really got a feel for the place! Some possible seven-day alternatives at the shoestring price level:

Alternative 1 Leave something out. Some people leave out Mandalay to have longer in Pagan; some deluded souls actually miss out on Pagan.

Alternative 2 Backtrack from Pagan to Mandalay to avoid the Pagan-Rangoon ordeal; flying Pagan-Mandalay is quite cheap.

Alternative 3 Flying one sector can generate a whole extra day of non-travel time – if you decide to do this, the Pagan-Rangoon or Heho-Rangoon sectors are the ones to choose for maximum time and energy savings.

Alternative 4 Take the night train to Mandalay on the day you arrive in Rangoon – bring the whole schedule back by one day.

Alternative 5 Do the normal seven-day trip suggested above but in the reverse order. So many people follow the same well-worn Rangoon-Mandalay-Pagan-Rangoon circuit that doing it Rangoon-Pagan-Mandalay-Rangoon is likely to be much less crowded.

Alternative 6 Fit in Inle Lake; one way of doing this is to take a bus (really a pick-up truck) from Pagan to Inle on day 6 and fly back to Rangoon on day 7.

Alternative 7 Leave out Pagan or Mandalay in favour of Inle Lake – an alternative that is becoming increasingly popular.

If you are not financially constrained to remaining at ground level, there are more possibilities of getting around. A possible Burma loop might be:

Day 1
    Arrive, book flight to Pagan, see Rangoon
Day 2
    Fly to Pagan in the morning, see Pagan
Day 3
    See Pagan
Day 4
    Fly to Mandalay in the morning, see Mandalay
Day 5
    See Mandalay in the morning, fly to Heho in the afternoon
Day 6
    See Taunggyi and Inle Lake, fly to Rangoon in the afternoon
Day 7
    Taxi to Pegu, back to Rangoon in the afternoon
Day 8
    Depart

Alternative 1 Cut out Taunggyi and Inle Lake, substitute a jeep up to Maymyo from Mandalay and a night there.
Alternative 2 Cut out Taunggyi and Inle Lake, have longer in Mandalay and Rangoon.

Whether you are travelling by land or air, I recommend that you leave Rangoon as soon as possible after arrival. There are two reasons for this: first, apart from the Shwedagon there is not a great deal of special interest in Rangoon in comparison to Mandalay or Pagan. Second, if there should be any problems in getting back to Rangoon you have longer to sort it out.

A number of travellers have suggested that speed at the beginning is all-important if you want to make the most of your seven days, although now that Tourist Burma is open till 8 pm (it used to close at 4) it is easier to make it in time, even when arriving in Rangoon in the evening – most, if not all, flights into Rangoon from abroad arrive well before 8 pm. If you don't get to the Tourist Burma office in time (and flights are

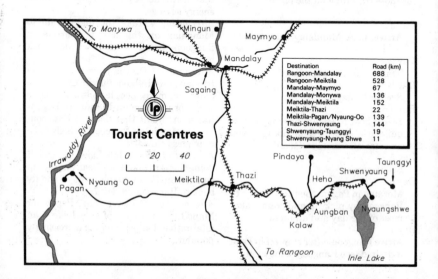

Destination	Road (km)
Rangoon-Mandalay	688
Rangoon-Meiktila	528
Mandalay-Maymyo	67
Mandalay-Monywa	136
Mandalay-Meiktila	152
Meiktila-Thazi	22
Meiktila-Pagan/Nyaung-Oo	139
Thazi-Shwenyaung	144
Shwenyaung-Taunggyi	19
Shwenyaung-Nyang Shwe	11

Tourist Centres

0   20   40

Top: The platform of the Swedagon (TW)
Left: Buddhist monk at Shwedagon (TW)
Right: Shwedagon & Elder or Naungdawgyi Pagoda (TW)

Top: Amusing scene on Shwedagon Pagoda Rd (TW)
Left: Chauk Htat Gyi in Rangoon (TW)
Right: Shwedagon statuette (TW)

sometimes late) to get on the night train to Mandalay, you may not even be able to get on the day train the next morning. Therefore it's wise to get the earliest possible flight into Rangoon, to exit the airport as quickly as possible and to go first to Tourist Burma in Rangoon before anything else.

One time-and-motion expert suggested getting a group together and appointing one person to travel sans-luggage. This person could then act as a forward scout, exit customs without delay and zip straight into town to get tickets lined up for the whole party, who would meet him or her later.

If you're flying you can try booking BAC tickets at the airport, but according to a recent letter, a new BAC policy was that flights must be booked (well, as 'booked' as you can get with BAC) by 2 pm and tickets will then be issued by 6 pm for flights the next day. This makes it impossible to book any flights for the next day on your day of arrival.

Being fast also gives you a better choice of hotel rooms in Rangoon, but my advice is not to worry too much about all this speed and efficiency. Burmese travel is notoriously unreliable, so whatever plans you make are almost bound to be comprehensively altered in any case. Only once has a trip around Burma gone exactly as I had planned, and on one occasion my neatly scheduled crack-of-dawn flight out of Bangkok ended up being delayed by seven hours.

Travel in Burma is likely to be uncertain at any time of year, but at the peak of the tourist season – the last two weeks of December – the chaos is at its peak. It's a nice time of year to be there, but people who brave Burma in the monsoon will find it much less crowded.

TOURS

Tourist Burma and BAC both operate tours in Burma, but the best 'experts' to consult outside Burma are probably Diethelm Travel in Bangkok. Their address is 544 Ploenchit Rd, Bangkok,

Thailand (tel 25 24041-9). Diethelm have regular five, six and eight-day tours to Burma costing US$670 to US$960. The tours include return fares between Bangkok and Rangoon, twin room accommodation at the better Burmese hotels (air-conditioned except in Kalaw) and all meals.

Itinerary on the five-day tour is:

Day 1
    Fly to Rangoon, afternoon free
Day 2
    Fly to Pagan, all-day tour
Day 3
    Fly to Mandalay, excursion to
    Sagaing
Day 4
    Sightseeing Mandalay, afternoon
    flight to Rangoon
Day 5
    Rangoon city tour, afternoon flight to
    Bangkok

On the six-day tour your itinerary will be:

Day 1
    Same as Day 1 of five-day tour
    above
Day 2
    Same as Day 2 five-day tour above
Day 3
    Fly to Mandalay, all-day tour
Day 4
    Fly to Heho, Inle Lake tour, overnight
    in Taunggyi
Day 5
    Local market tour in the morning, fly
    to Rangoon in the afternoon
Day 6
    Rangoon city tour; afternoon flight to
    Bangkok

And on the eight-day tour:

Day 1
    Same as Day 1 of tours above

Day 2
   All-day sightseeing tour of Rangoon
Day 3
   Fly to Pagan, all-day tour
Day 4
   More Pagan sightseeing, fly to
   Mandalay, Sagaing excursion, over-
   night in Mandalay
Day 5
   Mandalay tour, fly to Heho, Inle Lake
   tour, overnight in Taunggyi
Day 6
   Excursion to Pindaya Caves, overnight
   in Kalaw
Day 7
   Market tour, flight to Rangoon
Day 8
   Morning free, afternoon flight to
   Bangkok

Tourist Burma also does similar four and
seven-day tours.

It's a wise idea to book a room in Rangoon
for your return before heading 'up-
country'. Burma's occasional room
shortage is a circulating one – on a busy
day (when Thai International and BAC
both have flights into Rangoon during the
peak season, for example) the Rangoon
hotels can suddenly pack out – from the
YMCA right up to the Strand. Next day
people will disperse around the country
and the crush will disappear. But seven
days later! Travel as lightly as possible
out of Rangoon – most hotels will be quite
happy to look after your gear while you're
away, although some (like the Garden
Guest House) may make a small daily
storage charge.

TRAVELLING 'OFF-LIMITS'

You have to differentiate between what is
really 'off-limits' and what is only
vaguely so. Certain areas, mainly due to
the government's tenuous control there,
are totally forbidden, but others are
actually quite open – although you will
certainly not be encouraged to go there,
and perhaps you'll even be vaguely
discouraged. The discouragement is
usually through an official unavailability
of transport. This particularly applies to
places you have to fly to – since you have
to buy airline tickets officially, it's easy
for the government to prevent you from
flying there.

On the other hand, this discouragement
can easily be circumvented with rail
travel and exceedingly easily circumvented by road. Officially you are
supposed to buy rail tickets through
Tourist Burma, and certainly on the main
Rangoon-Mandalay line you'd have
trouble getting a ticket any other way.
But on lesser routes you should have no
trouble either buying a ticket yourself or
getting a friendly Burmese to buy tickets
for you.

For bus and boat travel, again apart
from major tourist routes like Mandalay-
Pagan, you generally have to get tickets
yourself in any case. So if you want to
travel to places which are only vaguely
off-limits – like Prome, Bassein, Moulmein,
Toungoo, Sandoway or the Kyaiktiyo
Pagoda – it's simply a matter of getting
out there and finding your own way.
Don't ask Tourist Burma first, they'll
only say no!

Rangoon

The capital of Burma is a comparatively young city – it only became the capital in 1885 when the British completed the conquest of upper Burma and Mandalay's brief period as the centre of the last Burmese kingdom ended. Rangoon lies in the fertile delta country of south Burma, on the wide Rangoon River about 30 km from the sea. Its population is a bit over three million, but it is a very different city than other Asian capitals of similar size.

Rangoon is easy-going to an extreme; the word 'rush' simply doesn't exist. There's none of the frenetic, neon-lit clamour of Bangkok to the east, nor the crowded squalor of Calcutta to the west. Surprisingly, Rangoon is also a very attractive city – if you can close your eyes to the neglect, the lack of upkeep, the decay, you'll probably agree that this could be one of the most charming cities in the east. The streets are wide and carefully laid out on a properly British colonial grid system. Many are tree lined and shady – you can almost picture pavement cafés along them. The architecture is of a piece; Rangoon is devoid of skyscrapers and other indications of the pace of modern life. The buildings are just as the British built them and left them. Most of them probably haven't even seen a fresh coat of paint since the colonial era closed. Probably the most annoying physical attribute of Rangoon is its torn and buckled sidewalks – it's hard to take in the sights when you have to keep your eyes on the ground in front of you to avoid a pedestrian accident.

Although Rangoon can be enjoyable and pleasant, once you've learned to look beyond the pervasive air of neglect it's definitely not Burma, and with your limited stay in mind you should depart the city as quickly as possible. Get up-country to the real Burma and leave Rangoon for the tail end of your stay. If you spend too long in Rangoon at the start of your visit you can easily find yourself running short of time when up-country.

Despite its short history as an important city, Rangoon has been in existence for a long time – although very much as a small town in comparison to places like Pegu, Thaton or Prome. In 1755 King Alaungpaya conquered lower Burma and built a new city on the site of Rangoon – which at that time was known as Dagon. Rangoon, or more correctly Yangon, means 'end of strife' – the king rather vainly hoped that with the conquest of lower Burma his struggles would be over.

In 1756, with the destruction of Syriam across the river, Rangoon also became an important sea port. In 1841 the city was virtually destroyed by fire; the rebuilt town again suffered extensive damage during the second Anglo-Burmese war in 1852. The British, its new masters, rebuilt the city to its present plan.

Rangoon's early history as Dagon is tied very closely to its beautiful monument, the Shwedagon Pagoda. It stands not in the city centre, but about three km to the north – despite which it totally dominates Rangoon.

Orientation

Rangoon is a relatively simple city to find your way around; the centre is quite compact and pleasant to explore on foot. The city is bounded to the south and west by the Rangoon River and to the east by Pazundaung Creek, which flows into the Rangoon River. The main streets in the centre are laid out in a grid system, with the minor north-south streets numbered in the American fashion. Many of the major streets were renamed after independence, but some of the old names persist and cause confusion. Pansodan St, for example, is still often called Phayre St

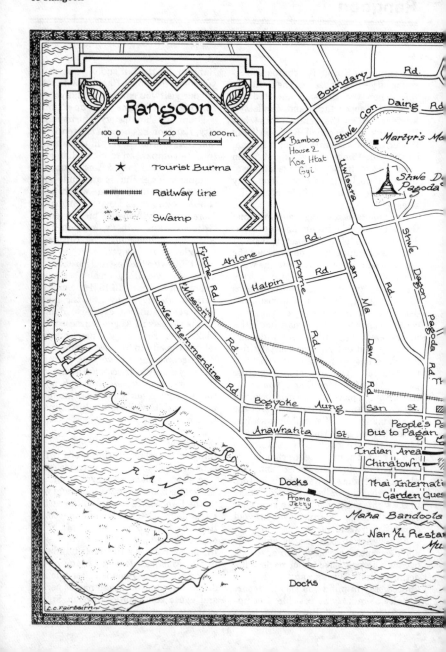

Rangoon

100 0   500   1000m.

★   Tourist Burma

▨▨▨▨▨   Railway line

Swamp

Boundary Rd.

Shwe Gon Daing Rd.

Bamboo House 2
Koe Htat Gyi

Martyr's Mo

Uwisara

Shwe D
Pagoda

Shwe Dagon Pagoda Rd.

Rd.

Ahlone

Fytche Rd.

Mission Rd.

Halpin

Prome Rd.

Lan Ma Daw Rd.

Rd.

Lower Kemmendine Rd.

Bogyoke Aung San St.

Anawrahta St.

People's Pa
Bus to Pagan

Indian Area
Chinatown

Thai Internati
Garden Gues

Maha Bandoola

Nan Yu Resta
Mu

R A N G O O N

Docks

Prome Jetty

Docks

C.C. Fairbairn

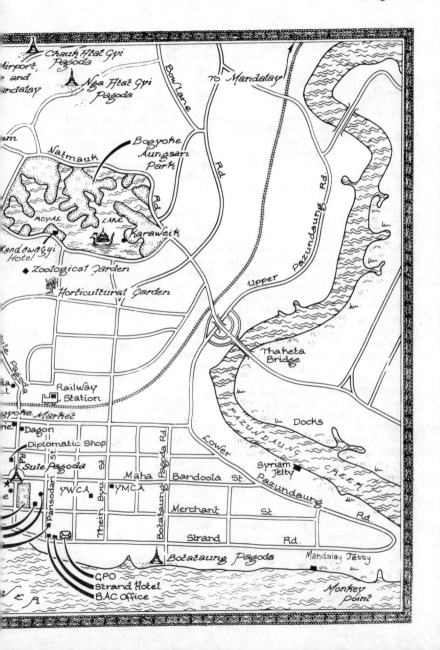

and has both new and old street signs. Other old and new central city names include:

Sparks St	now Bo Aung Gyaw St
China St	now Shwedagon Pagoda Rd
Latter St	now Latha St
Godwin Rd	now Lammadaw Rd
Dalhousie St	now Maha Bandoola St
Bigandet/ Fraser St	now Anawrahta St
Montgomery St	now Bogyoke Aung San St

Information

The centre of Rangoon is the Sule Pagoda, and for visitors that is also the centre of their Burma travels since the Tourist Burma office is right beside it. The BAC office is by the Strand Hotel, but foreign visitors are supposed to book flights through Tourist Burma. Thai International is by Tourist Burma, while Bangladesh Biman is at 106 Phayre (Pansodan) St. Most airline offices are closed Saturday afternoons and all day Sunday – bear this in mind for making reconfirmations.

The GPO is a short stroll east of the Strand Hotel on Strand Rd. Good bookshops in Rangoon include the Pagan Bookshop on 37th St and the many bookstalls around Scott Market, Bogyoke Market or along 37th St. See the introductory section on books and bookshops for more details. Good shopping places include the various markets and the entrances to the Shwedagon, particularly the east stairway. The Bogyoke Market is particularly good for crafts of all types – one visitor suggested Bonton at 149-150 Central Arcade in the market for lacquerware. Or have a look in Burma Handicrafts at 180 Sule Pagoda Rd. The Diplomatic Store is worth visiting; it's open 9.30 am to 4.30 pm daily but closed on Sundays and Mondays. Similar 'foreign currency only' goods can be bought at Tourist Burma outlets at the Inya Lake Hotel or the Strand. A couple of interesting galleries with pictures for sale are the Lovin Couple (YT) Gallery on Bahan Lane opposite the Royal Lake and the Za Bu Nyunt Gallery at 67 43rd St.

If you want medical attention in Rangoon try the Diplomatic Hospital, Kandawgyi Clinic near the Royal Lake. The Indigenous Burmese Massage House at the corner of Merchant St and Shwedagon Pagoda Rd, on the 1st floor, can be an interesting experience. Fear not, it's nothing like Bangkok massages.

Consulates & Embassies Rangoon is quite a popular place for collecting visas – because your stay is short some of the embassies co-operate by issuing visas very quickly. Plus the peculiarities of Burma's exchange rates make some of the visas surprisingly cheap. You could try here for Nepalese visas, for example. Some relevant embassies include:

Australia
   88 Strand Rd, Rangoon (tel 15711, 15076 & 15965)
Bangladesh
   340 Prome Rd, Rangoon (tel 23818 & 32900)
Germany (West)
   32 Natmauk St, Rangoon (tel 50477 & 50603)
India
   545-547 Merchant St, Rangoon (tel 15933, 16381 & 16383)
Indonesia
   100 Pyidaungsu Yeiktha Rd, Rangoon (tel 11714 & 11362)
Malaysia
   65 Windsor Rd, Rangoon (tel 31031 & 31677)
Nepal
   16 Natmauk Yeiktha, Rangoon (tel 50633)
Sri Lanka
   34 Fraser Rd, Rangoon (tel 12066)
Sweden
   48A Komin Kochin Rd, Rangoon (tel 50011)
Thailand
   91 Prome Rd, Rangoon (tel 12471 & 16555)

UK
　80 Strand Rd, Rangoon (tel 15700/1, 15138, 15812, 15616 & 12292)
USA
　581 Merchant St, Rangoon (tel 18055)

Shwedagon Pagoda

As the setting sun casts its last rays on the soft orange dome of the great Shwedagon Pagoda you can feel the magic in the air. In the heat of the day the pagoda glitters bright gold. It can be quiet and contemplative; colourful and raucous. The 'Golden Dagon' is the essence of Burma and a place that never fails to enchant.

The great golden dome rises 98 metres (326 feet) above its base. According to legends the pagoda is 2500 years old but, in common with many other ancient pagodas in earthquake-prone Burma, it has been rebuilt many times and its current form dates back only to 1769.

The legend of the Shwedagon tells of two merchant brothers meeting the Buddha, who gave them eight of his hairs to take back to be enshrined in Burma. With the help of a number of spirit *nats* the brothers and the king of this region of Burma discovered the hill where relics of the previous Buddhas had been enshrined. When the chamber to house the hairs was built and the hairs were taken from their golden casket some quite amazing events took place:

... there was a tumult among men and spirits ... rays emitted by the Hairs penetrated up to the heavens above and down to hell ... the blind beheld objects ... the deaf heard sounds ... the dumb spoke distinctly ... the earth quaked ... the winds of the ocean blew ... Mount Meru shook ... lightning flashed ... gems rained down until they were knee deep ... all trees of the Himalayas, though not in season, bore blossoms and fruit.

Fortunately hairs of the Buddhas are not unveiled every day.

Once the relics were safely enshrined, a golden slab was laid on their chamber and a golden pagoda built on it. Over this a silver pagoda was built, then a tin pagoda, a copper pagoda, a lead pagoda, a marble pagoda and finally an iron-brick pagoda. Or so the legend goes. Later, the legend continues, the pagoda at Dagon fell into disuse and it is said the great Indian Buddhist-emperor Ashoka came to Burma and found the site only with great difficulty, but subsequently had the encroaching jungle cleared and the pagoda repaired.

During the Pagan period the story of the pagoda emerges from the mists of legend and becomes hard fact. Near the top of the eastern stairway you can see an inscription recording the history of the pagoda up to 1485. King Anawrahta visited the Dagon from his capital at Pagan in the 11th century, while King Byinnya U, during his reign at Pegu (1353-1385), had the pagoda rebuilt to a height of 18 metres (60 feet). Succeeding kings alternately neglected, then improved the pagoda. During the 15th century it was rebuilt several times, eventually reaching 90 metres (302 feet), not far short of its present height.

During this period the tradition of gilding the pagoda also began – Queen Shinsawbu, who was responsible for many improvements to the pagoda, provided her own weight (40 kg or 90 lb) in gold, which was beaten into gold leaf and used to gild the structure. Her son-in-law, Dhammazedi, went several better by offering four times his own weight and that of his wife's in gold. He also provided the 1485 historical inscription on the eastern stairway.

In 1586 the English visitor Ralph Fitch made probably the best early European description of the great pagoda:

... it is called Dogonne, and is of a wonderful bignesse, and all gilded from the foot to the toppe ... it is the fairest place, as I suppose, that is in the world; it standeth very high, and there are foure wayes to it, which all along are set with trees of fruits, such wise that a man may goe in the shade above two miles in length

The pagoda suffered from a series of earthquakes that caused great damage during this time. In 1612 De Brito raided the pagoda from his base in Syriam and carried away Dhammazedi's great bell, with the intention of melting it down for cannons. As the British were to do later, with another bell, he managed to drop it into the river. During the 17th century the pagoda suffered earthquake damage on eight occasions. Worse was to follow in 1768, when a quake brought down the whole top of the pagoda. King Hsinbyushin had it rebuilt to virtually its present height, and its current configuration dates from that rebuild.

British troops occupied the pagoda for two years after the First Anglo-Burmese War in 1824. In 1852, during the Second Anglo-Burmese War, the British again took the pagoda, the soldiers pillaged it once more and it remained under military control for 77 years until 1929. In 1871 a new *hti*, provided by King Mindon from Mandalay, caused considerable head-scratching for the British, who were not at all keen for such an association to be made with the still independent part of Burma.

During this century the pagoda was the scene for much political activity during the Burmese independence movement and also suffered from a serious fire in 1931. It started at the bottom of the western stairway, which had been reopened to the public for less than two years after the British military occupation which had closed that entrance off. The fire rushed up the stairway and right round the northern side of the pagoda before being halted half way down the eastern stairway. The huge earthquake of 1930, which totally destroyed the Shwemawdaw in Pegu, only caused minor damage to the Shwedagon. After another minor earthquake in 1970 the pagoda was clad in bamboo scaffolding up beyond King Mindon's 100-year-old *hti*, and was refurbished.

There are four covered walkways up Singuttara Hill to the platform on which the Shwedagon stands. The southern entrance, from Pagoda Rd, is the one which can most properly be called the 'main' entrance. Here and at the northern entrance there are lifts available (10p) should you not feel fit enough for the stroll

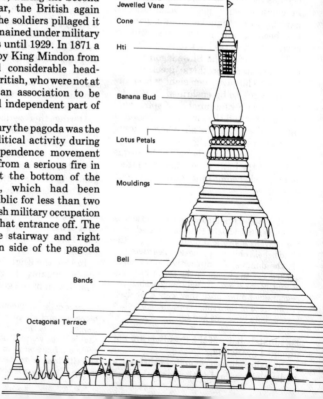

Diamond Orb
Jewelled Vane
Cone
Hti
Banana Bud
Lotus Petals
Mouldings
Bell
Bands
Octagonal Terrace

up the stairs. Two nine-metre-high (30 feet) chinthes, the legendary half lion, half griffin 'leogryphs', guard the southern entrance. You must remove your shoes and socks as soon as you mount the first step. A camera permit for the Shwedagon now costs K5, but you have to hunt them out to pay it and the fee is not usually enforced.

Like the other entranceways, the southern steps are lined with a whole series of shops. Here devotees can buy flowers, both real and beautifully made paper ones, for offerings. Or paper ceremonial umbrellas, Buddha images, golden thrones, ivory combs, books, antiques, incense sticks – they are all on sale. However hot it may be outside, you'll find the walkway cool, shady and calm. It's this quiet, subdued atmosphere on the entrance steps which makes the impact so great as you arrive at the platform. You emerge from semi-gloom into a visual cacophony of technicoloured glitter – for the Shwedagon is not just one huge, glowing pagoda. Around the mighty stupa cluster an incredible assortment of smaller pagodas, statues, temples, images, *tazaungs* and shrines. Somehow the bright gold of the main pagoda makes everything else also seem brighter and larger than life.

Pagodas, indeed all Buddhist structures, should properly be walked around clockwise, so at the top of the steps turn left, and like the crowds of Burmese start strolling. During the heat of the day you'll probably have to confine yourself to the mat pathway laid around the platform – unless your bare feet can take the heat of the uncovered marble paving.

The hill on which the pagoda stands is 58 metres (190 feet) above sea level and the platform is 5.6 hectares (14 acres) in area. Prior to the British takeover of lower Burma there had been Burmese defensive earthworks around the pagoda, but these were considerably extended by the British and their cannon emplacements can still be seen outside the outer wall.

The Shwedagon, which is completely solid, rises from its platform in a fairly standard pattern. First there is the plinth which stands 6.4 metres (21 feet) above the clutter of the main platform and immediately sets the Shwedagon above the lesser structures. Smaller pagodas sit on this raised platform level – four large ones mark the four cardinal directions, four medium-sized ones the four corners of the basically square platform and 60 small ones run around the perimeter.

From this base the pagoda rises first in three terraces, then in the 'octagonal' terraces and then in five circular bands – together these elements add another 30 metres (112 feet) to the pagoda's height. This is a normal solution to a standard architectural problem associated with pagodas – how to change from the square base to the circular upper elements. Here, as in many other pagodas, that transition is achieved with the help of the octagonal sections, which make a step between the square and the circle. Similarly, the circular bands make a transition from the horizontal design of these lower elements to the smooth vertical flow of the bell.

Earlier pagodas were commonly hemispherical; a good example in Burma is the Kaunghmudaw at Sagaing near Mandalay. The more graceful bell design, as seen here, is a comparatively recent development. The shoulder of the bell is decorated with 16 'flowers'. The bell is topped by the 'inverted bowl', another traditional element of pagoda architecture, and above this stand the mouldings and then the 'lotus petals'. These consist of a band of down-turned lotus petals followed by a band of up-turned petals.

The banana bud is the final element of the pagoda before the *hti* that tops it. Like the lotus petals below, the banana bud is actually covered with no less than 13,153 foot-square plates of gold – unlike the lower elements which are merely covered with gold leaf. The seven-tiered *hti* is made of iron and again plated with gold. Even without the various hanging bells it weighs well over a tonne. The seven tiers taper progressively and from the uppermost tier projects the shaft on which are hung gold bells, silver bells and various items of jewellery. The topmost vane with its flag turns with the wind. It is gold and silver plated and studded with 1100 diamonds totalling 278 carats – not to mention 1383 other stones. Finally, at the very top of the vane rests the diamond orb – a hollow golden sphere studded with no less than 4351 diamonds weighing 1800 carats in all. The very top of the orb is tipped with a single 76-carat diamond.

Around the Pagoda The mighty pagoda is only one of many structures on the hilltop platform. Reaching the platform from the southern stairway (1), you encounter the first shrine (2), which is to Konagamana, the second Buddha. Almost beside the shrine stands the planetary post for Mercury (3). If you were born on a Wednesday morning then this is your post and the elephant is your animal sign. Continuing around the plinth, you pass a double-bodied lion with a man's face, a laughing necromancer with his hands on his head and an earth goddess. At the south-west corner of the plinth you reach the planetary post for Saturn (4). Come here if you were born on a Saturday; your animal sign is the dragon. The pavilion (5) directly opposite has 28 images to represent the 28 'avatars' or previous incarnations of the Buddha.

Back towards the corner of the platform is a monument (6) with inscriptions in four languages, recounting a 1920 student revolt against British rule. Continuing around the platform, you come to a glass case with two figures of *nats* (7) – one is of the guardian *nat* of the pagoda. Close to these figures is a prayer pavilion (8), bare inside, but with fine wood-carving on the terraced roof. It is known as the Arakanese Pavilion since it was donated by brokers from the Arakan coast bordering Bangladesh. An eight-metre-long reclining Buddha can be seen in the next prayer hall (9). Next to this is the Chinese Merchants' *Tazaung* (10)

1	Southern stairway landing	17	Maha Gandha Bell	34	King Tharrawaddy's bell
2	Konagamana adoration hall	18	Wish fulfilling place	35	Pavilion with wood carvings
3	Planetary post for Mercury	19	Large pavilion	36	Planetary post for the Sun
4	Planetary post for Saturn	20	'Wonder working' image	37	Shan umbrellas
5	Prayer pavilion	21	North-west corner	38	East or Kakusandha adoration hall
6	Student monument	22	Chinese prayer hall	39	Eastern stairway landing
7	Guardian nat	23	Prayer hall with Indian figures	40	U Nyo pavilion
8	Arakanese pavilion	24	Northern stairway landing	41	Hintha prayer post
9	Prayer hall with reclining Buddha	25	Pavilion where *hti* was placed	42	Interesting bell
10	Chinese Merchants' Tazaung	26	Hair relics well	43	Bo tree
11	Mai Lamu & the king of the nats	27	Gautama adoration hall	44	Pagoda trustees' office
12	West of Kassapa adoration hall	28	Maha Bodhi-style pagoda	45	Curio museum
13	'Two pice' Tazaung	29	Small golden pagoda	46	Pavilion with wood carvings
14	Low pavilion	30	'Two pice' pavilion	47	Stairs to pagoda plinth
15	Pavilion with tall columns	31	Izza-Gawna pavilion	48	Tawa-gu 'wonder working' image
16	'Eight Day Pagoda'	32	Elder or Naungdawgyi Pagoda		
		33	Dhammazedi inscription		

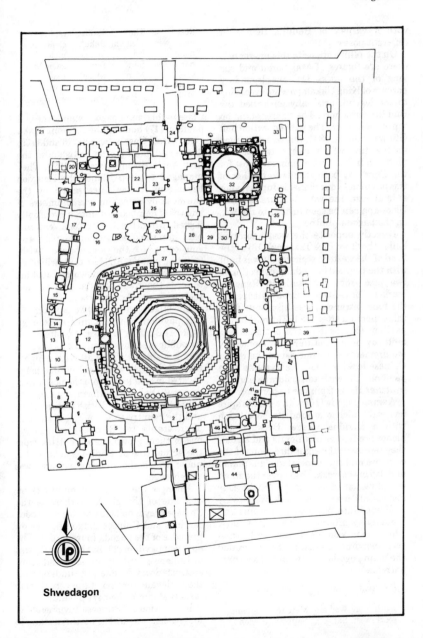

Shwedagon

with a variety of Buddha figures in different poses.

On the plinth opposite this prayer hall there are figures of Mai Lamu and the king of the *nats* (11), the legendary parents of King Ukkalapa who, according to the legend, originally enshrined the Buddha hairs here. The figures stand on top of each other. The west adoration hall (12) was built in 1841, but was destroyed in the fire which swept the pagoda platform in 1931. The planetary post for the Thursday-born stands to the left of this pavilion – your planet is Jupiter, your animal sign the rat. A figure of King Ukkalapa can be seen further to the left, on the pagoda plinth.

Directly opposite the west adoration hall is the 'Two Pice Tazaung' (13) at the head of the western stairway. It was built with the proceeds of a daily collection of two pice from the stalls in Rangoon market. The western stairway, steepest of the four entrances, was also built from this collection after the 1931 fire. The low pavilion (14) next to the entrance was built by manufacturers of monastery requirements – in contrast to the rather Chinese-looking roof. Next round is a pavilion (15) with tall columns and the *pyatthat* rising from the upper roof.

A small pagoda (16) with a golden spire has eight niches around its base, each with a Buddha image. Between the niches are figures of animals and birds – they represent the eight directions of the compass and the associated sign, planet and day of the week. To get over the small complication of having an 'Eight Day Pagoda' and a seven-day week, Wednesday is divided into Wednesday morning and Wednesday afternoon. The eight days, which can also be found with their corresponding planetary posts around the main pagoda, are (from the southern entrance):

Direction	Day	Planet	Sign
south	Wed am	Mercury	elephant
south-west	Sat	Saturn	dragon
west	Thu	Jupiter	rat
north-west	Wed pm	Rahu*	elephant
north	Fri	Venus	mole
north-east	Sun	Sun	galon bird
east	Mon	Moon	tiger
south-east	Tue	Mars	lion

*Rahu is the 'planet' that causes eclipses.

Close to this small pagoda stands the bell pavilion (17) housing the 23-tonne Maha Ganda Bell. Cast between 1775 and 1779, it was carted off by the British after the first Anglo-Burmese war in 1825. They managed to drop it into the Rangoon River and it was later raised by the Burmese by attaching vast numbers of lengths of bamboo to it until it eventually floated up from the river-bottom. Venturing back into the open area of the platform, you come to the star-shaped 'wish-fulfilling place' (18). Here there will often be devotees, kneeling down and looking towards the great pagoda, praying that their wishes will come true.

The large pavilion (19) across from the bell pavilion houses a nine-metre-high (30 feet) Buddha image and is often used for public meetings. Behind this pavilion stands a small shrine (20) with a highly revered 'wonder-working' Buddha image covered in gold leaf. From the north-west corner (21) of the platform you can look out over some of the British fortifications and the country to the north of the hill. There are also two Bo trees growing here, one of them grown from a cutting from the actual tree at Bodh Gaya in India, under which the Buddha sat and was enlightened.

Amongst the cluster of buildings on this side of the platform there is the Chinese prayer hall (22), with good wood-carvings and Chinese dragon figures on the sides of the pagoda in front of it. The adjacent pavilion (23) has life-size figures of Indians guarding the side and front entrance doors. No one quite understands their relevance or that of the very British lions that guard the next pavilion.

In 1824 a force of Burmese 'Invulnerables' fought their way up the northern stairs to the entrance (24) of the platform before being repulsed by the better-armed British forces occupying the pagoda. The crocodile-like stair bannister dates from 1460. The Martyrs' Mausoleum of Bogyoke Aung San and his compatriots stands on the western side of the hill reached from this stairway.

Walking back towards the pagoda, you pass the pavilion (25) built on the site where the great pagoda's *hti*, provided by King Mindon, was placed before being raised to the pagoda summit. The Hair Relics Well was located at the position of the Sandawdwin *Tazaung* (26) and is said to reach right down to the level of the Irrawaddy River and to be fed from it; the Buddha hairs were washed in this well before being enshrined in the pagoda. In the northern adoration hall (27) the main image is of Gautama, the fourth Buddha.

Modelled after the Mahabodhi temple in Varanasi, India, the temple (28) a few steps away is distinctively different from the general style of buildings on the platform. A small gilded pagoda (29) stands next to this temple, and next again is another 'two-pice' pavilion (30) enshrining a 200-year-old Buddha image. An opening behind this image is, according to legend, the entrance to a passage which leads to the chamber housing the Buddha hair relics. Although seen from the 'two-pice' pavilion, the image is actually in the adjacent pagoda.

Izza-Gawna (the name means Goat-Bullock) was a legendary monk whose powers enabled him to replace his lost eyes with one from a goat and one from a bullock. In his pavilion (31) the figure off to the left of the main Buddha image has eyes of unequal size as a reminder of this unique feat. The golden Elder Pagoda (32) is built on the spot where the hair relics were first placed before being enshrined in the great pagoda. A straight line drawn from the centre of this pagoda to the centre of the Shwedagon would pass through the small pagoda reputed to

be the entrance to the passage to the relic chamber. Women are not allowed to ascend to the platform around the Elder Pagoda, which is also known as the Naungdawgyi Pagoda.

Back in the corner of the platform is the Dhammazedi inscription (33), which dates from 1485 and was originally installed on the eastern stairway. It tells in three languages – Pali, Mon and Burmese – the story of the Shwedagon.

Cast in 1841, King Tharawaddy's bell is housed in an elegant pavilion (34). The Maha Titthadaganda or 'three-toned bell' weighs 42 tons. Note the cherubs floating around the ceiling. The adjacent small pavilion (35) has some good panels of wood-carvings. Back on the main platform the planetary post (36) for those born on Sunday stands at the north-east corner of the pagoda platform. Further round you will see golden Shan umbrellas (37) amongst the plinth shrines; there is also one over the Friday planetary post by the north pavilion.

Facing the eastern stairway, the east shrine hall (38) is said to be the most beautiful on the platform. It was renovated in 1869 but destroyed by the 1931 fire and subsequently rebuilt. The main image is that of Kakusandha, the first Buddha. The eastern stairway (39) is the longest and is lined with shops selling everyday articles as well as religious goods and antiques.

The graceful pavilion (40) beside the eastern entrance has a series of interesting wood-carved panels illustrating events in the life of Gautama Buddha. The prayer post (41) close to the south-east corner of the pagoda is topped by a mythological Hintha bird. An interesting bell (42) hangs near this prayer post.

In the corner of the platform stands another sacred Bo tree (43), also said to be grown from a branch of the original tree under which Gautama Buddha gained enlightenment in India. There is a good view from this corner of the platform over Rangoon and across the Rangoon River towards Syriam. You can, on a clear day, see the Kyaik-khauk Pagoda just beyond Syriam. The pagoda trustees have their office (44) on this side of the platform, and there's also a small curio museum (45). In front of the museum is a pavilion (46) with very fine wood-carvings. There is also a revolving *hti* and a telescope, possibly for looking at the real one on top of the pagoda.

Beside the southern shrine (2), the first stop on this circular tour, stairs (47) lead up onto the pagoda plinth. With permission from the pagoda trustees, men only are allowed to climb up to the plinth terrace. Men come up here to meditate; the terrace is about six metres wide – a circular walkway between the great pagoda and its 68 surrounding pagodas. There's a K5 fee for entering the terrace. Behind the eastern shrine there is a Buddha image (48) known as the Tawagu, which is reputed to work wonders.

Visiting the Shwedagon is far more than just wandering around and looking at the shrines, pavilions, images, bells and pagodas. It's a place you feel as much as see. There's a quite amazing atmosphere here – sometimes serene, sometimes exciting, but always enjoyable.

It's been said that a visit to Burma is incomplete without a visit to the Shwedagon, but I think that is quite incorrect. One visit is simply not enough – at the very least you should try to savour the difference in mood between the heat of the day and that electrifying period as the sun sets and the pagoda shifts from its daytime to nighttime character. It's definitely one of my 'wonders of the world', yet surprisingly my most lasting impression of the Shwedagon is of a moment when I was not even in Burma. From far above, in an aircraft flying from Bangkok to Kathmandu, I spotted a tiny golden dot, glittering miles below – magic!

Sule Pagoda

Situated in the centre of Rangoon – beside the Tourist Burma office – the Sule Pagoda is an excellent landmark. It is said to be over 2000 years old but, as with many other ancient Burmese shrines, it has been rebuilt and repaired many times over the centuries. The pagoda is said to enshrine a hair of the Buddha; its Mon name, Kyaik Athok, translates as 'the pagoda where a Sacred Hair Relic is enshrined'.

The golden pagoda is unusual in that its octagonal shape continues right up to the bell and inverted bowl. It stands 46 metres (152 feet) high and is surrounded by small shops and all the familiar non-religious activities which seem to be a part of every Burmese pagoda.

Botataung Pagoda

Bo means leader (usually in a military sense) and *tataung* is 1000 – the Botataung Pagoda was named after the 1000 military leaders who escorted relics of the Buddha brought from India over 2000 years ago. This ancient monument was completely destroyed during WW II. It stood close to the Rangoon wharves, and during an Allied air raid on 8 November 1943, a bomb scored a direct hit on the unfortunate pagoda.

After the war the Botataung was rebuilt in a very similar style to its predecessor, but with one important and unusual difference: Unlike most pagodas, which are solid, the Botataung is hollow and you can walk through it. There's a sort of mirrored maze inside the pagoda, with glass show cases containing many of the ancient relics and artefacts which were sealed inside the earlier pagoda. Above this interesting interior the golden pagoda spire rises to 40 metres (132 feet).

National Museum

Located on Pansodan (Phayre) St, close to the Strand Hotel, the building used to be the Bank of India premises. Inside, the pride of place goes to the eight-metre-high (27 feet) Lion Throne used by King Thibaw, the last Burmese king. It was taken from the Mandalay Supreme Court, outside the Mandalay Palace complex, after the British takeover. Thus it survived the destruction of the palace during WW II and after independence was returned to Burma from the Indian Museum in Calcutta. The carving on the throne depicts the Lokanat or 'World Preserver' legend from Burmese mythology, in which a battling lion and elephant cease fighting when a singing and dancing deva arrives on the scene.

Other exhibits include the Mandalay Regalia, a collection of gem-studded arms, swords, jewellery, bowls and other items. This too was taken by the British after the third Anglo-Burmese war, and was returned to Burma in 1964 from the Victoria & Albert Museum in London. The museum also contains King Mindon's queen's royal couch, a bronze cannon dating from 1757, the crocodile harp and other items, very few of which are labelled in English. The old photos of Mandalay Palace and Rangoon are interesting, but everything else is second best after the huge and intricately carved Lion Throne.

Note that the museum has a 2nd and 3rd floor which are very easy to miss. At one time you had to leave the main throne room on the ground floor, go out on to the street and re-enter the museum next door! There is now access from the ground floor, but you have to look for it. The only sign for the upstairs is in Burmese, and you have to first of all make your way through an empty room, round the lift shaft and climb some dingy stairs! Upstairs you'll find prehistoric and other early Burmese finds as well as traditional musical instruments. There are lots of English signs, though the excellent maps are mostly in Burmese. On the top floor there are modern Burmese paintings by the talented U Ba Nyan and others.

Admission is K1 and the museum is open from 10 am to 3.30 pm Tuesdays through Sundays. It is closed on Mondays and on 'government gazetted holidays'.

Just to the north of the museum, on the opposite side of the street, there's a gallery with modern, western-style paintings by Burmese artists. They're quite interesting and reasonably priced.

Kaba Aye Pagoda

The 'world peace' pagoda was built in 1952 for the 1954-56 Sixth Buddhist Synod. The 34-metre-high (111 feet) pagoda also measures 34 metres around its base. It stands about 11 km north of the city, a little beyond the Inya Lake Hotel. This attempt to construct a 'modern' pagoda was not terribly successful – it does not have much of the visual appeal of Burma's older, more graceful pagodas.

Maha Pasan Guha

The 'great cave' is a totally artificial one built close to the Kaba Aye Pagoda. It was here that the Sixth Buddhist Synod was held to coincide with the 2500th anniversary of the Buddha's enlightenment. The participants at the Synod were attempting to define a definitive text for the Buddhist scriptures known as the *Tripitaka*. The cavern measures 139 by 113 metres (455 by 370 feet).

Chauk Htat Gyi Pagoda

The reclining Buddha image here is even larger than the enormous figure in Pegu. The pagoda is on Shwegondine Rd, only a short distance beyond the Shwedagon Pagoda. Surprisingly, this huge figure is little known and hardly publicised at all – if you can't get to Pegu to see the Shwethalyaung, then don't miss this colossal image.

Other Temples

On Campbell Rd, south of the Chauk Htat Gyi Pagoda, there's a huge seated Buddha image at the Nga Htat Gyi Pagoda. It's appropriately known as the five-storey Buddha and is located in the Ashay Tawya Kyaung monastery. In Kemendine, in the west of the city, there's another huge seated Buddha in the Koe Htat Gyi Pagoda on Bargayar Rd; it stands (or sits) 20 metres (65 feet) high. There are many monasteries in the vicinity. Kemendine also has a busy night market.

Close to the airport, the Mae La Mu Pagoda has a series of images of the Buddha in his previous incarnations and also a reclining Buddha image. The pagoda is named after the mother of King Ukkalapa, the original founder of the city of Dagon. West of the airport in Insein the Ah Lain Nga Sint Pagoda has a five-storey tower and a particular connection with the *nats* and other spirit entities of Burmese Buddhism.

The Yau Kyaw Pagoda is a 30-minute drive from the city past the Kyaikkasan Pagoda. It's an interesting complex of pagodas with tableaux depicting Buddhist legends, pet monkeys, deer and peacocks and an interesting museum full of Burmese antiques. The pagoda is beside the Pazandaung Creek in a rural setting.

Martyrs' Mausoleum

Close to the Shwedagon, on a hill offering a good view over the city, stands this memorial to Bogyoke Aung San and his fellow cabinet officers who were assass-inated with him. It was here that a bomb set off by North Koreans killed a number of South Korea's top government officials in late '83.

Meditation Centres

There are several centres in Rangoon for the study and practice of *satipatthana vipassana* or insight-awareness meditation, based on instructions in the Maha Satipatthana Sutta (Sutra) of the Theravada Buddhist canon. This type of meditation is also commonly practised in Sri Lanka and Thailand, though the tradition of lay practice is probably stronger in Burma. Many westerners have come to Burma to practise at the various centres for periods of time ranging from 10 days to more than a year.

The most famous centre in Rangoon is Mahasi Meditation Centre (Mahasi Thathana Yeiktha in Burmese), founded in 1947 by the late Mahasi Sayadaw, perhaps Burma's greatest meditation teacher. Currently the resident master teacher is Sayadaw U Pandita, who is also highly thought of. The centre is on Thathana Yeiktha Rd (formerly Hermitage Rd) off Kaba-Aye Pagoda Rd, north of Royal Lake, about 10 minutes from the city centre or 20 minutes from the airport. Other centres include the International Meditation Centre, founded by the late U Ba Khin, a well-known lay teacher; Mogok Meditation Centre; and Chan Mye Yeiktha Meditation Centre. Instruction at all of the above centres is given to foreigners in English.

To obtain the necessary 'special-entry visa' for a long-term stay, applicants must receive a letter of invitation from the centre where they would like to study, which may in turn require a letter of introduction from an affiliated meditation centre abroad. This invitation is then presented to a Burmese consulate or embassy that will issue a visa for an initial stay of six to 12 weeks, as recommended by the centre. This may be extended in Rangoon at the discretion of the centre and Burmese immigration. Important points to remember: The special-entry visa takes eight to 10 weeks to be issued and cannot be applied for while a person is in Burma on a tourist visa. Food and lodging are provided at no charge at the centres but meditators must follow eight precepts, which include abstaining from food after 12 noon. Daily schedules are rigorous and may involve nearly continuous practice from 3 am till 11 pm. Students may be given permission to travel in Burma at the end of a long period of study but this is not automatic. Finally, westerners who have undergone the training say it is not recommended for people with no previous meditation experience.

For further information, write to:
    Mahasi Meditation Centre
    16 Thathana Yeiktha Rd
    Rangoon

    International Meditation Centre
    31-A Inya Myaing Rd
    Rangoon

    Chan Mye Yeiktha Meditation Centre
    655-A Kaba Aye Pagoda Rd
    Rangoon

    Mogok Meditation Centre
    82 Natmauk Rd
    Rangoon

For further information on Mahasi Sayadaw, U Ba Khin and Mogok Sayadaw, read *Living Buddhist Masters* by Jack Kornfield (Shambhala, Boulder, Colorado, 1984).

Other

The Zoological Gardens on King Edward Avenue are open from 6 am to 6 pm daily and have a collection of Burmese animals and an aquarium. The zoo is huge and has an entertaining elephant, monkey and snake-charmer performance at around 2.30 pm on Sundays after the monsoon. You can ride the elephants (and camels) at 4 pm, but the last white elephant died in 1979. The old Natural History Museum by the Royal Lake has had its exhibits removed to the Zoological Gardens and the building has been turned into a hotel.

The Royal Lakes are close to the city centre and are at their most attractive at sunset, when the glittering Shwedagon is reflected in their calm waters. The Karaweik, a reinforced concrete reproduction of a Royal Barge, sits (it certainly doesn't float) in the Royal Lakes. Apart from being something of a local attraction in its own right, the Karaweik, the legendary bird mount of the Hindu god Vishnu (Sanskrit: Garuda), is also a restaurant – see the 'Places to Eat'

Entry ticket to the Karaweik

section. Quite good dance performances are held here in the evenings. Rangoon has other lakes – the Inya Lakes are a popular weekend relaxation spot for local people. The Inya Lake Hotel stands beside the lakes.

The Bogyoke market appropriately is on Bogyoke Aung San St. Inside you'll find a whole variety of everyday requisites and interesting Burmese souvenirs, from lacquerware to Shan shoulder bags. There are other markets around such as the iron bazaar on the corner of Maha Bandoola St and Lammadaw Rd – here you can find all the items that go into Chinese cooking. Rangoon's waterfront makes an interesting if not altogether bustling scene, either from the park in front of the Strand Hotel or round at Pazundaung Creek. If anything, the latter seems to have more activity. The Independence Monument stands in the park near the Sule Pagoda.

Rangoon isn't a place you would usually think of for tailor-made clothes, but if you want a traditional national-style Burmese shirt (for men), try Ava Tailoring on Phayre (Pansodan) St near the railway station at the Anawrahta St intersection. Prices range from K60 to K130, depending on the material chosen. If you're measured the day you arrive, they'll have it ready by the time you return from up-country seven days later. For laundering, try Ava Laundry (same owner?) at 305 Mahabandoola Rd above 42nd St, where they even do 'judo' and 'safaree' suits, as well as Burmese overcoats and *longyis*.

Places to Stay

Things do change a bit in Burma. The odd hotel gets deleted from the approved list while another gets added. And recently even some of the bottom-end places have started to quote prices in US dollars, although this doesn't mean much because you still have to pay in kyats. A 10% service charge is tagged on the top at the more expensive places, which usually means the US dollar places.

Places to Stay - bottom end

Shoestring travellers in Rangoon generally head to the *YMCA*, which is reasonably priced, has pretty good food and is reasonably tatty. It is an excellent information source, however, both from your fellow travellers and from the management. Also, the rooms are large in comparison with other budget places in the city. There are singles/doubles with common bath at K40-50/55, singles/doubles with private bath at K50/65-75, and dorm beds for K25 each. On the top floor there are somewhat dismal rooms at K40 double or K49 triple. When full, the Y will allow visitors to sleep on the stage for K15.

If you want to be certain of accommodation when you return to Rangoon at the end of your seven days, they will even make an advance reservation for you for K5 – and it works! Depending on the time of year (the cool season seems to be quite OK), mosquitoes can be horrific at the Y; mosquito nets and/or screened windows seem to come and go. They do have fans, though, and the toilets work.

If the YMCA is full, as it often is, there are a number of alternatives. Next door to the Tourist Burma office on Sule Pagoda Rd is the *Garden Guest House*. It's a more modern establishment than the Y, and when first opened was spotlessly

clean although it soon became rather grubby. It has always lacked the Y's pleasant atmosphere, and its restaurant is nothing like the Y's. When I asked what was available for breakfast one morning, the answer was 'soup'. And it closes early in the evening. The dorm has comfortable beds with mosquito nets for K22, but you'll probably need your own sleeping bag since they don't supply sheets. Rooms cost from US$3.50/6 for a fan-cooled single/double up to US$7/9.50 for an air-con single/double. The rooms are clean, but very plain – they're just little cubicles with thin walls, small, spartan and not special value. There are no rooms with private bath. You can leave bags at the Garden Guest House for K1 per day.

On our last trip the up-and-coming guest house in town was *Pyin Oo Lwin* at 183 Barr St, two blocks east of the Sule Pagoda and Tourist Burma. It was new and clean, with friendly proprietors who went out of their way to help guests and even travellers who had come to hang out in the lounge while waiting for the night train to Mandalay – allowing them to shower and drink Chinese tea, etc. Singles/doubles/triples run K33/66/99 with shared bath.

The *YWCA* is open to women only – unlike the YMCA which is open to either sex although couples are supposed to be married if they share double rooms, a quaint custom for Asia. The YWCA is at 119 Brooking St and has just two singles and two doubles. Nightly cost is K24 single (with bathroom) or K36 double (without).

The old Orient at 256/260 Sule Pagoda Rd is now named the *Dagon* and for a time was a very pleasant place to stay. In recent years, however, it seems to have gone downhill and has become somewhat dilapidated and ill kept. Rooms at the front are also very noisy. It's a shame because this was a place with a bit of character – nice views from the balcony, good food in the restaurant downstairs (upstairs from the street) and a fine place for a beer. Rooms are US$3.50/6 or US$7/9.50 for singles/doubles.

There are, of course, a number of other hotels around town but they're not on the government-approved list, even though some of them are better than some of the places which are!

Places to Stay - top end

'When in Singapore stay at the Raffles' the saying used to go. (Actually it was 'feed at the Raffles' and stay somewhere else, but never mind.) Similarly, when you are in Rangoon the place to stay is the *Strand*. During its British heyday the Strand used to be one of those glorious outposts of Empire, east of Suez. Today in its sadder Peoples' Hotel role the Strand is just a rundown shadow of its former glory - certainly no competition for the well-kept likes of the *Raffles* or the *Oriental* in Bangkok. Yet somehow the old colonial era does live on in the Strand: you will just have to imagine the potted palms today, but if it's character you are after the Strand has plenty of it.

Even the top-notch air-conditioned rooms are a long way below the standards of other Asian first-class hotels, and the facilities for some of the cheaper rooms are less than you would expect in some shoestring travellers' places elsewhere in Asia. Shut your mind to these minor drawbacks and enjoy the Strand's other advantages - its conveniently central location, its pleasant bar and lounge area, its excellent and remarkably economical restaurant, and all-round cheerful service.

Staying at the Strand is full of amusing little touches - beside the reception desk there is a glass-faced cabinet labelled 'lost and found'. Most of the articles were clearly lost half a century ago; not many ladies carry delicate little folding fans around these days. The lifts are ancient, but smoothly operating. In the three-storey central lobby is an immense mural recently completed by one of Burma's leading painters, U Ba Kyi, entitled

'Road to Mandalay'. The scene depicts a wintry London gradually fading into tropical Moulmein with its pagoda 'lookin' lazy at the sea' - the odd return of colonialist Kipling. In the restaurant, the waiters may call everybody sir, male or female. Both the bar and restaurant close at 10 pm, but a small cache of Mandalay Beer from the Peoples' Brewery is kept behind the reception desk should you wish to continue drinking. By 11 pm you are likely to be feeling pretty lonely in the lounge area, though, just the occasional Strand rat scampering across the floor to keep you company. On the last night of one Burma visit, to my utter amazement hot water came from the shower when I turned on the tap. If you want to be sure of hot water, try early in the morning.

The Strand has 100 rooms of widely varying standard. Cheapest are the fan-cooled economy rooms which do not have their own bathrooms - singles/doubles cost US$11.50/14. The 2nd-floor rooms are better than those on the 1st floor, in as much as the tatty and dilapidated 2nd-floor bathrooms are at least less tatty and dilapidated than those on the 1st floor. With air-con, prices go up to US$23/26.50. There are also rooms with private bathrooms, but still fan cooled, for US$17.50/21. All of the rooms have wash basins, and towels and soap are provided.

More modern and equally conveniently located just across the railway line from the town centre - but completely impersonal in comparison - is the *Thamada* or *President Hotel*. Singles/doubles are US$12/20 with shower, US$20/23 with bath.

The *Kandawgyi* is on the Royal Lake, round from the Karaweik Restaurant and on the way to the Shwedagon. It was originally the British Boat Club and then became the Natural History Museum. The Kandawgyi is the training centre for all Hotel & Tourist Corporation staff - if you wander round the halls you may come across classrooms where they teach 'reception' and 'waiting service'. The rooms here cost US$15/17.50 facing the road, US$17.50/21 facing the lake, and are all air-con. There are also several spacious bungalows, newly built in 1986, right on the lake next to the hotel with colour TV, air-conditioning and refrigerators, possibly the most luxurious tourist quarters in Burma at the moment. They go for US$65 per night and are favoured by diplomats and development people in town for conferences. The hotel staff and trainees are friendly and the verandah bar is a good place to sip a beer, watch the sun set and gaze across at the Karaweik. The food is also quite good by Burmese standards, with the usual Strand Hotel-type selections (you'll find similar menus in all the upper-end HTC hotels in Burma). The museum is now housed at the zoo, but they left behind a huge six-metre-high Tyrannosaurus Rex in the hotel garden, rather startling when it's illuminated at night. Although not right in the centre, the Kandawgyi isn't too inconveniently situated and is in the vicinity of some of Rangoon's top restaurants.

Just fitting into the upper bracket is the *Sakantha*, located at the railway station with an entrance on the platform. With a post-colonial atmosphere reminiscent of the Strand, this place might be considered by travellers who have to make the 6 am express to Pegu, Thazi or Mandalay, saving time and taxi/trishaw fare. Big, fairly clean rooms with balconies, some of which overlook the trainyard (well, train buffs would like it), go for US$13/15 single/double with attached bath. The bar and restaurant downstairs are quite pleasant and service is attentive. Not many people seem to know about this place – at least there were no foreigners staying here at the height of the last tourist season. Even if you're not staying here, you might enjoy the bar or restaurant while waiting for trains.

The final upper-bracket hotel is both the least convenient and probably the worst value. The huge (by Burmese standards) *Inya Lake Hotel* has 222 rooms and is about six km from the centre, on the Inya Lake. Built with Russian aid and run, in its early days, by Israelis, the Inya Lake is big, imposing, dramatic and empty. Government VIPs and tour groups, who have no choice where they stay, are the only ones who use this hotel. Singles cost US$23 to US$30, doubles US$26.50 to US$39.50, but it's uninteresting and a glance at the visitors' book showed that not all the guests were very impressed. There were a lot of complaints about cleanliness and standards, including a comment from one visitor that his room offered something he'd

1	Peking Restaurant	15	Sule Pagoda	30	Museum
2	Sakantha Hotel	16	Dagon Hotel	31	Burma Airways
3	Hotel de City	17	Shwe Mya Bakery	32	Strand Hotel
4	Moulmein Buses (Ramanya Bus)	18	Bookstalls	33	Sarpay Beikman Library
5	Prome Buses	19	Independence Monument	34	Synagogue
6	Meiktila Buses (Road & Transport Corp.)	20	US Embassy	35	Australian Embassy
		21	Great Wall Restaurant	36	British Embassy
7	Nila Briwane Shop	22	Nan Yu	37	Post Office
8	Burma Patisserie	23	Mya Sabe Cafe	38	Ruby Restaurant
9	Gold Cup Cafe	24	Indian Embassy	39	Sein Win Restaurant
10	Yatha Restaurant	25	Customs House	40	YWCA
11	Diplomatic Shop	26	Bangladesh Biman Airways	41	YMCA
12	Thai International			42	City Hall & Library
13	Tourist Burma	27	Nilarwin Cafe	43	Pyin Oo Lwin Guest House
14	Garden Guest House	28	Pagan Bookshop		
		29	Palace Restaurant		

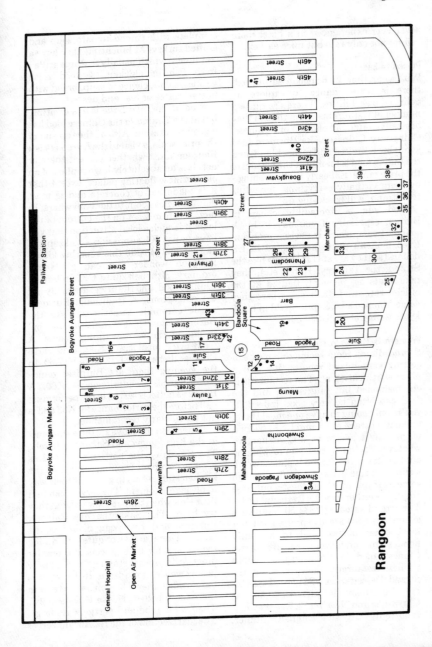

Rangoon

never ever experienced in a hotel room before: not only rats but mice as well.

Places to Eat

With your time in Rangoon so limited, there is little chance to explore its culinary possibilities. There are quite a number of restaurants, even though they basically offer a choice of Chinese, Chinese or Chinese. The Burmese food available is limited and rather bland, and the Indian food is mainly at the bottom of the price range. Eat early in the evening – by 9 pm virtually everything, including the Strand, will be closing up.

Food can be incredibly cheap in Burma, especially if you pay in black market kyats, which is never a problem. Even if menu prices are quoted in US dollars (as they are at HTC hotels like the Strand, the Taunggyi Hotel, etc), they take kyats as payment, figured at the official rate, and don't ask where they came from (so a US$3 price paid in black kyats is only about US$0.50).

Western & Hotels Although recently the *Strand* dining room seems to have been getting very mixed reports, it's still a place worth eating at. The restaurant is old fashioned but interesting, and the food can often be very good indeed. If you're only going to have one meal there, make it lobster – at around US$4.50 for a whole one it has to be a great bargain whatever exchange rate you're working on! Lobster at the Strand is almost worth a trip to Burma in its own right, although some fish fans say it's not lobster but large crayfish – either way it's fresh and tasty. The Strand's steaks (US$4.50, like nearly everything else) are also pretty good, but most other dishes tend to be fairly nondescript and you'll get far better Chinese food in Rangoon's numerous Chinese restaurants than you will at the Strand. Desserts cost US$1.50 to US$2.50, but ice cream is just US$0.50. At Christmas and New Year's Eve they now reportedly do an 'English' dinner,

complete with tinned tomato soup and stuffed turkey. At lunchtime they have a 'set lunch' which usually features grilled fresh fish or chicken, sauteed fresh veggies, salad, choice of soup, bread with butter, coffee or tea, and dessert.

Food at the *Inya Lake* is less exciting, but at the *Thamada* the Chinese food has a good reputation. Also at the top end of the price scale, a visit to the *Karaweik* is a Rangoon must whether you eat there or not. It is an absolutely huge replica of an old Burmese floating palace, except that it is made out of concrete and is most definitely not about to float anywhere. In fact, it is firmly set on the bottom of the lake. It is such a local attraction that you have to pay K1 admission – to keep the gawkers out. Inside this superbly kitsch Rangoon wonder you can get fairly ordinary, although quite OK, Indian or Chinese food; and the prices are really not too outrageous. A traditional Burmese music ensemble sometimes plays the Burmese equivalent of 'music to dine by' in one of the several dining rooms. A fixed-price meal costs K30; a la carte Chinese dishes cost K13.50 to K17.50. In the evening there are Burmese dance performances – admission is K60. A Burmese buffet is served in the performing hall before the performance for K38 and is not particularly recommended.

Better than the above are the restaurants at the *Kandawgyi* and *Sakantha* hotels. The Kandawgyi is particularly good as it's a government training centre and the kitchen staff seems to go out of their way to please customers. The service can be a little slow when they're crowded, but they try hard. The Sakantha has Chinese, Burmese and European dishes on its menu. There are two different dining rooms, one for hotel guests and one for diners/drinkers not staying there, usually people waiting for a train. If the latter is too crowded, they'll let you have a table in the room labelled 'House Guests Only'. The food is good and portions are large. The 'bar' section of the restaurant serves hard liquor only – Mandalay Gin or Mandalay Rum – if you want beer you must be served in one of the dining rooms. Meals are sometimes accompanied by someone playing the *pattala* or Burmese 'xylophone' in the foyer between dining rooms. Just outside the hotel on the railway platform is a table where you can get a very tasty boxed chicken biriyani for K12, catered by the Sakantha dining room, to take on the train.

Other more central and reasonably priced restaurants include the *Dagon's* pleasant, airy, upstairs restaurant at 256/260 Sule Pagoda Rd. Unfortunately TV has dealt this place a near mortal blow. It was always more a place for a beer than a meal, and these days the waiters (and from the quality of the food the cook too) seem more enthusiastic about watching the Dagon's TV than worrying about their customers. There's also a snack bar downstairs at street level.

The *YMCA* has a popular cafeteria with a large seating area serviced by several totally separate kitchen-counters engaged in spirited and most un-Burmese competition. Perhaps it's because the proprietors are mainly Indian! The result is a very wide choice of dishes from European to Indian and Chinese to Burmese, plus very low prices. The quality, however, is variable, and not everything is that good although few shoestring travellers complain. Meals typically cost K2 to K8.

Chinese Surprisingly, you can sample the whole range of Chinese cuisine in Rangoon – from the familiar Cantonese through the less well-known Shanghainese, Szechuan, Peking, Hokkien or Foochow dishes. One of the most popular is the *Palace* at No 84, 37th St, said by some locals to be the best restaurant in Rangoon. The food seems rather expensive at first glance, but in actual fact the servings are so generous that one dish here will be just as filling as two or three elsewhere. Count on K30 to K50 for two.

Popular specialties include sour-hot fish, which makes heavy use of garlic and costs about K25. The menu here has no prices; you have to enquire when ordering.

The *Nan Yu* at 81 Pansodan St has all the usual Cantonese specialties (including crabs' thumbs) plus specials that require 24 hours' notice – soups are particularly good here. At No 236 29th St the *Peking Hotel* is a Chinese Muslim restaurant where traditional Chinese dishes are prepared in Islamic fashion without pork. Next door to the Dagon Hotel on Sule Pagoda Rd the *Hai Khim* is basic in price but the food is quite good – try the fried prawns or sweet-and-sour fish.

Kan Bow Za at 120 Sule Pagoda Rd, close to the Sule Pagoda, is straightforward – meat dishes in the K12 to K20 range, although some cost less (such as fried rice with chicken or prawns). In properly Chinese fashion you get soup with it too. The *Great Wall* at 196 Pansodan is good; the menu features no less than 177 different items!

Sein Win at 112 Bo Aung Gyaw St, round the corner from the GPO, also has quite good Chinese food, as does the *Ruby* which is nearby at No 50 on the same street. At 147 40th St, between Mahabandoola and Merchant Sts, the *Queen Restaurant* gets very mixed reports – good food according to some, tasteless and dirty according to others.

A favourite of local residents is *Yan Kin*, an indoor/outdoor place near the Royal Lake on Shwe Gon Daing (Shwegondaing) Rd in the Bahan district. There is also a Chinese night market on Lanmadaw St around the corner from a Chinese temple.

Burmese Unfortunately the renowned *Burma Kitchen* on West Shwe Gon Daing Rd closed in 1986 when the owner died, and there are few remaining alternatives for good Burmese cuisine outside Burmese homes. The *Bamboo House* (tel 31934) is at 3 Thapye Nyo St, Shinsawpu – get there on a bus No 8 or 13 or take a taxi. There are

Chinese and Indian dishes as well as Burmese. A meal will be about K40 per person. Some dishes cost around K10 or less, lots fall between K20 and K30, and some go up to K40, K60, even K100 for shark's fin. The menu features 189 dishes, including four varieties of ducks' feet and even 'fried chicken fanny'.

'For real Burmese food', wrote a traveller, 'try the *Red Dragon* (Nagain in Burmese) at 186 33rd St'. Another suggestion is 'the nameless place at No 33, 12th St, where you can get a very filling meal for two for just K12 to K16, but although it is very clean it closes at 8 pm'. Apart from these, Burmese food in the capital of Burma is generally found at basic street stalls. The *mohinga* stall across from the Botataung market on Botataung Bazaar Rd is said by locals to serve the best *mohinga* (fish soup with rice noodles) in Rangoon.

Indian Along Anawrahta St, to the west of the Sule Pagoda, there are a number of small Indian biriyani stalls, and at night the *roti* (Indian bread) makers set up along the pavement. Indian food is probably the cheapest way of eating in Rangoon, particularly at the pavement cafés along Bo Aung Gyaw St. The biriyani, for K7, is certainly pretty good at the *Nila Briwane Shop* on Anawrahta St between 31st and 32nd. It's always crowded but the service is snappy.

At the *Coffee House Hotel* on Mahabandoola St near the Strand, the *Hotel de City* on Anawrahta St or the nameless pavement café on Shwebontha St near Mahabandoola, you can get a good meal for two for K12 to K20.

Japanese With all the Japanese aid projects going on in Rangoon, a good Japanese restaurant was bound to open up sooner or later. Just west of the defunct Burma Kitchen on Shwe Gon Daing Rd (No 16 bus) is the charming *Furusato*. You can get a *teishoku* or set dinner for K25 to K30.

Snack Bars For a cool drink or a light snack there are a number of places to consider. At 377 Mahabandoola St, about midway between the YMCA and the Sule Pagoda (between 37th and 38th St), you'll find the *Nilarwin Cold Drink Shop*. It's a clean little café where you can get yoghurt, *lassi* (a delicious Indian yoghurt drink) and milk. It's a good place for breakfast; plain lassi costs K3, with fruit K4. On the corner of Sule Pagoda Rd and Bogyoke Aung San St the *Burma Patisserie* is a cake-and-coffee place – it's also known as the Peoples' Patisserie – a wonderful idea, let them eat cake, etc. Because it is government-run, prices are lower than at many other large tea shops in town. The *Mya Sabe Café*, 71 Pansodan St (between Mahabandoola and Market Sts) is good for a drink or a cake.

In the park across the road from the Strand, and run by the Strand, is the *Nanthida*, an open-air kebab place where you can also get an open-air beer. The *Dagon* is a popular place for a cold bottle of the Peoples' Brewery's best ale. Or try the *Win Bar*, directly across the road from the Dagon, or the *Lay Nhin Tha* beside the Strand. Near the Tourist office, the *Yatha* is a white building where you can get drinks and ice cream. The friendly owner speaks excellent English.

On Sule Pagoda Rd, between Anawrahta and Bogyoke Aung San Sts, the *Gold Cup Café* is a lively and clean place for snacks and good pastries. On the other side of the road the *Shwe Mya Bakery* at 184/186 Sule Pagoda Rd does good baked goods. Finally, if you're waiting at Rangoon airport the upstairs restaurant-bar makes excellent iced tea, but keep some kyats to pay for it if you're departing.

Getting Around

Airport The standard taxi fare to and from the airport is K60 for the complete vehicle. BAC operate a bus service for their departing flights – but it departs for the airport so far ahead of time that if you have an early departure you will probably be willing to pay the extra and take a taxi. The very impecunious might find the local bus service to the airport for about a kyat. Coming from the airport, you have to get out to the main road, a couple of km from the terminal, to catch a No 9 (   ) bus.

Rail A circular train route loops out north from Rangoon to Mingaladon, Insein and the country and then back. A 2½-hour run around this loop (trains go hourly) will give you a cheap (about K2), but not particularly comfortable, look around.

Bus There are 17 numbered bus routes around Rangoon, but the buses are as ramshackle as anything else in Burma and impossibly crowded. A Burmese bus is not full until every available handhold for those hanging off the sides and back has been taken. Still, if you can find a space you can get anywhere in Rangoon for 50 pyas or less. Some useful routes:

to the Kaba Aye Pagoda and on to the Mae La Mu Pagoda – bus No 5 (၅)
to the Chauk Htat Gyi Pagoda – bus Nos 1 (၁), 13 (၁၃) or 14 (၁၄), then a 16 (၁၆) along Shwegondine Rd
to the airport – bus No 9 (၉)
to the Syriam jetty – bus Nos 9 (၉) or 12 (၁၂)
to Shwedagon Pagoda – bus No 10 (၁၀). This bus continues around the Royal Lake and loops back to the city.

Taxi There is often nothing to distinguish a taxi from any other vehicle in Rangoon. We've heard that taxis have red lettered license plates, private cars black. Another possible difference is that the taxis are the older vehicles. The best idea is to simply hail anything; if it doesn't stop then perhaps it is not a taxi. If it is a taxi it may have a meter but it certainly won't work. Most rides around town should only be about K10 to K15 – the Strand Hotel to the Shwedagon for example. If you're asked K25 or K30 they're trying a special 'tourist price' on you; wait for another.

Beware of the cab drivers at the station who will often try to overcharge you.

Three-Wheeler The little three-wheel, two-stroke, taxi trucks are close relatives of Indonesian bemos or Thai samlors. You can take a complete one just like a taxi and pay a kyat or two less than the equivalent taxi fare for most rides. Around town most rides will be K5 to K10; you can even take one out to the airport for K20 to K30. Some seem to run along like buses, picking up and dropping off people as they go – fares are K1 to K2 around the city.

Trishaw Every Asian country seems to have its own interpretation of the bicycle trishaw. In some countries the passengers sit beside the rider, side by side in a sort of sidecar. In others they sit in front or in back. In Burma, trishaw passengers ride beside the rider, but back to back – one facing forward, one backward. Most trips around town cost K5 per person. It's a leisurely way of getting around and quite manageable in Rangoon's light traffic flow.

Boat The Tinbonseik jetty for ferries across the river to the 'Syriam side' is about 1½ km east of the Strand; the cost is K2.75 to cross over. You can hire sampans from the wharf directly across the park from the Strand if you just want to have a look at the river life.

There are a number of other wharfs around Rangoon for the various steamer services. The Mandalay Steamer Jetty is east of the Strand Hotel, beyond the Botataung Pagoda. Near that pagoda is the Syriam Jetty, confusingly named since the Syriam ferries do not depart from there. West of the Strand are the jetties for boats to Twante and Bassein (Mawtin St Jetty) and to Prome.

Tours Daily three-hour tours of Rangoon depart from the major city hotels in the morning and cost K50.

Around Rangoon

SYRIAM & KYAUKTAN

If you've got a morning or afternoon to spare in Rangoon, you can make an excursion across the river to Syriam and on to a little pagoda at Kyauktan. The journey involves a ferry trip down the Pazundaung Creek, then along and across the Rangoon River to Syriam. This was the main port until the British came along and shifted things over the river to Rangoon. Although Rangoon is no longer anywhere near as busy a port as it was in the British days, there is still plenty to be seen on this short but interesting river trip.

Syriam was the base during the late 1500s and early 1600s for the notorious Portuguese adventurer, De Brito. Officially a trade representative for the Arakanese, he actually ran his own little kingdom from Syriam, siding with the Mons (when it suited him) in their struggle against the Burmese. In 1599 his private army sacked Pegu, but in 1613 the Burmese besieged Syriam and De Brito received the punishment reserved for those who defiled Buddhist shrines – death by impalement. It took him two days to die, due, it is said, to his failure to take the recommended posture where the stake would have penetrated vital organs. Syriam continued as a major port and trading centre until it was destroyed by Alaungpaya in 1756, after which Rangoon took over its role.

Today there is nothing of this ancient city to be seen in Syriam, but a short bus ride out of town will take you to the large, golden Kyaik-khauk Pagoda, rising on a hillock to the north of the road. Just before this pagoda are the tombs of two famous Burmese writers – Natshingaung and Padethayaza.

If you continue further, until the road terminates at a wide river you can visit the Ye Le Paya or 'middle stream' pagoda at Kyauktan. It's appropriately named since the complex is perched on a tiny island in the middle of the river. In the temples there are pictures of other famous pagodas from Burma and elsewhere.

Getting There

Take a No 12 (၁၂) or a No 9 (၉) bus running along Bogyoke Aung San St and ask to get down at the Tinbonseik Ferry Terminal – make sure they know where to put you down or you'll sail straight by.

Ferries depart every hour (at least) and cruise down the Pazundaung Creek and across the Rangoon River to Syriam. Fare is K2.50 and the 45-minute trip is pleasant and interesting. Going on to Kyauktan (say 'chowk tahn'), take a bus (or rather a truck with wooden board seats along each side) from the road in front of the ferry pier. The trip takes about 45 minutes to an hour and costs about K1. It's the end of the road so you can't miss it.

Walk to the right a couple of hundred metres to the pagoda crossing – it'll cost you K1 each way to be rowed out to the small island. The last ferry back from Syriam to Rangoon departs at 8 pm. Buses from Syriam don't necessarily depart after every boat arrival, so you can easily spend two to three hours getting from Rangoon to Kyauktan and it's wise to allow plenty of time for this trip. It's also possible to hire jeeps from Syriam, but they're rather expensive.

TWANTE

It's an interesting day trip from Rangoon to Twante, a small town noted for its pottery and also with a pagoda worth seeing. The boat trip to Twante takes two to three hours each way and the wharf is 1½ km west of the Strand Hotel. Boats continue on from Twante to Bassein, an 18-hour trip.

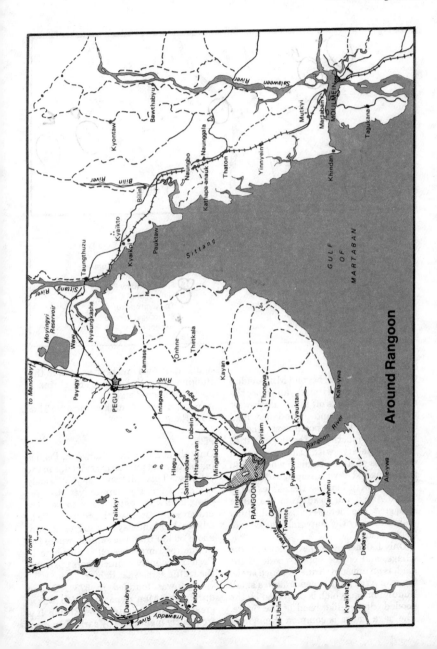

Around Rangoon

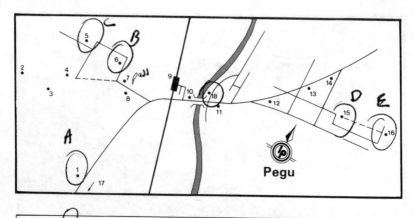

1 Kyaikpun
2 Mahagi Pagoda
3 Gothaingotan Pagoda
4 Shwegugale Pagoda — stairs
5 Mahazedi Pagoda — boys–monks
6 Shwethalyaung Buddha
7 Four Figures Pagoda
8 Kalyani Sima
9 Railway Station
10 Rangoon Buses

11 Shwe Mikntha Cold Drinks
12 Rangoon Buses
13 Shwewatan Restaurant
14 Moulmein Buses
15 Shwemawdaw Pagoda
16 Hinthagone
17 To Payathonzu,
   Shwegugyi Pagoda &
   Rangoon
18 Market

HTAUKKYAN

On the road to Pegu, beyond Mingaladon Airport, you reach Htaukkyan where the road to Prome forks off to the north-west while the Pegu and Mandalay road continues on to the north-east. Shortly beyond the junction is the huge British War Cemetery with the graves of thousands of Allied soldiers who died in the Burma and Assam campaigns of WW II. The memorials here list the names of the 27,000 Allied war dead from the bitter struggle. The cemetery is beautifully maintained by the Imperial War Graves Commission.

Only 100 metres further on towards the village, and on the opposite side of the road, is an unusual shrine. A coiled snake figure or *naga* is entwined around a small Buddha image which is protected by the hooded, dragon-like head of the figure. The naga image is common throughout South-East Asia and is often seen in this Buddha-protecting pose. The shrine is about six metres high.

You can get to Htaukkyan on a No 9 bus from Rangoon.

PEGU

Only about 80 km from Rangoon, Pegu is one of the most interesting sidetrips in the country. This pleasant city is easily reached from the capital yet just far enough off the beaten track to be very untouristed. By road the route to Pegu follows the Mandalay road to Htaukkyan, about 30 km from the capital, where the Prome road branches off. From here to Pegu the country is much more open and the traffic somewhat lighter.

Pegu was founded in 573 AD and during the Mon dynasty period was a great city and capital of lower Burma. It is frequently mentioned by early European visitors as an important seaport. In 1740 the Mons, after a period of submission to Toungoo, re-established Pegu as their capital, but in 1757 King Alaungpaya sacked and utterly destroyed the city. King Bodawpaya, who ruled from 1782 to 1819, rebuilt it to some extent, but when the river changed its course the city was cut off from the sea and lost its importance as a seaport. It never again reached its previous grandeur.

✷ Shwemawdaw

The 'Great Golden God Pagoda' stands north of the railway station on the far side of town from Rangoon. You can't miss it since its height of 114 metres (374 feet) completely dominates the town. The Shwemawdaw is over 1000 years old and was originally built to a height of 23 metres (75 feet) to enshrine two hairs of the Buddha. In 825 AD it was raised to 25 metres (81 feet) and then to 27 metres (88 feet) in 840. In 982 a sacred tooth was added to the collection; in 1385 another tooth was added and the pagoda was rebuilt to a towering 84 metres (277 feet). In 1492, the year Columbus sailed the Atlantic, a wind blew down the *hti* and a new one was raised.

King Bodawpaya, in the reconstruction of Pegu after the ravages of Alaungpaya, rebuilt the pagoda to 91 metres (297 feet) in 1796, but from that point it has had a rather chequered career. A new *hti* was added in 1882, but a major earthquake in 1912 brought it down. The pagoda was repaired, but in 1917 another major quake again brought the *hti* down and caused serious damage. Again it was repaired, but in 1930 the biggest quake of them all completely levelled the pagoda and for the next 20 years only the huge earth mound of the base remained.

Reconstruction of the Shwemawdaw commenced in 1952 and was completed in 1954, when it reached its present height. The glittering golden top of the pagoda reaches 14 metres (47 feet) higher than the Shwedagon in Rangoon. Shady trees around the base make it a pleasant place to stroll or simply sit and watch the Burmese. At the north-east corner of the pagoda a huge section of the *hti* toppled by the 1917 earthquake has been mounted into the structure of the pagoda. It is a convincing reminder of the power of such geological disturbances.

Like the Shwedagon, the pagoda is reached by a covered walkway lined with stalls – a number with interesting collections of antique bits and pieces. Along the sides of the walkway a collection of rather faded and dusty paintings illustrates the terrible effects of the 1930 earthquake and shows the subsequent rebuilding of this mighty pagoda.

✷ Hintha Gone

Behind the Shwemawdaw, this small pagoda has good views over Pegu from the roofed platform on the hilltop. According to legend this was the one point rising from the sea when the mythological bird known as the *hintha* landed here. A statue of the bird, looking rather like the figures on opium weights, tops the hill. The pagoda was built by U Khanti, the hermit monk who was also the architect of Mandalay Hill. You can walk to it by taking the steps down the other side of the Shwemawdaw from the main entranceway.

✷ Shwethalyaung

To the south of the Rangoon-Pegu road, only a little over a km on the Rangoon side of the railway station, the Shwethalyaung is a huge reclining Buddha. Measuring 55 metres (180 feet) long and 16 metres (56½ feet) high, it is a good five metres longer than the reclining Buddha at Wat Po in Bangkok. The corrugated iron shed which houses it may be rough and ready, but it is spacious and airy and gives you a far better view than most reclining Buddhas in their cramped cells offer. The Shwethalyaung is reputed to be the most lifelike of all reclining Buddhas as well as one of the largest. The walkway up to the platform is crowded with souvenir and handicraft stalls.

Originally built in 994 AD, the Shwethalyaung was allowed to deteriorate and was then restored several times during its existence before the destruction of Pegu in 1757. The town was so completely ravaged that the huge Buddha was totally lost and overgrown by jungle. It was not found until the British era, when an Indian contractor, digging in a large earth mound for fill to be used in the construction of the railway line, rediscovered the image. It was restored and covered with the present ugly iron *tazaung*.

Kalyani Sima

This 'sacred hall of ordination' was originally constructed in 1476 by Dhammazedi. It stands beside the road en route from the railway station to the Shwethalyaung. It was the first of the 397 similar *simas* he built around the country, to plans brought back from Ceylon. De Brito, the Portuguese adventurer, burnt it down in 1599 during his period of plunder, and during the sack of Pegu it was destroyed once again.

Subsequently it suffered from fires or quakes on a number of occasions before being levelled by the disastrous 1930 quake. As with the Shwemawdaw, reconstruction was completed in 1954. Next to the hall are 10 large tablets with inscriptions in Pali and Mon.

Across the road from the Kalyani Sima, by the corner, is a curious pagoda with four Buddha figures standing back to back, in somewhat similar fashion to the four seated Buddhas at the Kyaik Pun on the outskirts of town. An adjacent open hallway has a small reclining Buddha image, thronged by followers, and some macabre paintings of wrongdoers being tortured in the afterlife.

Mahazedi Pagoda

Continuing beyond the Shwethalyaung brings you to the Mahazedi or 'great pagoda'. Originally constructed in 1560, it was destroyed during the 1757 sack of Pegu. An attempt to rebuild it in 1560 was unsuccessful and the great earthquake of 1930 comprehensively levelled it, after which it remained a ruin. Recently construction recommenced and was completed in the last few years. Stairways lead up the outside of the pagoda, and from the top there are fine views over the surrounding area. Note the model pagoda by the entrance.

The Mahazedi originally had a Buddha tooth, at one time thought to be the actual Buddha tooth of Kandy, Sri Lanka. After Pegu was conquered in 1599 the tooth was later moved to Toungoo and then to Sagaing near Mandalay. Together with a begging bowl supposed to have been used by the Buddha, it remains in the Kaunghmudaw Pagoda near Sagaing to this day.

Shwegugale Pagoda

A little beyond the Mahazedi, this pagoda has a dark 'tunnel' running around the circumference of the structure. Inside are 64 seated Buddha figures. From here you can take a short cut back to the corner in the road, just before the Shwethalyaung.

Kyaik Pun

❦ Kyaik Pun

About three km out of Pegu on the Rangoon road, and then a couple of hundred metres to the north of the road, stands the Kyaik Pun. Built in 1476 by King Dhammazedi, it consists of four 30-metre-high sitting Buddhas placed back to back around a huge, square pillar. According to a legend, four Mon sisters were connected with the construction of the Buddhas; it was said that if any of them should marry, one of the Buddhas would collapse. One of the four did and thus the fourth Buddha has disintegrated, leaving only a brick outline.

En route to the Kyaik Pun you can detour to the prettily situated Gaung-Say-Kyan Pagoda, reached by crossing a wooden bridge over a small lake.

Other

Pegu has a very interesting market just across the river from the railway station. Take some time to wander around the various market buildings. The market serves as a distribution point for cloth, household items and other 'imports' from Thailand and beyond.

Places to Stay & Eat

Although there is a government rest house in Pegu, you are highly unlikely to be allowed to stay overnight. There is a rather run-down *rest house* on No 2 St, parallel to the railway tracks about 50 metres from the station. A bare and basic double will cost K20.

There are a number of food stalls around the marketplace or close to the Shwemawdaw Pagoda, including good Indian biriani stalls alongside the market. The *Shwewatan Restaurant* on the Mandalay road is a fairly new, and usually less than busy, garden restaurant.

Getting There

You can get to Pegu by either rail or road; in either case the trip takes about two hours. It's very easy to day-trip to Pegu from Rangoon, but allow the whole day. An early start is probably the best idea since Pegu can get very hot around mid-day.

Rail It is possible to visit Pegu by hopping off the Rangoon-Mandalay train and taking a later one. It is wiser to do this coming down from Mandalay rather than going up from Rangoon because of the difficulties of getting a seat from Pegu to Mandalay. From Pegu to Rangoon you could easily stand, wait for another train or change to the bus. Note also that the overnight Mandalay-Rangoon train does not stop in Pegu, although when I took it on my most recent visit to Burma it went through the station so slowly that hopping off was no problem.

From Rangoon there are about 10 trains a day from around 5 am. Although I easily bought a Pegu-Rangoon ticket in Pegu, I am told that it is not possible to buy tickets in Rangoon because Rangoon-Pegu is not on Tourist Burma's itinerary! In that case you will have to get a helpful Burmese to buy tickets for you, or else take the bus.

Bus The buses from Rangoon operate approximately hourly from 5 or 6 am and

SHWE THA LYAUNG IMAGE
(RECLINING BUDDHA)
CONSTRUCTED IN 998 A-D BY
KING MIGA DEPA (JUNIOR)

DIMENSIONS

Length	180 ft.
Height	52½ ft.
Face	22½ ft.
Ear	15 ft.
Eye	5½ ft.
Eye brow	7½ ft.
Eye lid	7½ ft.
Nose	7½ ft.
Lip	7½ ft.
Neck	7½ ft.
Shoulder to waist	53½ ft.
Waist to knee	47½ ft.
Knee to foot	40½ ft.
Elbow to tip of finger	47½ ft.
Little finger	10 ft.
Sole of foot	25½ ft.
Great toe	9 ft.
Palm of hand	22 ft.

1 METRE = 3.28 ft.

depart from 18th St. The company is Oakthadagon, the fare is K5 and this can be a reasonably manageable bus trip. Avoid Sundays, however, when Pegu is a very popular excursion from Rangoon and the buses get very crowded. It can also be difficult to get back to Rangoon because the buses will be booked out until late in the evening.

Taxi A third, more expensive, but also more convenient, alternative is to take a taxi from Rangoon. Start negotiating at around K250, or pay about US$20 if you want to do it on the 'black market'.

Taking a taxi or taxi-truck has the additional advantage of giving you transport from place to place once you get to Pegu. Some drivers may feel that getting you to Pegu and back, and to the two big attractions – the Shwemawdaw and the Shwethalyaung – is quite enough for one day. Don't accept feeble excuses that other sites are 'too far off the road', are down tracks 'only fit for bullock carts', or are simply 'closed'. A good place to hire taxis for a Pegu trip is near the Strand. Choose a driver with reasonable English-language skills.

Top: Strawberries in Mandalay market (TW)
Left: Kyaikpun in Pegu (TW)
Right: A Burmese reminder (TW)

Top: Young monks after breakfast (TW)
Left: Woodcarvings on Shwenandaw Monastery (TW)
Right: Handcranked softdrink vendor (TW)

Mandalay

Mandalay was the last capital of Burma before the British took over, and for this reason it still has great importance as a cultural centre. It's the most Burmese of cities, the place where you'll come closest to the 'real' Burma. It lies in the centre of Burma's dry zone and is a surprisingly sprawling place – you'll find wandering around the city, if you're here in the hot season, a dry and dusty experience.

Mandalay is a comparatively young city and its period as the capital of the last Burmese kingdom was a short one. Most of the monuments and buildings are therefore fairly recent, although some pagodas long pre-date the city. For centuries this area of Burma was the site of capitals of Burmese kingdoms, and while in Mandalay you can easily visit three former royal cities – all now deserted.

King Mindon founded the city in 1857 and began construction of his new capital. The actual shift from Amarapura to the new royal palace took place in 1861. In true Burmese tradition the new palace was constructed mainly from the dismantled wooden buildings of the previous palace at Amarapura. Mandalay's period of glory was short – Mindon was succeeded by the disastrous Thibaw and in 1885 Mandalay was taken by the British, Thibaw and his notorious queen were exiled and 'the centre of the universe', 'the golden city', became just another outpost of the British Empire.

The city takes its name from Mandalay Hill, the 236-metre-high (775 feet) hill that rises just to the north-east of the palace. Today the population is about 400,000, the largest in the country after that of the capital, Rangoon, 716 km to the south. Mandalay still has considerable cultural and religious significance and its Buddhist monasteries are amongst the most important in the country.

Mandalay is a rather more easy-going town than Rangoon, if that can be imagined! Although it suffered considerable damage in the fierce fighting at the end of WW II, particularly the royal palace which was completely burnt out, there is still much to be seen both in Mandalay and in the surrounding deserted cities.

Orientation & Information

The Tourist Burma office is in the Mandalay Hotel. Although it's a nuisance having to get over there to pay for the cheaper hotels, they are pretty helpful. Many people only spend a day in Mandalay – arriving by train in the morning and then camping out on the Pagan ferry that night – and the tourist office will store your gear for you during the day. Tourist Burma also have a desk at the airport to meet flights and at the station to meet tourist trains – in order to steer you towards their approved hotels and guest houses.

Most of the other offices, including BAC ('the only airline office I've seen with birds nesting in the ceiling,' reported one traveller) and the post office, are over towards the river in the same area as the cheap guest houses.

The hill with the huge grounds of the old royal palace at its base is the natural focus of Mandalay. The city sprawls away to the south and east of the palace, bounded on the east by the busy Irrawaddy River. The city streets are laid out on a grid system with numbered streets running north-south and numbered roads running east-west – plus some important east-west roads which are named A Rd, B Rd and so on.

Mandalay's typical Burmese wooden architecture is still highly inflammable. On 12 May 1981 a disastrous fire raced up and down the

Burma fire

RANGOON. — About 35,000 people were left homeless in a fire yesterday which killed five and ravaged a large section of Mandalay, Northern Burma, officials reported today.

The fire broke out at an illicit petrol shop, and gutted more than 6100 buildings including schools, shops and Government offices in Burma's second largest city, 640 kilometres north of Rangoon.

riverbank in the north-west part of the town and left 35,000 people homeless. In addition, over a dozen monasteries, eight schools, four rice mills and many other buildings were destroyed. Fortunately none of the most important temples and monasteries were damaged.

Mandalay Hill

Since it's such a natural focus for the city, and the only place with a good view over the pancake-flat central plain, the hill is where most people start their visit to Mandalay. The hermit monk, U Khanti, is credited with inspiring the construction of many of the buildings on and around the hill in the years after the founding of the city. From the south two covered stairways wind their way up the hill, meeting about half way up. Another path ascends more steeply from the west. It's a pleasant stroll, with plenty of places to stop for a rest. From the top you'll have a fine view back over the battlements of the palace to the city of Mandalay, while to the east you can see the hazy blue outline of the Shan hills. Shoes must be removed as you enter the walkways.

Close to the top of the hill you come to a huge standing Buddha image looking out towards the royal palace with an outstretched hand pointing in that direction. This image, known as the Shweyattaw, represents a rather interesting legend. The Buddha, accompanied by his disciple Ananda, was said to have climbed Mandalay Hill while on one of his visits to Burma. In the 2400th year of his faith, he prophesied, a great city would be founded below the hill. By our calendar that 2400th year was 1857 – the year King Mindon decreed the move from Amarapura to Mandalay. The statue represents the Buddha pointing to where the city would be built.

The first temple you come to, half way up the hill, should be given much more importance than it appears to be given. It contains the so-called 'Peshawar Relics', three bones of the Buddha that may actually be just that. When there are so many Buddha teeth and Buddha hairs scattered so widely around the world and treated with such veneration, it's unusual that these relics are ignored.

The relics were originally sent to Peshawar, now in Pakistan, by the great Indian emperor Ashoka himself. The stupa into which they were built was destroyed in the 11th century, but in 1908 the curator of the Peshawar Museum discovered the actual relic casket during excavations. Although Peshawar had once been a great Buddhist centre, it had by that time been Muslim for many centuries; so the British government presented these important relics to the Burmese Buddhist Society, and this relatively neglected temple was built to house them.

Those interested in military history can also find, in a small building attached to one of the pagodas at the top of a wide, steep flight of steps, a monument to the British regiment which retook the hill from the Japanese in fierce fighting in 1945.

Kyauktawgyi Pagoda

Close to the southern entrance to the hill stands the Kyauktawgyi Pagoda, construction of which commenced in 1853 and was completed in 1878. It was originally intended that this pagoda, like its namesake a few km south in Amarapura, would be modelled after the Ananda Temple of Pagan, but due to a palace rebellion this grand plan was not carried through.

It is chiefly interesting for the huge seated image of the Buddha carved from a single block of marble. The marble block from the mines of nearby Sagyin was so colossal that it required 10,000 men labouring for 13 days to transport it from a canal to the pagoda site. The image was completed and dedicated in 1865. Around the shrine are figures of the Buddha's 80 *arahats* or disciples, arranged 20 on each of the four sides.

In mid-October Mandalay's biggest festival is held here for seven days to commemorate Thadingyut.

Sandamuni Pagoda

To the south-east of the hill, close by the bus stop, is the Sandamuni Pagoda, which was built on the site of King Mindon's temporary palace – used while the new Mandalay Palace was under construction. King Mindon had come to power after the successful overthrow of King Pagan, an operation in which he had been assisted by his younger brother Prince Kanaung.

Mindon tended to concentrate on religious matters and leave the niceties of secular rule to his brother, but in 1866 Prince Kanaung was assassinated in an unsuccessful revolt inspired by Prince Myingun. The Sandamuni Pagoda was built as a memorial to Prince Kanaung on the spot where he was killed.

The Sandamuni Pagoda enshrines an iron image of the Buddha cast in 1802 by Bodawpaya and transported here from Amarapura in 1874. Around the pagoda a large collection of marble slabs is inscribed with commentaries on the Buddhist canon. They were another project of the venerable U Khanti. Do not confuse them with the 729 inscribed marble slabs of the Kuthodaw Pagoda which stands to the east of the Sandamuni.

Kuthodaw Pagoda

Also known as the Maha Lawka Marazein Pagoda, this construction was modelled after the Shwezigon at Nyaung-Oo near Pagan. Building commenced in 1857, at the same time as the royal palace. The pagoda has been dubbed 'the world's biggest book', for around the central pagoda are arranged 729 marble slabs on which are inscribed the entire Buddhist canon or *Tripitaka*. Each slab is housed in its own individual small temple and is of considerable interest to scholars of Buddhism.

It took an editorial committee numbering over 200 to produce the original slabs, and it has been estimated that, reading for eight hours a day, one man would take 450 days to read the complete 'book'. King Mindon convened the Fifth Buddhist Synod and used a team of 2400 monks to read the whole book in a non-stop relay lasting nearly six months! In 1900 a paper edition of the stone original was printed in 38 volumes, each with about 400 pages. A 730th slab in the corner of the inner enclosure tells of the construction of this amazing book.

Atumashi Kyaung

The ruins of the 'Incomparable Monastery' stand a little to the south of the Kuthodaw Pagoda. Built at the same time as the Kuthodaw Pagoda, this monastery was of traditional Burmese monastic construction – a masonry base topped by a wooden building, but instead of the usual multi-roofed design it consisted of graduated rectangular terraces. Inside was a famous Buddha image, clothed in the king's silk clothing and with a huge diamond in the forehead. The image was stolen in 1885, during the British takeover of the city.

In 1890 the monastery caught fire and, together with its contents which included four complete sets of the *Tripitaka* in teak boxes, it was completely gutted. Today only the huge brickwork platform with the main stairway and fine stucco carvings remain, but in the nearby Shwenandaw Monastery you can see an early photograph of the Atumashi Kyaung prior to its destruction.

Shwenandaw Kyaung ✳ *excellent*

Close to the Atumashi Kyaung stands the Shwenandaw Kyaung; this monastery is of great interest for not only is it a fine example of a traditional Burmese wooden monastery, it is also a fragile reminder of the old Mandalay Palace. At one time this building was part of the palace complex and was used as an apartment by King Mindon and his chief queen, and it was in this building that he died. After Mindon's death, King Thibaw had the building dismantled and reassembled on its present site in 1880 as a monastery. It is said that Thibaw used the building for meditation, and the couch on which he sat can still be seen.

The building is covered inside and out with carved panels; unfortunately, though, many of the exterior panels have weathered badly and some have been prised off and removed. At one time the building was gilded and decorated with glass mosaics. The carved panels inside are still in excellent condition, particularly the 10 scenes from the *Jataka*.

Mandalay Palace

On 20 March 1945, in fierce fighting between advancing British and Indian troops and the Japanese forces which had held Mandalay since 1942, the royal palace caught fire and was completely burnt out. The traditional wooden construction of Burmese palaces had often in the past led to severe damage by fire, and this – the last and most magnificent palace complex – was no exception. All that remains of the palace today are the huge walls and moat, the base on which the wooden palace buildings and apartments stood, and a few masonry buildings or tombs.

Mandalay Palace is immense – the walls are eight metres high and three metres thick at the bottom, tapering to 1½ metres thick at the crenellated top,

and are made of burnt brick backed by earth ramparts. Each of the four sides – the palace is a perfect square – is two km long; the surrounding moat is 70 metres (225 feet) wide and over three metres deep. A channel from the Mandalay irrigation canal fills the moat.

There are three gates to the palace on each of the walls. Originally there were five bridges into the palace, four running to the main gates. Each of the gates was topped by a *pyatthat*, or wooden pavilion. Smaller *pyatthats* stood at each corner and between the large ones – making 32 in all. Apart from some damage repaired after the war and

Palace watchtower, destroyed in 1945

changes made when the railway was directed through the palace grounds, the wall and its pavilions are original.

The palace was far more than just royal living quarters – it was really a walled city within the city. Today you enter by the main south gate; since the palace is now a military encampment you must be accompanied when visiting it, so you collect a 'guide' at the guardhouse. There is also a small collection of trishaw riders waiting here to pedal you from the gate to the old palace site.

Where the palace once stood there is today just a large empty space on a raised plinth. Steps up to this platform, flanked by cannons at the end, are all that remain of the original palace apartments. In the middle of the platform there is a modern museum with a miserable collection of assorted odds and ends. It is planned to eventually combine this museum with the equally drab museum and library on 80th St, outside the palace walls. Don't hold your breath. A little to the west of the palace platform, a small open building houses a large-scale model of the palace as it was prior to the war. This and some black-and-white photographs are all you can see of what must have been, at one time, a magnificent complex.

Slightly to the east of the platform you can see the ruins of a clock tower, the better preserved tooth relic tower and the tomb of King Mindon. The latter was once gilded and decorated with glass mosaics but an 1898 restoration obliterated all traces of the earlier craftsmanship. The large open sheds here contain over 600 inscribed stone slabs which were collected by King Bodawpaya and were later moved to the palace from Amarapura just before WW II. Other reminders of the former glory of the old palace are the Royal Mint and the Sabbath Hall, which are also close by. During the British period the palace was known as Fort Dufferin.

Mandalay City

The sprawling grid of Mandalay city lies west and south of the palace walls. Mandalay's 'centre' is a short walk west from the south-west corner of the palace. Here you will find the clock tower and the extensive Zegyo Market. Designed in 1903 by Count Caldari, the Italian first secretary of the Mandalay Municipality, the market is a fascinating collection of stalls selling every sort of Burmese ware you could imagine – and a fair assortment of smuggled goods from outside Burma. In the usual Asian manner there are sections for everything from jewellery or materials to books or hardware. In the evening busy night markets spring up along 84th St & 26th Rd and 79th St & 29th Rd.

If you continue down 26th Rd beyond the market you will eventually come to the river foreshore, a scene of constant activity and interest; something is always happening down here. It is to the boat landings at the end of 26th Rd that you must come for the riverboats heading upriver to Mingun. You can see working water buffaloes at the bottom of C Rd. North of the Mingun jetty a bit is an area where people come to do their laundry, very colourful.

Something is also always happening on the streets of Mandalay – horse carts trot by or those strange Burmese trishaws with the passengers sitting back to back wind through the crowds. Rattling jeeps of WW II vintage start off on the uphill haul to Maymyo or even beyond to forbidden Lashio. Equally ancient buses, their tops hidden under mounds of goods, wait for departure at odd hours to equally odd places. Mandalay is one of those places that seems like a key to so much more - unfortunately, in present-day Burma, it's so much more that you won't be allowed to explore.

Shwekyimyint Pagoda

On 24th Rd between 82nd and 83rd Sts, a little north-east of Zegyo Market or the

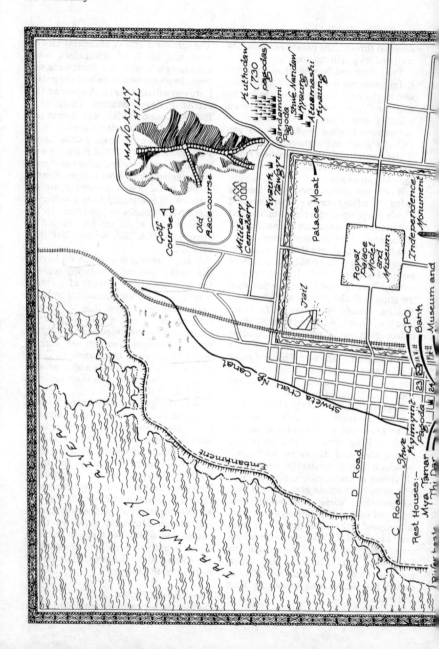

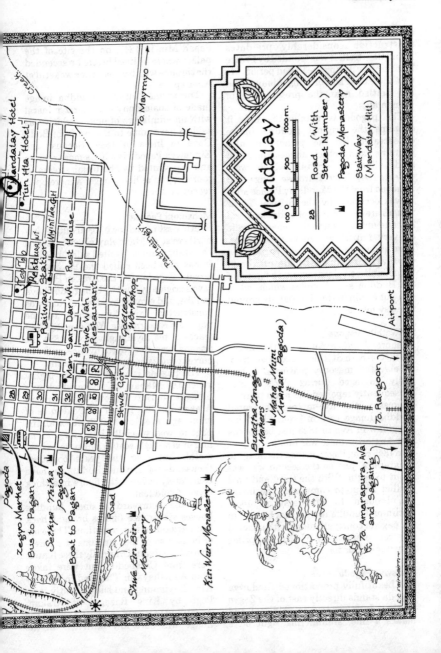

clock tower, this pagoda's original construction considerably pre-dates Mandalay itself. It was founded by Prince Minshinzaw during the Pagan period. He was the exiled son of King Alaungsithu and settled near the present site of Mandalay.

The pagoda is notable because it contains the original Buddha image consecrated by the prince. It also contains many other images, made of gold, silver or crystal, which were collected by later Burmese kings and removed from the Mandalay Palace after it was occupied by the British. These images are generally kept under lock and key and only shown to the general public on very important religious occasions. Here and at the Setkyathiha Pagoda you can find the ridiculous in close proximity to the sublime – glass cases with figures of the Buddha and disciples which, when you put a coin in the slot, parade around to noisy music.

Setkyathiha Pagoda

A short distance south of the Zegyo Market on 85th St, this pagoda rises from an elevated masonry platform. It was badly damaged during WW II, but subsequently repaired. Its main point of interest is the five-metre-high seated Buddha image cast in bronze by King Bagyidaw in Ava in 1823 just before the first Anglo-Burmese war broke out.

In 1849 King Pagan moved the image to Amarapura, just as the second war was about to begin. With the third and final conflict about to commence the image was brought to Mandalay in 1884. Reclining Buddha images can be seen in the pagoda courtyard along with a sacred Bo tree planted by U Nu, ex-prime minister of Burma.

Eindawya Pagoda

The beautifully proportioned Eindawya Pagoda stands directly east of the Zegyo Market. It is covered in gold leaf and makes a fine, shimmering sight on a sunny day. The pagoda was built by King Pagan Min in 1847, on the site of the palace where he lived before he ascended the throne – which at that time was still at Amarapura.

The shrine houses a Buddha image made of chalcedony – a quartz mineral with an admixture of opal – which was said to have come to Burma from Bodh Gaya in India in 1839. Because the Eindawya Pagoda is a little more remote and less visited by the usual stream of tourists, you're likely to get a more open reception here.

Mahamuni Pagoda

South-west of the town, or about 1½ km north-west of Mandalay airport, stands the Mahamuni or 'exalted saint' pagoda. It has also been called the Payagyi, or 'great', Pagoda, and the Arakan Pagoda. It was originally built by King Bodawpaya in 1784, and a road paved with bricks was constructed from his palace to the pagoda's eastern gate. You can still find traces of his royal highway. In 1884 the pagoda was destroyed by fire and the current one is comparatively recent.

The pagoda is notable for the highly venerated Mahamuni image which was brought to Burma from Myohaung in Arakan in 1784. It was believed to be of great age even at that time, and the pagoda was specially built for it. The four-metre-high seated image is cast of metal, but over the years countless thousands of devout Buddhists have completely covered the figure in a thick layer of gold leaf.

In the courtyard a small building houses six bronze figures brought back from Arakan at the same time. Three are of lions, two of men and one of a three-headed elephant. Originally these figures were from Cambodia, but were taken from Ayutthaya in Thailand in 1663 by King Bayinaung and subsequently from Pegu by King Razagyi of Arakan. According to legend, rubbing a part of the image will cure any affliction on the corresponding part of your own body – knee and stomach ailments seem to be the main preoccupation of the Burmese, who have polished these parts to a high gloss.

The pagoda courtyard contains more inscription stones collected by King Bodawpaya, who appears to have had quite a thing about this hobby. Another small building, next to the one containing the bronze figures, has two large statues shouldering a pole between them, from which is slung a traditional Burmese gong said to weigh five tonnes. There are many interesting shop stalls at the entranceway to the pagoda.

During the Mahamuni Pagoda Festival in early February people from nearby districts make pilgrimages to the Mahamuni. The temple is always a centre of activity and during this festival it explodes with energy.

Crafts

In a street close by the Mahamuni Pagoda is a whole series of stone-carvers' workshops. Here Buddha images of all sizes are hewn from solid stone slabs. If you have a dilapidated pagoda in need of refurbishing, then head for the west exit of the Mahamuni – here you will find workshops manufacturing all sorts of pagoda paraphernalia. If the *hti* has toppled from the top of your pagoda then this is the place to come for a new one.

Also on this side of the city you can find wood-carvers. Mandalay's gold-leaf makers are concentrated in the south-east of the city. Sheets of gold are beaten into paper-thin pieces which are sold in packets to devotees to use for gilding images or even complete pagodas. Gilding a Buddha image or a pagoda with gold leaf brings great credit to the gilder, so there is a steady growth of gold leaf on many

Father Lamont's Catholic Church

images in Burma. Other crafts you may be able to see around Mandalay include silk weaving and ivory carving.

Across from the Aung Ti Yi Guest House on 80th St is a shop which specialises in weaving *longyis*. All varieties can be found here, from everyday cotton plaids for around K75 to fancy silk *longyis* for special occasions at K200. The black-indigo-green plaids are Kachin designs and cost K120; Malaysian sarongs, highly valued by the Burmese, are K150 up. Prices are fixed and it costs K2 to have a *longyi* sewn into a 'tube' for wearing. The staff can show you the proper ways to tie them.

There are many little shops around central Mandalay and near the Mya Mandalar and Mandalay hotels selling a mixture of gems, carvings, silk, *kalaga* tapestries and other crafts. If you enter without a tout (most of the younger trishaw or horsecart drivers are into this), you'll get better deals than with a tout, as they are usually paid high commissions. Mandalay is a crafts centre and you can get some really good bargains if you know what you're looking for.

Churches
Mandalay has some churches amongst the many temples. At the corner of 80th St and 34th Rd the Catholic church of the Frenchman Father Lamont seems to have had a mainly Chinese congregation, judging from the Chinese lettering on the intricate church front. The uninteresting Anglican Church of Our Lord, tucked away at the junction of C Rd and 85th St, is on the site of an earlier church which predates the arrival of the British.

Places to Stay – bottom end
Mandalay has a lot of hotels and rest houses in the bottom-end bracket, but they're uniformly spartan and basic, and Tourist Burma hardly encourages any improvement. Since you have to book them through the inconveniently located tourist office in the Mandalay Hotel (or at

the station if you arrive by train), you often find yourself simply 'assigned' to one particular hotel so there is little incentive for managers to improve their places. Worse still, some places not on the Tourist Burma approved list are better than some that are. However, Tourist Burma approval is not something Mandalay guest houses actively seek; TB simply assigns them that status if they are considered 'convenient' enough for tourists. Many Burmese guest houses try to avoid being selected, as the staff don't want to deal with foreigners and their peculiar demands as guests (Pagan is an exception to this since without foreign tourists there would be no guests). To top it off, there are actually fewer places where you are officially allowed to stay in Mandalay than when the last edition of this book came out. At the height of the tourist season Mandalay can get really packed out and you may simply have to stay at one of the unapproved places.

The shoestring hotels are all around the town centre area, to the south-west of the palace. With one exception they charge an identical K21/36 for singles/doubles and offer similar standards – bare little cubicles for rooms, and narrow, hard beds – fortunately usually with mosquito nets. There's some movement in and out of the approved list at Mandalay. While some places like the Man San Dar Win have seemingly always been OK, others come and go from the list. There may be additions and deletions to the places that follow, but Tourist Burma will have a blackboard up listing the currently favoured places and whether they have rooms free or not.

The relatively new *Aung Na Wayard* is probably the best of the bunch – it's on 31st Rd near 80th St, next door to the grubbier *Man Shwe Myo*. All rooms have fans, the beds are slightly softer than the Mandalay standard, and windows are screened. Unlike the other Mandalay guest houses, this one charges K25/50 for singles/doubles.

The *Man San Dar Win* (tel 23317) is at 177 31st Rd, across the street from *Man Shwe Myo* and *Aung Na Wayard* between 81st and 80th Sts. The longest-running of the cheapies and a friendly place, it seems to have gone downhill since the last edition – even the hard beds need sweeping.

On the east side of the railway, towards the Mandalay Hotel, is the *Myintida* (Myint Thida) guest house on 29th Rd between 73rd and 74th Sts. Its main advantages are its proximity to Tourist Burma and location in a quiet, tree-studded neighbourhood.

Places to Stay – top end

There are just a couple of places aspiring to the top-end tag in Mandalay. The Tourist Burma hotel, used by most package-tour groups in Mandalay, is the *Mandalay Hotel*, on the road beside the south moat of the palace and very close to the south-east corner. Which means it is a good long way from the town centre – not a great problem since everything seems to be a good long way from everything in Mandalay.

The hotel is fairly featureless and dull, although quite comfortable. There are 60 rooms and four suites. 'Standard' singles cost US$14, doubles US$19.25; 'superior' (air-conditioned) rooms are US$23 for both singles and doubles. There are also a few cramped 'economy' rooms for US$8/10. The Tourist Burma office is in the lobby area, behind which is the large dining room. There is another, Chinese-style, restaurant near the front gate. Breakfasts are quite good in the Mandalay, but the other meals are not great value. Apart from the hotel dining room there is a second restaurant (with Chinese food) outside the main building, by the entrance gate to the hotel.

The second hotel used to be the one place in Mandalay with a distinctive character, but it was inevitable that a privately run place would be taken over by the government and stamped with the same dull pattern as their other places. So the Tun Hla has now become the *Mya Mandalar* and is not the place it once was. It's a block back from the palace moat and a couple of blocks towards the city from the Mandalay Hotel. The rooms here are much more colonial Burmese, less a Burmese interpretation of a modern, western hotel. In other words it has (or had) a lot more character.

There are only 10 rooms, four at K99/121 for singles/doubles and six lesser-quality rooms for K72 single or double. They all have attached bathrooms, and with recent renovations even the cheaper ones are fairly good. There's quite a good dining area, but since the government takeover the menu has become much more limited – fried rice or fried noodles is about it. Like the Mandalay Hotel, western breakfast is what they do best.

On the wall in the bar area there's a framed account of the 1939 anti-British riots in which 17 people were killed, including the 12-year-old son of U Tun Hla. Prior to the government takeover another son ran the hotel and made British visitors feel just as welcome as any other nationality. The bar is a favourite watering hole for the local Burmese upper class and can get quite crowded in the evening. This is (or was) also the only place in town where you could find a Mandalay map, and it has a swimming pool, very pleasant if you are there in the summer heat.

Places to Eat

There are a fair number of restaurants around Mandalay, most of them Chinese for, as in Rangoon, it's hard to find real Burmese food apart from at street stalls. *Shwe Wah*, a grubby-looking little restaurant on 80th St between 32nd and 33rd Rds has long been popular with shoestring travellers. The quality of food turned out far exceeds the visual expectations; in my opinion the food in this little place can be better than that in the Tourist Burma Mandalay Hotel.

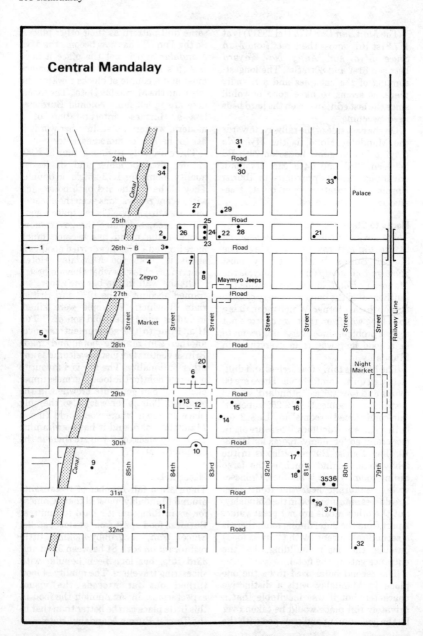

Central Mandalay

The menu includes fresh lime juice (K2) and fruit salad (K3), plus all the regular Chinese dishes – not to mention cold pigs' stomach or special pigs' feet. Main courses are generally K8 to K12. The numbers on the menu vary from one copy to another so don't put too much trust in ordering by number! Here, as in other places in Mandalay, you can get excellent fresh prawns in season. Tell them to go easy on the 'sweet' in sweet-and-sour dishes, though. The English-speaking manager is a good information source and has a jeep which can be hired for sightseeing. Not far away, the Chinese *Htaw Yin* restaurant at 396 81st St, near 31st Rd, is also good apart from actually looking healthier.

On 83rd St, between 26th and 25th Rds (close to the Zegyo Market), there's quite a selection of eating places. Here you'll find the *Mann Restaurant* – no English menu, but they'll usually fix you something that's both good and cheap; most dishes are K8 to K15. Across the road at 176 83rd St there's the very popular *Nylon Ice Cream Bar* – it's a strange name (actually Nai Lon), but the ice cream is excellent and seems to be safe. In the evening you can sit out at the pavement tables and try strawberry, pineapple or orange ice cream at K2 for a large serving.

Next door is the *Olympia Café* – popular for light snacks at any time of day. For breakfast or lunch ask for a 'pauk-see' and get (for K2) a meat-and-vegetable mixture cooked up in a sort of bread roll. Next door again there's the equally popular *Orient* – light snacks and drinks again. The nearby *Min Min*, on 83rd St between 26th and 27th Rds, has Chinese Muslim food – it's reasonably cheap, with most dishes K8 to K10, and the food is excellent. Next door to Min Min is the *Taj*, which serves passable Indian food for K6 to K10 per set meal. Better Indian food is served at *Chiddy* on the corner of 81st St and 27th Rd.

On 29th Rd, particularly between 83rd and 84th Sts, there is a whole parcel of Chinese eateries. I thought the Chinese food was very good in the *Shanghai Restaurant* at 172 84th St, between 31st and 32nd Rds, where they have a real English menu with most dishes K7 to K20. The chicken and chillies at K10 is excellent, and you can always supplement the menu with the old 'point and ask for it' routine. Unfortunately a recent report indicates that the Shanghai has suffered a sharp drop in standards and is known as a gathering place for heavy tipplers.

For true local delicacies, try *Too Too* on the south side of 27th Rd between 74th and 75th (two blocks from Myintida Rest House), which serves Burmese food; and *Kyaukmei*, a Shan restaurant on the east side of 80th between 38th and 39th. Shan food is very similar to northern Thai cuisine – try Shan-style rice noodles with curry *(khowsen)* or the same noodles fried *(khowsen jo)*. The Kyaukmei also serves *shwe le maw*, orange brandy produced in the Shan State.

The food stalls strung along 26th Rd, beside the Zegyo Market, have good food at very cheap prices. Along the east side of 80th St between 28th and 30th many food stalls open up at night, selling everything from *mohinga* and chicken biriyani to moonshine *(ayet piu*, K3 a shot or K10 per bottle) and tea. Food is generally quite tasty here and you'll meet interesting people – less insular than most indoor restaurants in town.

Towards the end of the dry season Mandalay is a very dusty, thirsty place. All over town there'll be the sugar-cane squeezers with their big, heavy crushing wheels ready to fix you a glass of iced sugar-cane juice (with a dash of lime). Very refreshing and it seems to be fairly safe for K1. In season there is a collection of strawberry vendors on the corner of 84th St and 28th Rd. The baskets of delicious strawberries (from Maymyo?) sell for 50p, K1 or K2. Take a basket to one of the ice cream bars and have strawberries and ice cream!

Getting There

For information on travel between Mandalay and Pagan or Mandalay and Taunggyi, see the Pagan or Inle Lake sections. From Rangoon you can either fly or rail 'up-country'. Kipling never actually took the 'road to Mandalay' and if Tourist Burma have their way, neither will you.

Air There are usually at least a couple of flights a day on this sector. Rangoon-Mandalay straight through costs K461 and takes about 1½ hours by F-27; by F-28 it takes about an hour. Some of the F-27 flights go via Magwe or Heho, which will add an hour or more to your trip in either case. Air fare from Pagan is K152 and the flight takes only 30 minutes.

Rail Although there are a number of trains each day between the two cities, you should only consider the day or night express since the other trains are everything that can be wrong with Burmese rail travel – slow, crowded, uncomfortable and so on. Additionally, it is possible to reserve a seat on the express services (through Tourist Burma), and on these special 'impress the tourists services' you really do get a seat – not a half or a third of a seat. Upper class even has reclining seats and is quite comfortable.

Trains leave both ends at the same time and should arrive at the same time. They are generally admirably punctual, although you should reserve your seat as early as possible. Get an excellent chicken biriyani wrapped in a banana leaf

5 up	3 up	*		4 down	6 down	*
6.15 pm	6.00 am	9.00 pm	Rangoon	7.45 pm	8.15 am	11.30 am
	7.40 am		Pegu	5.59 pm		8.56 am
9.33 pm		0.18 am	Nyaunglebin		4.52 am	
	10.46 am		Pyu	2.54 pm		
0.16 am	11.59 am	3.05 am	Toungoo	1.36 pm	2.07 am	5.33 am
2.18 am	2.04 pm	5.07 am	Pyinmana	11.34 am	12.05 pm	3.31 am
4.17 am		7.06 am	Yamethin		10.19 pm	
	4.19 pm		Pyawbwe	9.23 am		1.20 am
5.31 am	5.00 pm	8.30 am	Thazi	8.43 am	9.04 pm	0.00 am
	6.47 pm		Kyaukse	6.59 am		
8.35 am	8.00 pm	11.30 am	Mandalay	6.00 am	6.15 pm	9.00 pm

*this train always seems to be referred to as 'the 9 pm train'.

for lunch at one of the stations on the way or, if you take the night train, on the Rangoon platform. Avoid the crunchy roast cricket kebabs I saw for sale at one station. Sleepers on this route are now impossible to get, but you can book two seats at night and stretch across them or simply sleep under a bench. Schedules and costs are:

fares:	ordinary class	K44
	upper class	K110
	1st class	K88

Getting Around

Bus Mandalay's buses are virtually always crowded, particularly during the 7 to 9 am and 4 to 5 pm 'rush hours'. Somehow it feels rather strange to be talking about a rush hour in Burma. The buses are also surprisingly friendly – so if that's more important to you than smooth comfort, you'll probably quite enjoy bussing around Mandalay. Some of the useful services include:

1 (၁)

to the Mahamuni Pagoda

2 (၂)

to the river end of B Rd (departure point for boats to Mingun) and out by the railway station and airport. Painted blue

4 (၄)

to Mandalay Hill from the clock tower

5 (၅)

also to Mandalay Hill, goes by the Mandalay Hill

7 (၇)

to the other side of Mandalay Hill, to the Institute of Indigenous Medicine

8 (၈)

via the Mahamuni Pagoda and Amarapura to Ava; starts from the corner of 27th and 84th

Jeep There aren't any taxis in Mandalay; jeeps or Japanese pick-ups are what you take. There are always some waiting at

Bus ticket

the airport – standard K20 for the whole jeep into town, although BAC tickets now include bus transport to the Mandalay Hotel. You'll also find them around Zegyo Market. They operate to surrounding towns, Maymyo in particular, on a depart-when-full basis. It's possible to hire jeeps or pick-ups by the day for tours around Mandalay, but they must have Tourist Burma stickers. Count on around K350 to K400 for a trip to Amarapura and Sagaing that includes an English-speaking guide; the trucks will take up to eight people so it needn't be expensive.

Trishaw & Tonga The familiar back-to-back trishaws or the horse-drawn tongas are the usual round-the-town transport. Count on K2 or K3 for a short ride in a trishaw, K4 or K5 for a longer one – say from the Mandalay Hotel to one of the restaurants or guest houses in town. For about K60 two people could hire a trishaw for the whole day and all their sightseeing. Tongas (horsecarts), which will take up to four passengers, are about double the cost of a trishaw, but you can hire one all day for sightseeing for K80 – definitely a more comfortable way to spend the day than in a cramped trishaw. If you're looking for a French-speaking tonga guide, Than Tun's your man. Best place to look for tongas/trishaws for day hire is outside the Mandalay or Mya Mandalar hotels. You must bargain for your fare, and either form of transport will be cheaper if a local negotiates the price for you.

Foot Mandalay is a surprisingly sprawling place. Think three times before setting out on a little stroll around the palace walls or out to Mandalay Hill.

Top: Street signs in Mandalay (TW)
Left: Palace moat from Mandalay Hill (TW)
Right: Mandalay palace moat (TW)

Top: Novice monks queue for alms (TW)
Left: On Sagaing Hill (TW)
Right: Shweyattaw image on Mandalay Hill (PC)

Deserted Cities

Within easy reach of Mandalay are four 'deserted cities'. After the fall of Pagan, right up to when the third and last Anglo-Burmese war reached its final, and for the Burmese disastrous, conclusion in 1885, the capital of a Burmese kingdom stood close to Mandalay. Perhaps it's part of the Buddhist belief in the temporary nature of life, but many kings developed an overpowering urge to start their reign with a new capital and a new palace. Thus the capital seemed to play musical chairs around the countryside.

Additionally, masonry or brick construction was reserved almost solely for religious buildings. The palaces may have been magnificent and extensive, but they were made of wood. When the shift was made to a new capital the wooden palace buildings were often dismantled and taken along. When the royal entourage departed the mighty cities soon reverted to farming villages – with neglected pagodas picturesquely dotting the fields.

In the chaos after the fall of Pagan it was Sagaing that first rose to power in the early 1300s, but in 1364 it was succeeded by Ava. Not until 1760 was the capital shifted back across the river to Sagaing, where it remained for just four years. Ava regained its pre-eminent position only from 1764 to 1783, when Amarapura became the capital. In 1823 Ava was again the capital, but following the terrible earthquake of 1838, which caused great damage to all these cities, the capital was moved back to Amarapura in 1841. Amarapura was again capital for only a short period and in 1860 the seat of power was transferred to Mandalay, where it remained until the British finished their conquest of Burma 25 years later.

Three of the ancient cities are south of Mandalay. Amarapura and Ava are on the east (Mandalay) side of the Irrawaddy,

while Sagaing lies to the west of the river but is easily reached by the long Ava Bridge. Mingun, which was never a capital although other cities also enjoyed that distinction for shorter periods, is on the west bank of the Irrawaddy to the north of Mandalay. It's easily reached by frequent riverboats from Mandalay.

The Last Kings
Alaungpaya founded the last dynasty (the Konbaungset dynasty) of Burmese kings in 1752. It ended only 133 years later when Thibaw was deposed by the British and exiled to India. Two of the kings, Hsinbyushin and Bodawpaya, were Alaungpaya's sons. The kings were:

Alaungpaya	1752-1760
Naungdawgyi	1760-1763
Hsinbyushin	1763-1776
Singu Min	1776-1782
Bodawpaya	1782-1819
Bagyidaw	1819-1837
Tharawaddy Min	1837-1846
Pagan Min	1846-1853
Mindon Min	1853-1878
Thibaw Min	1878-1885

AMARAPURA
Situated 11 km south of Mandalay, the modern town of Amarapura is often referred to as Taungmyo, 'the southern city', to distinguish it from Mandalay, the northern city. The old name means 'city of immortality', but Amarapura's period as capital was brief. Amarapura was founded by Bodawpaya as his new capital in 1783, soon after he ascended the throne, but in 1823 Bagyidaw moved back to Ava. In 1841 Amarapura again became the capital but in 1857 Mindon decided to make Mandalay the capital and the changeover was completed in 1860.

Today little remains of the old Amarapura palace area, although there

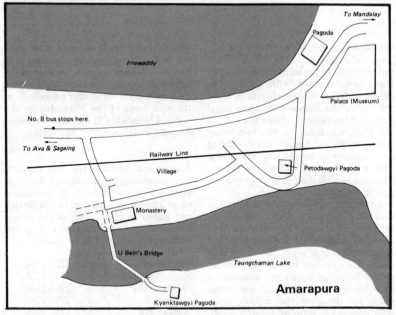

are several interesting sites to be seen. They are widely scattered, so if you've not got transport allow enough time and energy for walking. The city walls were torn down to make quarry material for railway lines and roads, while most of the wooden palace buildings were dismantled and taken to the new palace in Mandalay. Amarapura was also the site for the first British embassy in Burma in 1795.

Patodawgyi Pagoda
Built by Bagyidaw in 1820, this well-preserved pagoda stood outside the old city walls. The lower terraces have marble slabs illustrating scenes from the *Jataka*. You'll have a fine view over the surrounding countryside from the upper terrace. An inscription stone, within the temple precincts, details the history of the pagoda's construction.

Palace Ruins
Little remains of the old Amarapura palace, but you can find two masonry buildings – the treasury building and the old watch tower. King Bagyidaw and King Bodawpaya were both buried here and their tombs also remain. The corner pagodas still stand at the four corners of the once square city.

U Bein's Bridge
South of the Patodawgyi Pagoda the shallow Taungthaman Lake is crossed by a long and rickety teak bridge. During the dry season the bridge crosses dry land. U Bein was the 'mayor' at the time of the shift from Ava, and he wisely salvaged material from the deserted Ava Palace to build this km-long footbridge. It has stood the test of time for two centuries.

At the start of the bridge there's a monastery with whimsical monks' quarters in the shape of a row of (concrete) paddle steamers. There is also a new, and rather ugly, temple with a gigantic seated Buddha.

Kyauktawgyi Pagoda

If you stroll across the bridge – there are fine views across the lake to the Patodawgyi Pagoda and rest places where you can shelter from the sun – you'll come to the Kyauktawgyi Pagoda. Constructed in 1847 by King Pagan, it is said to have been modelled on the larger Ananda Temple at Pagan, but it has the look of a Tibetan or Nepali temple, with its five-tiered roof.

While the pagoda does not have the perfectly vaulted roofs or the finer decorations of the original, it does have an excellent seated Buddha image and interesting and well-preserved frescoes in the four entrance porches. Religious buildings, zodiac charts, scenes from everyday life are all illustrated in the frescoes. You can even find some suspiciously English-looking figures in the crowds – they were beginning to make their presence felt at the time of the pagoda's construction. In 1979 the Kyauktawgyi was repainted in a most un-Burmese-looking shade of baby blue.

U Bein's Bridge

The atmosphere around Kyauktawgyi is very peaceful and shady, and this is a good place to be at sunset when people, bicycles and bullock carts pass on their way back from a day's work in the fields surrounding the pagoda. There are several smaller overgrown pagodas in the vicinity, including a unique 'honeycomb' design stupa covered with Buddha niches. Lay people come here to practise meditation away from the worldly distractions of Mandalay. There are a couple of traditional outdoor tea shops where those with time on their hands sit on woven mats around low tables, drinking small pots of Chinese tea and eating snacks like fried gourd, soy cake and fried lentil balls dipped in tasty tamarind sauce.

Other

On the Irrawaddy bank, across from Sagaing, stand two 12th-century pagodas which were built by a king of Pagan – the Shwe Kyetyet and the Shwe Kyetkya. Amarapura also has a Chinese joss house – when the decision was made to shift to Mandalay the Chinese traders preferred to remain. Amarapura is noted for silk and cotton weaving, and as you wander through the wooden buildings of the modern town you'll hear the steady clackety-clack of the looms. Bronze casting is also carried on in Amarapura.

Getting There

A No 8 (၈) bus from in front of the Shwekyimyint Pagoda will take you to Amarapura and on to Ava if you wish. Get off the bus when you come to the palace wall on the left of the road and a pagoda guarded by elephants on the right, with the Irrawaddy visible behind it. From here you can walk to the Patodawgyi Pagoda and through the village of Taung Thaman to U Bein's bridge. You can also get there by tonga from Mandalay.

AVA

A few km south of Amarapura the Ava

Bridge spans the Irrawaddy to Sagaing. It's the only bridge across the Irrawaddy. Just south of the bridge the Myitnge River flows into the Irrawaddy, and south of this river stands the ancient city of Ava. A channel, known as the Myittha Chaung, was cut across from the Myitnge to the Irrawaddy to make Ava into an island.

From 1364, apart from brief interludes, Ava was the capital of a Burmese kingdom for nearly 400 years until the shift was made to Amarapura in 1841. Although Burma was known to the outside world as Ava until comparatively recently, the classical name of the city was Ratnapura – 'city of gems'.

Sagaing had been the capital of the central Burmese kingdom prior to 1364, but after it fell to the Shans the capital was moved across the river. The kings of Ava set about re-establishing Burmese supremacy which had been in decline since the fall of Pagan. Although the power of Ava soon extended as far as Prome, the Mon rulers of Pegu were a match for the Burmese.

In 1555 Ava fell to another Burmese kingdom, that of Toungoo, and in 1636 the capital of Toungoo was transferred to Ava, but this period as capital of the entire Burmese kingdom lasted only a century. The Mons again rose up and took and destroyed Ava in 1752. Only a few years later Alaungpaya vanquished the Mons forever, and after a period with Shwebo in the north as capital, Ava once again became the centre of the Burmese kingdom.

Bodawpaya moved the capital to Amarapura, but his successor Bagyidaw shifted it back to Ava. Then the disastrous earthquake of 1838 caused serious damage and the city was finally abandoned as a capital, in favour of Amarapura, in 1841.

Although there is not a great deal to be seen within the city, the massive old city walls are still easily traced. To the south of the city an ancient brick causeway

leads from the city gate towards the town of Tada-u. Inside the city walls a number of small villages have sprung up and peasants till the soil where once the palace used to stand.

Watch Tower

The 27-metre-high (90 feet) masonry watch tower, the Nanmyin, is all that remains of the palace built by Bagyidaw. The upper portion was shattered by the 1838 earthquake and the rest has taken on a precious tilt – it's the 'leaning tower of Ava'.

Maha Aungmye Bonzan

Also known as the Ok Kyaung, this is a masonry monastery built by the chief queen of Bagyidaw for her royal abbot Nyaunggan Sayadaw in 1818. Monasteries were normally built of wood and were prone to deterioration from the elements or destruction by fire. Although this monastery was built in imitation of the traditional wooden style, its masonry construction has ensured its survival. The 1838 earthquake badly damaged it, but in 1873 it was restored.

Judson Memorial

Near the monastery a huge block of white stone sits on a platform as a memorial to the American missionary Dr Adoniram Judson. This was the site of the Let Ma Yoon (no-holds-barred) prison where Judson was imprisoned from June 1824 to May 1825. During the first Anglo-Burmese war Judson had thought that the Burmese would realise Americans and British were not alike and leave him alone. He was wrong.

Other

Farms, villages, monasteries and ruined pagodas are scattered around the area within the old city walls. The walls are in particularly good condition near the northern gate, facing the Irrawaddy. This was known as the Gaung Say Daga or 'hair-washing' gate since kings had their

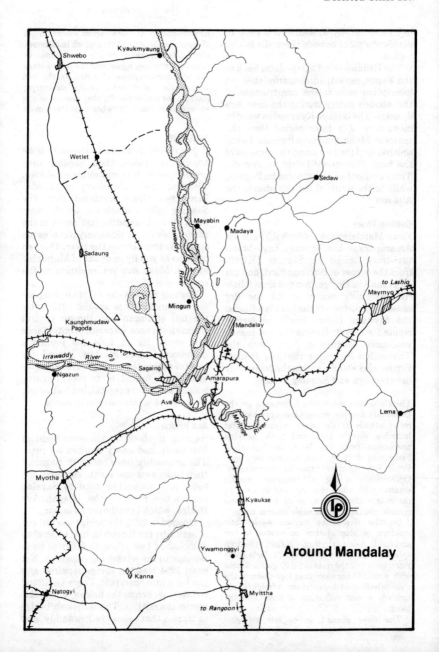

Around Mandalay

hair ceremonially washed at this gate. In places the moat outside the walls is also visible.

The Htilaingshin Pagoda dates back to the Pagan period; in a nearby shed an inscription records the construction of the wooden palace during the first Ava dynasty. The Bagaya Kyaung is a wooden monastery of a later period than the masonry Maha Aungmye Bonzan. To the south side of the city stand the remains of the huge four-storey Leitutgyi Pagoda. There is also the Lawkatharaphu Pagoda, while to the south of the city stands the Ava fort.

Getting There

From Mandalay take a No 8 (၆)) bus via Amarapura to Ava, or take a Zaya-Mann taxi-truck bound for Sagaing (K1.40) from the corner of 29th and 83rd, and get off at the Ava Bridge. You can then follow the extremely dusty (if it's the dry season) track down to the ferry landing on the Myitnge River. You'll be ferried across for a kyat. During the wet season you have to take a ferry from the Thabyedan Fort near the Ava Bridge. Ferries also shuttle across the Irrawaddy between Ava and Sagaing for 35p.

There's always something happening on the Irrawaddy. Canoes, strange boats in which the rower stands at the rear, or small motor launches shuttle back and forth carrying passengers from one bank to the other. Fishermen drift by, casting their nets out. Ferries forge up-river or speed by downstream. Occasionally a big, old-fashioned paddle steamer – its wheel chunkin' and thunkin' at the rear – churns past on its way to some remote and unpronounceable upriver town.

On the riverbanks women wash their children or slap clothes on stones in the standard Asian rhythm. Naked children splash noisily in the shallows. Ox-carts come right down into the river to fill 50-gallon drums with water. Other oxen drag logs down to the river to be floated downstream. A freight barge unloads a vast collection of pots onto the bank.

The river doesn't follow one straight-

forward course. At times it splits into a number of separate channels that surge off in different directions, separated by low sand banks or islands. Later they rejoin, and the river widens out to a huge expanse of water. In the wet season the lower sand banks submerge; towards the end of the dry they rise out of the water and the bigger ferry boats get stuck more often.

SAGAING

If you're unable to get to Pagan to poke around the ruins, then Sagaing may provide you with an interesting substitute. There are certainly plenty of pagodas here, and those scattered over the Sagaing hills – which rise on the west bank of the Irrawaddy, just north of the modern town – provide a very picturesque spectacle from across the river. Or even more so as you fly in or out of Mandalay airport. Make sure you're sitting on the correct side of the plane.

Sagaing became capital of an independent Shan kingdom around 1315, after the fall of Pagan had thrown central Burma into chaos. Its period of importance was short, for in 1364 the founder's grandson, Thado Minbya, moved his capital across the river to Ava. For four brief years, from 1760 to 1764, Sagaing was once again the capital, but its historic importance is comparatively minor.

Ava Bridge

Sagaing is about 20 km south-west of Mandalay and easily reached by road. The Irrawaddy flows south by Sagaing, then turns west and north, enclosing the town in a loop. The road to Sagaing crosses the river on the 16-span Ava Bridge, which is well over a km long.

Opened in 1934, the bridge was put out of action by the British in 1942 when they demolished two spans in order to deny passage to the advancing Japanese. Not until 1954 was the bridge repaired and put back into operation. There's a K2 toll to take cars across the bridge, which also carries the rail line. This is the only bridge in Burma that spans the Irrawaddy, and because of its strategic importance taking photos is supposedly illegal.

Thabyedan Fort

Just to the left of the bridge, on the Mandalay and Ava side, is the fort of Thabyedan which was built as a last-ditch defence by the Burmese before the third Anglo-Burmese war. It was taken by the British with little effort.

Kaunghmudaw Pagoda

Kaunghmudaw Pagoda

Best known of the Sagaing pagodas, this huge edifice is actually 10 km beyond the town of Sagaing. The enormous dome rises 46 metres (151 feet) in the shape of a perfect hemisphere and was modelled after the Mahaceti Pagoda in Ceylon – although legend also says that it

represents the perfect breast of a well-endowed Burmese queen. Also known as Rajamanicula, the pagoda was built in 1636 to commemorate Ava's establishment as the royal capital of Burma.

Around the base of the pagoda are 812 1½-metre-high stone pillars, each with a small niche cut in it for an oil lamp. Images of *nats* can be seen in 120 niches which also circle the base. A nearly three-metre-high polished marble slab stands in a corner of the pagoda grounds – the 86 lines of Burmese inscriptions on the slab record details of the pagoda's construction.

Tupayon Pagoda

Constructed by King Narapati of Ava in 1444, the Tupayon is of an unusual style for Burma; it consists of three circular storeys each encircled with arched niches. A temporary wooden bridge was constructed across the Irrawaddy when the *hti* was raised, and a huge festival was held. The 1838 earthquake toppled the pagoda, and although it was partially repaired in 1849 the reconstruction was never completed.

Aungmyelawka Pagoda

Situated on the riverfront, near the Tupayon, this pagoda was built in 1783 by Bodawpaya on the site of his residence before he became king. It is built entirely of sandstone in imitation of the Shwezigon Pagoda at Nyaung-Oo in Pagan. It is also known as the Eindawya Pagoda.

Other Pagodas

The Datpaungzu Pagoda is comparatively recent, but houses many relics from other, older pagodas which were demolished when the railway was built through Sagaing. The Ngadatkyi to the west of Sagaing was built in 1657 and houses a fine and very large seated Buddha image. The Hsinmyashin Pagoda is on the way to the Kaunghmudaw Pagoda and is known as the Pagoda of Many Elephants. Built in 1429, it was badly damaged in an earthquake in 1485. Although subsequently repaired, it suffered even worse damage in a 1955 earthquake.

Sagaing Hill

The hill itself has a number of pagodas and monasteries – some of which are comparatively recent. The Padamyazedi dates from 1300, while the Onhmin Thonze or '30-caves' pagoda has many Buddha images in a crescent-shaped colonnade. The impressive Soon U Ponya Shin Pagoda nearby was constructed in 1312 and reaches 29.3 metres high with a 7.8-metre *hti* beyond that; in front of the principal altar, large bronze frogs on wheels serve as collection boxes. The view of Sagaing from Soon U Ponya Shin and its approaches is outstanding. Mural paintings can be seen in the Tilawkaguru cave temple which was built around 1672. The Pa Ba Gyaung is typical of the many monasteries on the hillside.

Sagaing also has the remains of a fort by the riverbank. At the nearby village of Ywataung you can see silverworkers producing bowls and other silver items by traditional methods.

The village at the foot of Sagaing Hill makes an interesting visit, chock-a-block with markets, shops and restaurants.

Getting There

The Sagaing taxi-truck will take you right to the middle of town for K1.50 from Mandalay. If you want to continue to the Kaunghmudaw Pagoda it will cost you another K1.60 for a taxi-truck ride.

MINGUN

If I had to choose just one of the four ancient cities around Mandalay to visit, I think it would be Mingun. Not only are there some very interesting things to see within a comparatively compact area, but getting there is half the fun. Mingun is about 11 km up-river from Mandalay on the opposite bank of the Irrawaddy and accessible only by river. It's just long enough a trip to give you a pleasant feel for the river without being so long that

Mingun

you'll worry how much of your precious seven days you're using up – as can happen on the Mandalay-Pagan riverboat (particularly if you get stuck).

A footpath parallel to the river that runs the length of the ruins area and beyond makes an interesting walk and is less dusty than the main road in dry weather. The Mingun Sanitarium (also called the Buddhist Infirmary), a nursing home for the elderly, is worth checking out. The head nurse here is Than Than Sue – she speaks excellent English and is happy to impart info on the Mingun area. You might be able to put up here for the night if there's room.

At the restaurants along the second Mingun landing you can get a tasty lunch of Indian tea, roti and chickpeas.

Mingun Pagoda

If King Bodawpaya had succeeded in his grandiose scheme, Mingun might now have had the world's largest pagoda. At 150 metres (500 feet) high it would have towered 20 metres above the colossal pagoda at Nakhon Pathom in Thailand. When Bodawpaya died in 1819 construction was abandoned, and all that remains today is the world's largest pile of bricks.

But what a pile of bricks – the base of his projected pagoda, badly cracked by the earthquake of 1838, stands 50 metres high overlooking the river. A pair of commensurately large griffins are crumbling away at their guard posts closer to the river. They too were badly damaged by the 1838 'quake.

Each side of the enormous base measures 72 metres (235 feet), and the lowest terrace measures 140 metres (450 feet). There are projecting arches on each of the four sides. Beautiful glazed tiles in brown, pale brown, cream and green were intended to be set in panels around the terrace; some of these tiles can be seen in the small building in front of the enormous ruin.

Despite its dilapidated state you must still go barefoot if you intend to climb the base. You can climb the pagoda on the crumbled corner, and from the top you have a fine view of the Hsinbyume Pagoda.

Pondawpaya

Closer to the riverbank, a little downstream from the Mingun Pagoda, is this five-metre-high (15 feet) working model for the gigantic structure. It gives a clear picture of just what Bodawpaya intended to achieve. During the 15 years it took to build the base of his pagoda he frequently set up residence on an island in the Irrawaddy to supervise the construction.

Mingun Bell

In 1790 Bodawpaya had a gigantic bell cast to go with his gigantic pagoda. Weighing 90 tonnes, it is claimed to be the largest hung, uncracked bell in the world. There is said to be a larger bell in Moscow, but it is cracked.

The same earthquake that shook the pagoda base also destroyed the bell's supports so it was hung in a new *tazaung* (shed) close to the riverboat landing. The bell is about four metres high and over five metres (15 feet) in diameter at the lip. You can scramble right inside it and some helpful bystander will give it a good thump so you can hear the ring from the interior.

Hsinbyume or Myatheindan Pagoda

Built by King Bagyidaw in 1816, three years before he succeeded Bodawpaya as king, the pagoda was constructed in memory of his senior wife, the Hsinbyume princess. It is built as a representation of the Sulamani Pagoda which, according to the Buddhist plan of the cosmos, stands atop Mt Meru. The seven wavy terraces around the pagoda represent the seven mountain ranges around Mt Meru, while the five kinds of mythical monsters can be found in niches on each terrace level. This pagoda, too, was badly damaged in the 1838 quake, but King Mindon restored it in 1874.

Settawya Pagoda

Close to the riverbank, downstream from the Pondawpaya model, this hollow, vaulted shrine has a footprint of the Buddha which was brought to Mingun by King Bodawpaya when the relic chamber in the base of his huge pagoda was sealed up. The temple was built in 1811.

Getting There

Riverboats to Mingun depart from the bottom of 26th St with reasonable frequency. The up-river journey usually takes about 45 minutes, though sometimes it can take as long as two hours. Depending on the currents, coming back may be rather quicker. It's best to get a boat out of Mandalay between 7 and 8 am; arrange transport to the jetty the night before – from the Myintida or Mandalay Hotel, a tonga or motor trishaw would be K15, a pedal trishaw K5 to K10. The last boat back to Mandalay from Mingun usually leaves around 3 pm, so don't start this trip too late in the day. The cost is K4.

It's a pleasant, interesting trip with plenty to see along the way – fishing villages, bullock carts, corn fields, market boats, laundering. The boat stops at a sandbank at the southern end of the Mingun area, then continues to the main landing place beyond the Mingun Pagoda base. Get off the ferry and walk past the restaurants straight through the Buddhist Infirmary to the big bell.

Tourist Burma also runs a boat trip to Mingun every Sunday and Thursday for K60, which includes lunch but is considerably more expensive than doing it on your own, especially since the fee must be entered on your currency form.

MONYWA

Not exactly a deserted city, Monywa is a worthwhile trip for true Burmese pagoda enthusiasts or others who just want to go where few travellers go. Monywa is 136 km north-west of Mandalay along the Mandalay-Ye U branch railway line and is a trade centre for the Chindwin Valley. The big attraction here is the magnificent Thanboddhay Pagoda, a Mt Meru-type structure with no less than 582,357 Buddha images ensconced thereon – conceptually reminiscent of Borobudur in Indonesia. Nobody seems to know its age, but it's in very good condition so either it's rather new or the locals have taken especially good care of it. Nearby Kyaukka village is a centre for the crafting of lacquerware.

Getting There

You can catch a bus to Monywa at the corner of 84th and 30th. Buses leave about every 45 minutes between 4 am and 3 pm, cost K25, and take around three hours to reach their destination. You can also get a Ye-U train from the Mandalay station for only K8, but that will take four to five hours.

Maymyo

Named after a British Colonel May ('Maytown') in 1886, Maymyo was long a British hill station where, during the hot season, the servants of the Raj went to escape the heat of the plains. It is 67 km beyond Mandalay and, standing at 1070 metres, considerably higher. The altitude makes all the difference. Even at the height of the hot season Maymyo is pleasantly cool and at certain times of the year it can get quite chilly.

Getting to Maymyo is half the fun. From Mandalay you take a rough old jeep which chugs its way across the plains, then up the winding road into the hills. There's no hurry about the trip, which is interspersed with stops to top up the jeep's radiator. At the half way mark you pass 'View Point' with spectacular views.

Getting around Maymyo can be equally enjoyable; the standard transport around town is a miniature, enclosed wagon pulled by a pony. You're never sure if it's a half-scale replica from the Wells Fargo days of the American West or something from the British 'stand and deliver' era. The place to stay can be most fun of all – see Candacraig in the accommodation details, or read Paul Theroux's delightful account of Maymyo in his book *The Great Railway Bazaar*.

Around Town

Maymyo has a notable 200-hectare botanical garden and is also a centre for growing many 'English' vegetables which do not flourish in the hotter conditions of the plains. Surprisingly, strawberries are one of the products of this higher altitude – in season (February, March) they're cheap and delicious. The town itself is easy-going and full of interest – a good place for an evening stroll or an interesting morning around the market. There are still many English signs around

Maymyo. A few minutes' walk from Candacraig there's a colourful and interesting Chinese temple.

Just north of the town there's a good view from the Naung Kan Gyi pagoda on the hill top. You can leave your bicycle at the shops at the bottom of the hill.

Out of Maymyo

There are a number of picturesque waterfalls around Maymyo. The Pwe Kauk Falls are about eight km from town on the Lashio Rd. You can swim in the upper reaches, but not at the bottom where the undertow can be dangerous.

More spectacular are the Anisakan, although a fairly long walk is required to get to them – you should allow half a day for this trip. At the village of Anisakan, about eight km down towards Mandalay, turn right at the railway station, continue about 600 metres to the railway crossing, then turn left on a dirt road for about 800 metres to a fork where you again take a left turn. After about a half km you reach a parking place from where you continue on foot. The falls are in five parts; the third is particularly spectacular. There are also the Wetwun Falls, about 24 km out of Maymyo.

Gokteik

The unusual Gokteik railway viaduct is 55 km (34 miles) out of Maymyo en route to Lashio, but this is well into 'forbidden' territory. Trains and jeeps run up the spectacular route to Lashio, but you can't go. At Sakhantha, just beyond Gokteik, there is one of the best examples of Shan architecture – the palace or *Haw* of the Sawbwa of Hsipaw.

Places to Stay

Half the reason for coming to Maymyo is to stay in *Candacraig* – even if it is now officially known as the *Maymyo Govern-*

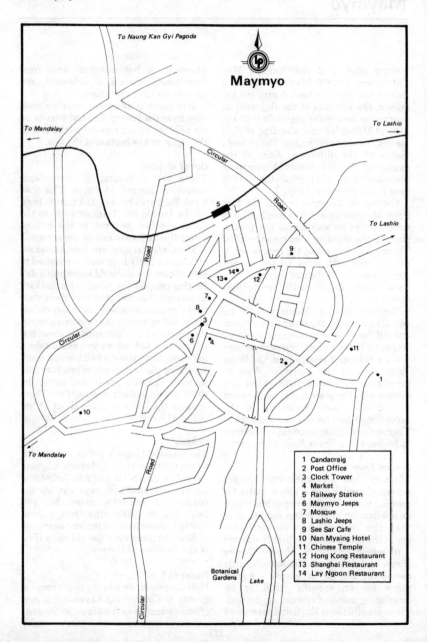

To Naung Kan Gyi Pagoda

Maymyo

To Mandalay

To Lashio

Circular Road

To Lashio

Circular Road

To Mandalay

Botanical Gardens

Lake

1	Candacraig
2	Post Office
3	Clock Tower
4	Market
5	Railway Station
6	Maymyo Jeeps
7	Mosque
8	Lashio Jeeps
9	See Sar Cafe
10	Nan Myaing Hotel
11	Chinese Temple
12	Hong Kong Restaurant
13	Shanghai Restaurant
14	Lay Ngoon Restaurant

ment Rest House. In the colonial era this was the 'chummery' or bachelor quarters for employees of the Bombay Burmah Trading Company. This trading firm was engaged in extracting teak in upper Burma, and the chummery was built in 1906 in the form of an English country mansion – constructed, naturally, of the finest teak. Today you can sweep up the imposing staircase to the upper landing where you will find huge, old-fashioned rooms, the doubles each with their own bathrooms and curtained-off dressing area. If it gets chilly at night they will even light a fire in the fireplace. The cost is K29 for singles, K55 for doubles.

Much of Candacraig's appeal was that Mr Bernard, the chummery cook back in the British era, ran the place exactly as if the British had never left. Unhappily Mr Bernard has now departed this world, but roast beef still appears on the menu some nights and most travellers find it a great place to stay. You can sip a beer in front of the roaring log fire in the lounge, and at breakfast or lunch they may put a table out on the lawn so you can dine in open-air splendour. Candacraig has 19 staff members and often very few guests – the last night I was there we numbered six (two Australians, two French, an American and myself).

Tourist Burma have a second place in Maymyo, on your left just as you enter town from Mandalay. The *Nann Myaing* has standard singles/doubles at US$7.50/9 or larger 'superior' rooms for US$10/17. Actually Candacraig is officially an annex to the Nann Myaing; Tourist Burma will try to send you there first of all.

For the impecunious, Maymyo also has the *YMCA* which costs K10, or guest houses like the *Shwe Yema* or the *Ububahan* which charge an identical K11 single, K22 double.

Places to Eat

Apart from Candacraig there are a number of assorted eating places in the town centre, including two restaurants reputed to have the best Chinese food in Burma, outside of Rangoon. The *Shanghai Restaurant* is a block east of Purcell's Tower (the clock tower) on the Mandalay-Lashio road. It specialises in Shanghainese and Szechuan food. A further half-block east, the *Lay Ngoon Restaurant* specialises in Cantonese food. Along the Lashio road a km or so you can get cold drinks at the *See Sar* (Dawn) café.

Getting There

Jeep A taxi-jeep is the usual way to climb the hills to Maymyo. They depart from several places around the centre of Mandalay from before 7 in the morning until about 3 in the afternoon. As soon as a full load of eight passengers has fitted itself on board, your jeep will depart; for comfort and view you are better off grabbing the front seats and letting the hardier Burmese cram themselves into the back. Cost is K28 (K30 to Candacraig) and the trip takes two to 2½ hours up, 1½ to two hours down – barring breakdowns of course, which in Burma are quite likely.

Burma's jeeps are mainly of decidedly ancient vintage, and at the very least will require a couple of radiator refilling stops on the way up. Chartering a whole jeep will cost you K200+. Some of the jeeps continue on beyond Maymyo all the way to Lashio – foreigners are not permitted to continue beyond Maymyo, but if you were, the ride would cost K35 each.

Rail There is also a daily train up to Maymyo from Mandalay, but this is more for railway enthusiasts than a sensible means of transport. The train departs Mandalay at 5 am and climbs the hills by a switchback system, arriving four to five hours later. Cost is just K5; for a further K45 the locals can go on to Lashio.

Getting Around

You can hire bicycles at Candacraig, and also from the See Sar Cafe on the Lashio road.

Pagan

It's the most amazing sight in Burma, if not South-East Asia. Across 40 square km of country, stretching back from the Irrawaddy, stand hundreds of pagodas and temples. Everywhere you look stand ruins of all sizes – huge and glorious temples like the Ananda soar towards the sky; graceful small pagodas stand alone in fields. There are places full of history, others which are identified only by a number.

History

The extraordinary religious fervour that resulted in this unique collection of buildings lasted barely two centuries. Although the kingdoms of Pagan date back almost to the beginning of the Christian era, Pagan only entered its golden period with the conquest of Thaton in 1057 AD. Just over 200 years later, in 1287, Pagan was abandoned and overrun by the Tartar hordes of Kublai Khan. But what fantastic effort went into those two centuries – it's as if all the medieval cathedrals of Europe had been built in one small area, and then deserted, barely touched over the centuries.

Pagan's prime started with Anawrahta's ascent to the throne in 1044. At this time, Burma was in a period of transition from Hindu and Mahayana Buddhist (the greater vehicle) beliefs to the Theravada Buddhist (the lesser vehicle) beliefs that have since been characteristic of Burma. A monk was sent by the Mon king of Thaton, Manuha, to convert Anawrahta; he met with such success that Anawrahta asked Manuha to give him a number of sacred texts and important relics. Manuha, uncertain of the depths of Anawrahta's beliefs, refused the request. Anawrahta's reply to this snub was straightforward – he marched his army south, conquered Thaton and carted back to Pagan everything worth carrying,

including 32 sets of the *Tripitaka* (the Buddhist religious writings), the city's monks and architects and, for good measure, King Manuha himself.

Immediately Anawrahta set about a great programme of building, and some of the greatest Pagan edifices date from his reign. Amongst the better-known monuments he constructed are the beautiful Shwezigon Pagoda, considered a prototype for all later Burmese stupas; the Pitakat Taik, built to house the scriptures carried back from Thaton by 30 elephants; and the elegant and distinctive Shwesandaw Pagoda, built immediately after the conquest of Thaton.

His successors continued this phenomenal building programme, particularly Kyanzittha, Alaungsithu and Narapatisithu, although the building must have been virtually non-stop throughout the period of Pagan's glory. Then the threat of invasion from China by Kublai Khan threw the last powerful ruler of Pagan into a panic – after a great number of temples were torn down to build fortifications, the city was suddenly abandoned. It is not even certain if the Tartars actually sacked Pagan, or merely took over an already deserted city. Although some minor rebuilding and maintenance continued through the centuries, the city was effectively finished. Today a few farmers are the only occupants of the great city. Grain fields stand where once there were palace grounds.

It's hard to imagine Pagan as it once was because, like other Burmese royal cities, only the religious buildings were made of permanent materials. The kings' palaces were all constructed of wood, and even most monasteries were partly or wholly wooden. So what remains today is just a frail shadow of Pagan at its peak.

The kings who reigned over Pagan during its golden period were:

Anawrahta	1044-1077
Sawlu	1077-1084
Kyanzittha	1084-1113
Alaungsithu	1113-1167
Narathu	1167-1170
Naratheinkha	1170-1173
Narapatisithu	1174-1211
Htilominlo (Nantaungmya)	1211-1234
Kyaswa	1234-1250
Uzana	1250-1255
Narathihapati	1255-1287

The 1975 Earthquake

In 1975 Pagan was shattered by a powerful earthquake. At first it was thought that this 1000-year-old wonder was totally ruined, but in actual fact the story was not nearly so disastrous. Only a limited number of the most important temples have been regularly maintained down through the centuries. Many of these were badly damaged, but reconstruction started almost immediately and all the major restoration work has now been completed. Since renovation of those important pagodas and temples has been an ongoing project for many centuries, the old skills have not been lost and they were all rebuilt by totally traditional means. You certainly won't see any modern construction equipment in Pagan. As for the hundreds of lesser temples – anything that was likely to fall off in an earthquake would have fallen off centuries ago. While it was quite evident which of the major temples was under repair, Pagan never looked like a huge building site. I've been to Pagan both before and several times after the earthquake, and the difference was not enormous.

Fortunately the earthquake took place in the middle of the hot season so there were few visitors at Pagan at the time. The quake took place at sunset, yet miraculously nobody was up in the temples catching the sunset that evening. There was no loss of life. The Gawdawpalin, the most seriously damaged of the major temples, is a favourite sunset view point.

A guide told me that for some reason he didn't feel like taking his visitors up to a temple for the sunset that evening and suggested they view it with a cold beer at the Thiripyitsaya instead! He was walking down towards the Irrawaddy for a swim when the quake took place, and he remembers a strange noise before the ground actually started to move. Afterwards the air was filled with dust, and since the power failed everything was soon plunged into darkness. The epicentre was 39 km away.

Architectural Styles

There are a number of distinct architectural styles at Pagan, and it is also possible to trace the developments of temple design over the two centuries. Buildings are primarily solid pagodas or hollow temples. A pagoda customarily houses some relic from the Buddha, while the focal point of a temple will be a Buddha image. There are also some unique structures – like the Pitakat Taik library or the Upali Thein ordination hall. These are buildings that would normally have been constructed of wood and therefore would have disappeared. There are also a number of Indian-style cave temples, particularly around the town of Nyaung-Oo.

The pagodas can be seen in an earlier, more bulbous style and in a clearly Sinhalese design before they evolved into the more distinctively Burmese pattern. Early temples were heavily influenced by the Mon architects imported from Thaton after its conquest. These early temples are characterised by their perforated windows and dark, dimly lit interiors. Later temples added Indian design elements to the mix to produce a truly Burmese design in bright and well-lit temples like the Gawdawpalin, Htilominlo and Thatbyinnyu. The Ananda and Dhammayangyi are examples of the transition phase; indeed, the Ananda is thought to have been built by imported Indian labour. The temples can be divided into two types – those having one entrance to a vaulted inner area and those having four entrances with images around a central cube.

Orientation & Information

Although the whole area is known as Pagan, the actual village of Pagan is just one of many in the area. The main town is Nyaung-Oo, about five km (three miles) up-river from Pagan. Although the airport is near Nyaung-Oo and this is also the place for buses and riverboats, the 'tourist centre' is in Pagan village – here you will find all the accommodation, the BAC office and the Tourist Burma office, which is open 8 am to 8 pm daily. You can change money at the Thiripyitsaya Hotel.

Pagan is on a curve of the Irrawaddy River. A road follows the river bend from Nyaung-Oo, through Pagan to Myinkaba and Thiripyitsaya – other small villages. At times this road was a dusty track, as are most trails between the villages.

Round towards the Co-Op there's a small Burmese puppet theatre. Shows for visitors last about half an hour and cost K8. The puppets are very interesting and the shows are well worth seeing.

What to See?

What you will be able to see is very much limited by the amount of time at your disposal and how you intend to use it. If you can afford to hire a jeep and a guide, you'll be able to visit more temples, particularly those further off the beaten track. The availability of bicycles to rent also makes the temples much more accessible than on foot.

Thatbyinnyu Temple

Top: Thatbinnyu, Pitakat & Taik (TW)
Left: Shwezigon in Nyaung-Oo (PC)
Right: Transport around Pagan (TW)

Top: On the shores by Mingun Pagoda (TW)
Bottom: Decaying pagodas around Pagan (TW)

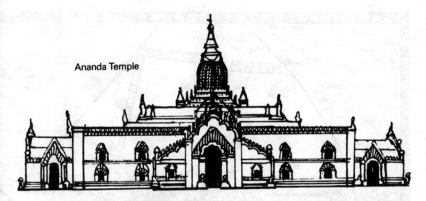

Ananda Temple

If your time is very limited – just an afternoon or a day, for example – I suggest that you restrict yourself to the temples close to Pagan village. This is where the greatest concentration of temples and pagodas can be found, plus the small Pagan museum. You can spend an interesting day wandering around the major buildings here and catch the sun, sinking dramatically behind the hills over the Irrawaddy, from one of the great temples or, with a cold one from the Peoples' Brewery & Distillery, from the verandah of the Thiripyitsaya Hotel.

If you have more time at your disposal, then go further afield – visit the important Shwezigon in Nyaung-Oo and the other interesting temples along the road from Pagan. Head out of Pagan to the nearby village of Myinkaba (you can walk there) and see the lacquerware workshops and my favourite temple – the Manuha. With even more time, and wheels, you could continue on to Thiripyitsaya or head well off the road to Pwasaw or Minnanthu. If you're going to these very remote centres, be a little cautious – I have heard of a woman being 'mugged' (a very un-Burmese thing to happen) when visiting a remote temple by herself.

PAGAN
Although Pagan is not the major population centre in the area, it is the tourist centre so it will be the place where you spend the most time. There are quite a few places to stay and eat, and lots of lacquerware shops too. Pagan is right on the bend of the Irrawaddy – sometime during your stay wander down to the waterfront and watch the coming and going of river trade. Boats will be passing by or pausing to unload goods, villagers will come down to the river with oxen carts to collect water. You can even take a boat across the river to the village on the other side. Note how Pagan's water supply is pumped up from a point just down below the Irra Inn. Pagan also has an interesting little market, close to the main road near the old city gates.

Pagan Museum
The small but interesting Pagan Museum is in a new building near the Co-Operative guest house – across from the Gawdawpalin. It contains a large number of images and other fine works found in temples around Pagan. There is also a small exhibit on the '75 earthquake. It makes an interesting introduction before you start exploring the actual temples. The museum is open 9 am to 4.30 pm, Tuesday to Sunday.

Sarabha Gateway
The ruins of the main gate on the east wall

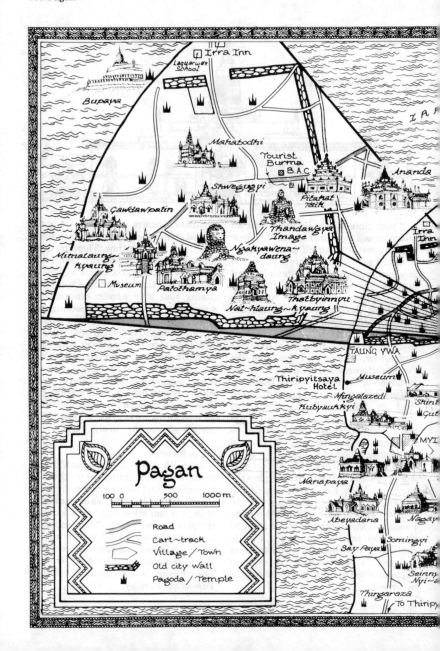

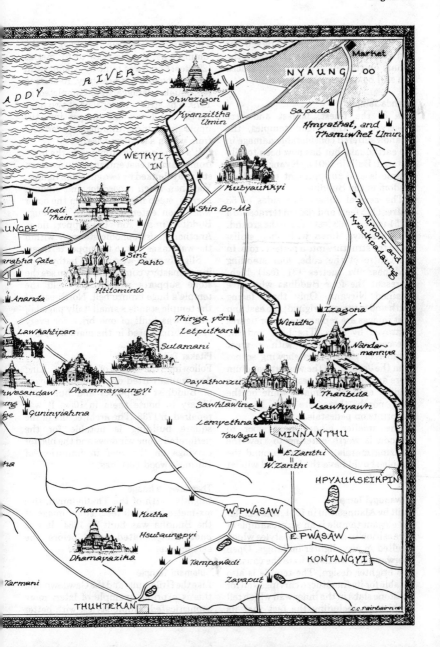

are all that remain of the old 9th-century city wall. The gate is guarded by brother and sister *nats*, the male on the right, the female on the left. Traces of old stucco can still be seen on the gateway.

Ananda Temple

One of the finest, largest and best preserved of the Pagan temples, the Ananda suffered considerable damage in the earthquake but has now been totally restored. Built in 1901 by Kyanzittha, the temple is said to represent the endless wisdom of the Buddha.

The central square has sides of 53 metres (175 feet) and rises in terraces to a *hti* 51 metres (168 feet) above the ground. Entranceways, lined with shop stalls, make the structure into a perfect cross. In the centre of the cube, four standing Buddhas, 9½ metres (31 feet) high, represent the four Buddhas who have attained Nirvana. Only those facing north and south are original; the east and west images are replacements for figures destroyed by fires. The base and the terraces are decorated with a great number of glazed tiles showing scenes from the *Jataka*. In the western sanctum there are life-size statues of the temple's founder and his primate, while on the west porch there are two Buddha footprints on pedestals.

The smaller *vihara* next door to Ananda is worth entering to view the amazing murals – someone around the temple should have the keys and will let you in.

Shwegugyi Temple

Built by Alaungsithu in 1311, this smaller but elegant temple is an early example of a transition in architectural styles which resulted in airy, lighter buildings. Open doorways and windows were the cause of this brighter design. The temple is also notable for its fine stucco carvings and for the stone slabs in the inner wall which tell its history, including the fact that its construction took seven months.

Thatbyinnyu Temple

The highest temple in Pagan, the 'omniscient' temple rises to 61 metres (200 feet) and was built by Alaungsithu around the mid-12th century. Repairs to earthquake damage were completed in 1979. The structure consists of two huge cubes; the lower one merges into the upper with three diminishing terraces from which a *sikhara* rises.

It's quite a maze climbing to the top – from the main east entrance you ascend a stairway flanked by two guardian figures. You then reach a corridor and climb a narrow, steep flight of steps in the outer wall, then external steps to the huge Buddha image on the upper floor. Another claustrophobic stairway within the wall takes you to the upper terraces.

Slightly south-west of the Thatbyinnyu in a monastery compound you can see the stone supports which once held the temple's huge bronze bell. North-east of the temple stands a small 'tally pagoda', which was built of one brick for every 10,000 bricks used in the main temple.

Pitakat Taik

Following the sack of Thaton, King Anawrahta carted off 30 elephant-loads of Buddhist scriptures and built this library to house them in 1058. It was repaired in 1738. The architecture of the square building is notable for the perforated stone windows and the plaster carvings on the roof in imitation of Burmese wood-carvings.

Thandawgya Image

Slightly north of the Thatbyinnyu, this six-metre-high (19 feet) stone image of the Buddha was built in 1284. It was badly deteriorated even before the earthquake.

Sulamani Temple

Like the Htilominlo and the Gawdawpalin, this is a prime example of later, more sophisticated temple styles, with better internal lighting. It stands beyond the

Dhammayangyi Temple and was built in 1181 by Narapatisithu. The temple has two storeys and small stupas at the corner of each terrace. Buddha images face the four directions from the ground floor. The image at the main east entrance sits in a recess built into the wall. The interior was once painted with fine frescoes, but only traces can be seen today – the walls have been painted over with later, inferior, though nevertheless interesting frescoes. You can get very close to the top of this temple, where the views are superb.

Nathlaung Kyaung

Slightly to the east of the Thatbyinnyu, this is the only Hindu temple remaining in Pagan. It is said to have been built in 931 by King Taunghthugyi; this was about a century before the southern school of Buddhism came to Pagan, following the conquest of Thaton. The temple is dedicated to the Hindu god Vishnu. Around the outside wall are figures of the '10 Avatars', of whom Gautama Buddha was said to be the ninth.

The central brick pillar suppo[rts] dome and crumbled *sikhara*, and had figures of Vishnu on each of the sides. The temple may have been built Indian settlers in Pagan – possibly the skilled workers brought to construct other temples.

Gawdawpalin Temple

One of the largest and most imposing of the Pagan temples, the Gawdawpalin was built during the reign of Narapatisithu (1174-1211) but was very badly damaged in the '75 earthquake. Reconstruction of the Gawdawpalin was probably the largest operation undertaken following the earthquake, and it was into the '80s before it was completed.

In plan the temple is somewhat similar to the Thatbyinnyu – cube-shaped with Buddha images on the four sides of the ground floor. The top of the stupa, which toppled off in the earthquake, reaches 55 metres (180 feet) in height. The top terrace is an excellent place to catch the sunset over the Irrawaddy. The passageways leading to the top get very dark after

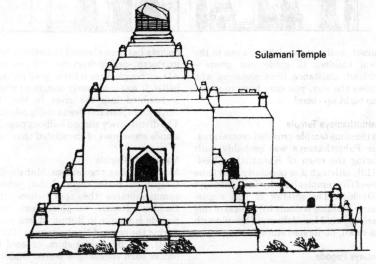

Sulamani Temple

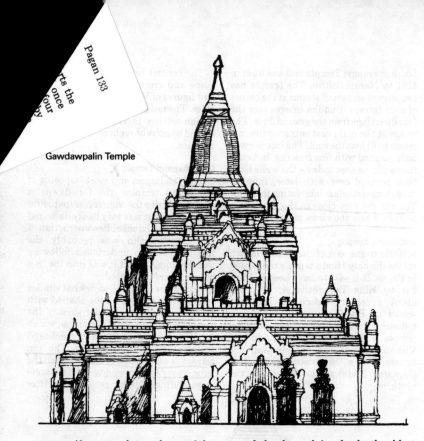

Gawdawpalin Temple

sunset, so if you stay late, ask one of the local children to guide you down – without assistance from someone who knows the way, you may have to spend the night up there!

Pahtothamaya Temple

In the same temple-crowded central area, the Pahtothamaya was probably built during the reign of Kyanzittha (1084-1113), although it is popularly held to be one of five temples built by Taunghthugyi (931-964). The interior of this single-storey building is dimly lit, typical of this early type of Mon-influenced temple with its small, perforated stone windows.

Bupaya Pagoda

Right on the bank of the Irrawaddy, this

pagoda has been claimed to be the oldest in Pagan, dating from the 3rd century AD, although there is little proof for this belief. It was completely destroyed when it tumbled into the river in the '75 earthquake, but has been totally rebuilt. The distinctively shaped bulbous pagoda stands above rows of crenellated terraces.

Mahabodhi Pagoda

Modelled after the famous Mahabodhi temple in Bodh Gaya, India, which commemorates the spot where the Buddha attained enlightenment, this pagoda is unique in Burma. It was built during the reign of Nantaungmya (1211-1234). The pyramidal spire, covered in niches each enclosing a seated Buddha figure, rises from a square block.

Mahadodhi Pagoda

Shwesandaw Pagoda

Following his conquest of Thaton, this very graceful circular pagoda was built by Anawrahta in 1057. The five terraces once had terracotta plaques showing scenes from the *Jataka*, but traces of these, and of other sculptures, were covered by rather heavy-handed renovations. The pagoda bell rises from two octagonal bases which top the five square terraces.

In the earthquake the *hti* was brought down and can still be seen lying on the far side of the pagoda. It was repaired soon after the quake. Close to the Shwesandaw stands the Lawkahteikpan Temple – small, but interesting for its excellent frescoes and inscriptions in both Burmese and Mon.

Shinbinthalyaung

Situated beside the Shwesandaw, this long, brick-built, shed-like structure houses an 18-metre-long (60 feet) reclining Buddha from the 11th century.

Dhammayangyi Temple

Similar in plan to the Ananda, this later temple is much more massive looking. It was built by Narathu (1160-65), who was also known as Kalagya Min, the 'king killed by Indians', although other sources say it was invaders from Ceylon who slew him.

The interior of the temple is blocked by brickwork. If you climb to the upper terraces, make sure you know how to get back down – it's quite a maze on top, with many false paths hiding the single stairway built into the outer wall. The Dhammayangyi is said to have the finest brickwork in Pagan.

Mingalazedi Pagoda

Close to the riverbank, a little south of the Thiripyitsaya Hotel, the Mingalazedi Pagoda was built in 1284 by Narathihapati. It was one of the last to be built before the Tartar invasion ended the real power of the Pagan empire; it's said to be one of the finest pagodas in Pagan and represents the final flowering of Pagan's architectural skills. The Mingalazedi is noted for its fine proportions and for the many beautiful, unglazed terracotta tiles around the three square terraces, illustrating legends. Although many have been damaged or stolen, there are still a considerable number left.

Ngakywenadaung Pagoda

Close to the Thatbyinnyu Temple, this

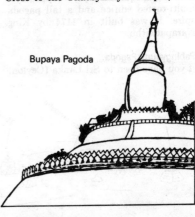

Bupaya Pagoda

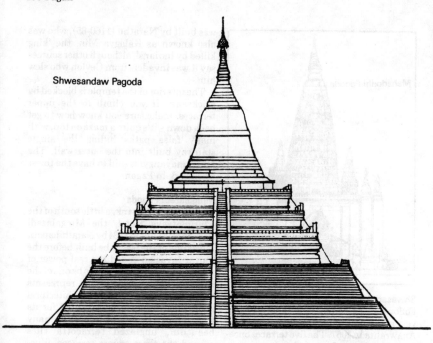

Shwesandaw Pagoda

ruined 12th-century stupa has an unusual bulbous shape. Many of the green-glazed tiles that covered it can still be seen.

Mimalaung-Kyaung Temple

This small, square temple is topped by a multi-roofed edifice and a tall pagoda spire. It was built in 1174 by King Narapatisithu.

Pebingyaung Pagoda

If you have been to Sri Lanka (Ceylon)

you'll recognise the distinctly Sinhalese character of this small pagoda. It was probably built in the 12th century and stands towards the river, near the Bupaya Pagoda.

NYAUNG-OO

This is the major village in the Pagan area; you'll pass through Nyaung-Oo whether you arrive in Pagan by road, air or river. It's an interesting little place for a wander around – lots of shops (look out

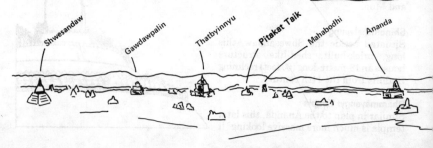

Shwesandaw
Gawdawpalin
Thatbyinnyu
Pitakat Taik
Mahabodhi
Ananda

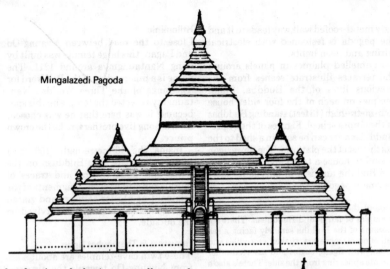

Mingalazedi Pagoda

✗ for the cigar dealers), an excellent and colourful market and even a Burmese billiard hall.

Although some of the monuments here are close to the village, or conveniently situated between Nyaung-Oo and Pagan, others are rather inconveniently far east of the village. You'll probably see some of them from the river or as you fly in or out of Pagan.

Shwezigon Pagoda
Close to the village of Nyaung-Oo, this circular pagoda was commenced by Anawrahta but not completed until the reign of Kyanzittha (1084-1113). Unfortunately, some misguided and rather ham-fisted renovations have rather spoilt what is basically a very fine pagoda – an

Shwezigon Pagoda

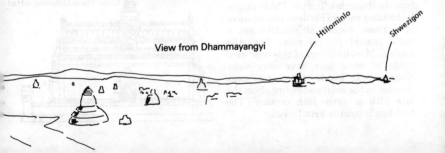

View from Dhammayangyi

Htilominlo

Shwezigon

ugly metal-roofed walkway leads to it and the pagoda is festooned with electrical wiring and neon lights.

Enamelled plaques in panels around the terraces illustrate scenes from the previous lives of the Buddha. Small temples on each of the four sides house four-metre-high (13 feet) standing Buddhas of the Gupta school. Figures of the 37 pre-Buddhist *nats* can be seen in a shed to the north-east of the platform. The Shwezigon is said to house a tooth and a bone from the Buddha and is a prototype for later Burmese pagodas.

Around the Shwezigon there are also a few examples of fairground Buddhism. There's a diorama of the Buddha serenely facing a sea full of ogres, monsters, snakes, crocodiles and so on, with tigers, eagles and assorted other threats appearing from the side. There's also a revolving 'wishing pagoda' complete with *nats* who bow as they go around, and labelled bowls into which you can try tossing money for 'a win at the lottery', 'meeting with your loved ones', 'good luck' or even 'a pass at the examinations'.

Kyanzittha Umin

Although officially credited to Kyanzittha, this cave temple may actually date back to Anawrahta. Built into a cliff face close to the Shwezigon, the long, dimly lit corridors are decorated with frescoes, some of which were painted by Pagan's Tartar invaders during the period of Tartar occupation after 1287.

Upali Thein

Named after Upali, a well-known monk, this ordination hall was built in the mid-13th century and stands across the road from the Htilominlo Temple. The rectangular building has roof battlements imitative of Burmese wooden architecture and a small central pagoda rising from the rooftop. Most buildings of this type were made of wood and have long since disappeared. Inside there are some frescoes on the walls and ceilings from the late 17th or early 18th century. The building is usually kept locked.

Htilominlo

Close to the road between Nyaung-Oo and Pagan, this large temple was built by King Nantaungmya around 1211. The name is a mis-reading of the Pali word for 'Blessings of the Three Worlds'. Nantaungmya erected the temple on this spot because it was here that he was chosen, from among five brothers, to be the crown prince.

Inside the 46-metre-high (150 feet) temple there are four Buddhas on the lower and upper floors, and traces of murals can still be seen. Fragments of the original fine plaster carvings and glazed sandstone decorations have survived on the outside.

Hmyathat & Thamiwhet Umin

These twin cave-temples are about a km from Nyaung-Oo towards the airport – but off the main road. Dug into hillsides, the caves date from the 13th century.

Kubyaukkyi Temple

Close to Wetkyi-In village, this 13th-century temple has an Indian-style spire like the Mahabodhi Temple in Pagan. It is interesting for the fine frescoes of scenes from the *Jataka*, but unfortunately in 1899 a German collector came by and surreptitiously collected many of the panels the frescoes were painted on.

Kubyauknge Temple

Close to the Kubyaukkyi Temple, this temple has some excellent stucco carving on the outside walls.

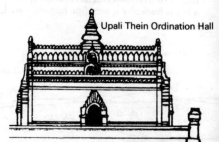

Upali Thein Ordination Hall

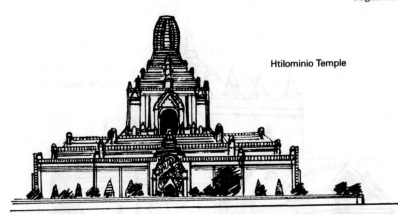

Htilominio Temple

Sapada Pagoda

Close to the road as you approach Nyaung-Oo from Kyauk Padaung or the airport, this 12th-century pagoda was built by Sapada, who came from Bassein but became a monk in Ceylon. His pagoda is Sinhalese in style, with a square relic chamber above the bell.

Other Temples

Closer to the river, about three km from Nyaung-Oo, you can find the 13th-century Thetkyamuni and Kondawgyi temples. The 11th and 12th-century Kyaukgu cave temple is further from the river and is built into the side of a ravine.

MYINKABA ☥

Only a km or two south of Pagan,

Myinkaba has a number of interesting temples and pagodas in or around it, but it is also worth visiting for its lacquerware workshops. Some of these accomplish the complete process of producing lacquerware in one centre, while others specialise in a single phase of the production – for example, making the bamboo frames on which the lacquer is coated.

Myinkaba Pagoda

In the village of Myinkaba, this 11th-century pagoda was built by Anawrahta to expiate the killing of his half-brother, the preceding king, Sokkade, in man-to-man combat. It stands at the Myinkaba stream, along which Sokkade's body and saddle floated by. Since it was built before Anawrahta's conquest of Thaton, it is also an interesting example of pagoda

Sapada Pagoda

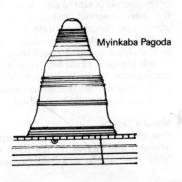

Myinkaba Pagoda

Manuha Temple

architecture before the influence of the southern school of Buddhism had made itself felt.

Kubyaukkyi Temple

Situated just to the left of the road as you enter Myinkaba, this temple was built in 1113 by Kyanzittha's son Rajakumar, on his father's death. An inscription dedicated by him is of considerable linguistic and historical importance since it relates the chronology of the Pagan kings in Mon, Pali, Burmese and Pyu.

The temple is also of great interest for the well-preserved paintings inside, which are thought to date from the original construction of the temple and to be the oldest remaining in Pagan. The temple is typical of the Mon style in that the interior is dimly lit; you need a powerful light to see the ceiling paintings clearly. It is generally kept locked.

Manuha Temple

One of my favourite Pagan temples, Manuha was named for the Mon king from Thaton who was held captive in

Pagan by Anawrahta. He was allowed to build this temple in 1059, and it was constructed to represent his displeasure at captivity. The exterior is uninteresting, but inside are three seated and reclining Buddhas. All are far too large for their enclosures, and their cramped, uncomfortable positions indicate the stress and lack of comfort the 'captive king' had to put up with.

It is said that only the reclining Buddha, in the act of entering Nirvana, has a smile on its face, showing that for Manuha only death was a release from his suffering. But from stairs at the entrance to the reclining Buddha chamber, in the back of the temple, you can climb to the top. Through a window you can then see the face of the sitting Buddha, and from up at this level you'll realise that the gigantic face, so grim from below, has an equally gigantic smile! In the earthquake the central roof collapsed, badly damaging the largest, seated Buddha, but it has now been repaired.

Nanpaya Temple

Close to the Manuha Temple, this former Hindu temple is said to have been used as Manuha's prison. His captors thought using it as a prison would be easier than converting it to a Buddhist temple. In the central sanctuary the four stone pillars have finely carved bas-relief figures of four-faced Brahma. The perforated stone windows are typical of earlier Pagan architecture, and there are interesting arches over the windows. This temple is generally kept locked up.

Nagayon Temple

Slightly beyond the village of Myinkaba, this elegant and well-preserved temple was built by Kyanzittha. It is generally kept locked to protect its interesting contents. The main Buddha image is twice life size and shelters under the hood of a huge *naga* or serpent. This reflects the legend that Kyanzittha built the temple on the spot where he was sheltered while fleeing from his angry brother and predecessor Sawlu – an activity he had to indulge in on more than one occasion.

The outer, dark corridor has many niches with images of the earlier Buddhas. Paintings also decorate the corridor walls. The central shrine has two smaller, standing Buddhas as well as the large one. Nearby stands the small but uniquely designed Pawdawmu Pagoda.

Abeyadana Pagoda

While Kyanzittha sheltered, during his flight from Sawlu, at the the site of the Nagayon Temple, his wife Abeyadana waited for him a short distance away. At that site he subsequently built this temple, which is similar in plan to the Nagayon. The inner shrine contains a large, brick-built seated Buddha image, but the fine frescoes are the main interest here. They illustrate the gods of the Mahayana school, including Brahma, Vishnu, Shiva and Indra. This temple is usually kept locked.

Seinnyet Ama Temple & Seinnyet Nyima Pagoda

This temple and pagoda stand side by side and are traditionally assigned to Queen Seinnyet in the 11th century, although the architecture points to a

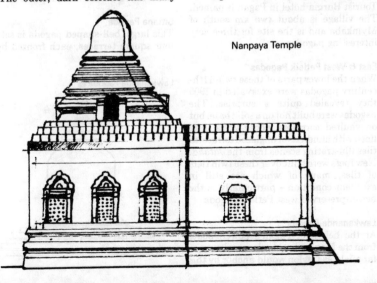

Nanpaya Temple

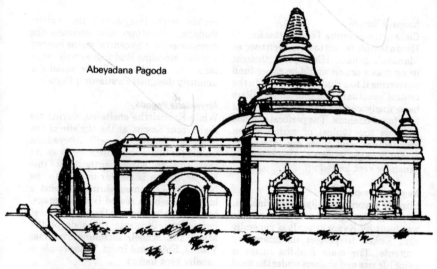

Abeyadana Pagoda

period two centuries later. The pagoda rests on three terraces and is topped by a stylised umbrella.

THIRIPYITSAYA

A small village stands at the former site of a Pagan royal palace – after which the Tourist Burma hotel in Pagan is named. The village is about two km south of Myinkaba and is the site for three very interesting pagodas.

East & West Petleik Pagodas

When the lower parts of these twin 11th-century pagodas were excavated in 1905 they revealed quite a surprise. The pagodas were built not on a solid base, but on vaulted corridors whose walls were lined with hundreds of unglazed terracotta tiles illustrating scenes from the *Jataka*. New roofs were built over these twin tiers of tiles, many of which are still in excellent condition – particularly in the better-preserved west Petleik Pagoda.

Lawkananda Pagoda

At the height of Pagan's power, boats from the Mon region, Arakan and even as far afield as Ceylon would anchor by this distinctive riverside pagoda. It was built in 1059 by Anawrahta, who is also credited with the Petleik Pagodas, and has a distinctive elongated cylindrical dome. It is still used as an everyday place of worship and is thought to house an important Buddha-tooth replica.

Sittana Pagoda

This large, bell-shaped pagoda is set on four square terraces, each fronted by a

Lawkananda Pagoda

standing Buddha image in brick and stucco. The pagoda was built by Htilominlo and stands slightly south of Thiripyitsaya.

Somingyi Monastery

This is a typical monastery of the Pagan period. Most Pagan monasteries were wooden and have long since disappeared.

MINNANTHU

Situated more or less directly south of Nyaung-Oo, the monuments here are of a later period than those in the central Pagan area. The Sulamani is the most important and also the closest to the central area of Pagan – see the Pagan temple section for details. Other temples here are quite a way off the 'beaten track', and the track to the village can be very sandy, making bicycle riding difficult. These temples are generally locked up, because of their frescoes.

Lemyethna Temple

Built in 1222, this east-facing temple has interior walls decorated with well-preserved frescoes and stands on a high platform. It is topped by an Indian-style spire rather like that on the Ananda.

Payathonzu Temple

This complex of three temples was abandoned shortly before its construction was completed – possibly due to the invasion of Kublai Khan? The small, square temples are interconnected by narrow passages.

Thambula Temple

This square temple is decorated with frescoes and was built in 1255 by Thambula, the wife of King Uzana.

Nandamannya Temple

Dating from the mid-13th century, this small, single-chambered temple has very fine frescoes and a ruined, seated Buddha image. Nearby is a strange, subterranean monks' retreat.

PWASAW

Situated between Myinkaba and Minnanthu, Pwasaw was the site of the royal palace after it was transferred from Thiripyitsaya and before it was moved to Pagan in 874 AD.

Dhammayazika Pagoda

This circular pagoda is similar to the Shwezigon or the Mingalazedi, but has an unusual and rather complex design. The pagoda, which was built in 1196 by Narapatisithu, rises from three five-sided terraces. Five small temples, each containing a Buddha image, encircle the terraces. An outer wall also has five gateways.

Places to Stay - bottom end

Down from the government-run hotels there is a string of small places along the main road of Pagan – all very spartan and bare, but all popular with shoestring travellers. You are really camping out in these places, but somehow that feels just right in Pagan. Most people even find the old-fashioned outhouses and outdoor cold showers quite OK. They all cost K12/24 and are supposed to be booked through the Tourist Burma office. In early '87 six Pagan guest houses were censured for renting rooms to visitors without stamping their currency forms. Each was ordered to close for a certain length of time, some for one month, others two and three months. Because closing all six at the same time would have created a severe accommodation shortage, they were penalized in shifts, three at a time. At this writing, every guest house in town is very strict about stamping; this will probably vary from season to season, depending on Tourist Burma politics.

These privately run cheapies seem to rise and fall in favour – the popular places one year may end up at the bottom of the list a year later. *Sithu Guest House* is one of the most popular; it's friendly and helpful (even by Burma's high standards in that department), and the rooms have mattresses, mosquito nets and fans plus good showers in the yard and western-style toilets with even toilet paper supplied. There's a fridge with bottles of cold water always available.

The *Burma Guest House* is on the same side of the road and a little further down. Once again there are mosquito nets and friendly people, and a pot of Chinese tea is plonked down in front of you every time you sit down. It's very welcome after a

couple of hours' sightseeing. The beds are very hard, though. A couple of doors down is the *Aung Thahaya*, where again the people are friendly and helpful. The Thatbyinnyu Temple is right behind it. All the beds here have mosquito nets and mattresses, and the building is a little more substantial than some at Pagan. There is also a very nice garden in front with tables and chairs.

Next door to the Aung Thahaya is the

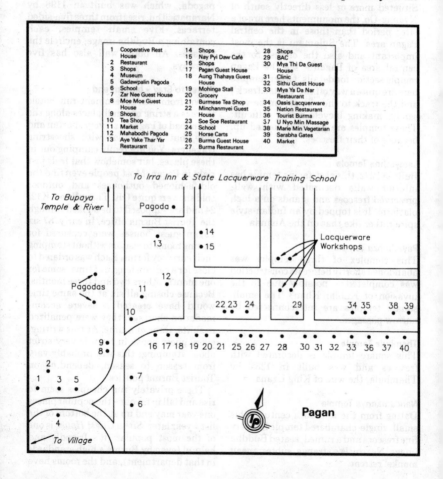

1	Cooperative Rest House	14	Shops	28	Shops
2	Restaurant	15	Nay Pyi Daw Café	29	BAC
3	Shops	16	Shops	30	Mya Thi Da Guest House
4	Museum	17	Pagan Guest House		
5	Gadawpalin Pagoda	18	Aung Thahaya Guest House	31	Clinic
6	School			32	Sithu Guest House
7	Zar Nee Guest House	19	Grocery	33	Mya Ya Da Nar Restaurant
8	Moe Moe Guest House	20	Mohinga Stall		
		21	Burmese Tea Shop	34	Oasis Lacquerware
9	Shops	22	Minchanmyei Guest House	35	Nation Restaurant
10	Tea Shop			36	Tourist Burma
11	Market	23	Soe Soe Restaurant	37	U Nyo Min Massage
12	Mahabodhi Pagoda	24	School	38	Marie Min Vegetarian
13	Aye Yake Thar Yar Restaurant	25	Horse Carts	39	Sarabha Gates
		26	Burma Guest House	40	Market
		27	Burma Restaurant		

To Irra Inn & State Lacquerware Training School

To Bupaya
Temple & River

Pagoda •

• 14
13 • • 15

Lacquerware
Workshops

12 •

Pagodas
11 •

10 •

22 23 24   29   34 35   38 39

9 •
8 •

16 17 18 19 20 21 25 26 27 28 30 31 32 33 36 37 40

2 •
1 • 3 • 5 •   • 7

• 6

Pagan

• 4

← To Village

Top: Htilominlo (TW)
Left: Novice smoker (TW)
Right: Detail from a Pagan pagoda (TW)

Top: Mahazedi, Pegu (TW)
Left: Thatbinnyu (TW)
Right: Street music in Nyaung-Oo (TW)

newer *Pagan*, which was one of the more popular places in town during our last visit, although the roof leaked a bit during rainstorms. The staff is very friendly, and like Aung Thahaya the Pagan has a garden in front and laundry facilities.

Next door to the Soe Soe Restaurant on the other side of the road is *Minchanmyei*, which is pleasant enough when it's not raining – the grounds tend to flood in heavy rains (the *Pagan* and the *Minchanmyei* were the only places that seemed to have rain-related problems). Further up the road, around the bend and close to the fire station, is the *Moe Moe Inn*, the longest-running of the Pagan cheapies. A bit further, just across the road from the Gawdawpalin Temple and next door to a school, is the nicely kept and popular *Zar Nee Rest House*.

The *Co-Operative*, which is government run, is directly behind the Gawdawpalin Temple and across the road from the museum. Opinions vary on the Co-Op, but for just a bit more than the other guest houses (singles/doubles are K16.80/26.40) you get a real room – that is, one separated from other rooms by more than a woven bamboo partition. Beds are a bit softer, too, and every room has a fan. It can also be a bit quieter since it is removed from the main drag, and there is a relatively large bar and restaurant next door which is popular with locals. On the downside, the staff don't speak much English, and service can be rather indifferent. This is the only guest house in town where there are Burmese as well as foreign guests.

Places to Stay - top end

Pagan's top-end places consist of one real top-ender and one aging colonial-style hotel. The Tourist Burma top-class hotel is the *Thiripyitsaya Hotel*, which does manage to take some advantage of its location and look like it belongs to an exotic place like Pagan – something which certainly cannot be said of most of Tourist Burma's new hotels. There are six

separate bungalows, each with its own little verandah. Rooms have private bathrooms and fridges and are air-conditioned. They are quite a wonder of modern technology to the locals – the doorman showed me round one room with evident pride, even swinging open the door to the closet with awe: 'and a shelf for your handkerchiefs!' A recent visitor reported that it was becoming a little run down and that his bathroom had most unusual plumbing: 'When the shower was turned on, the hot-water tap in the basin ran, but the latter would not run under any other circumstance'!

Nightly cost is US$18.50/24.50/31.50 singles/doubles/triples. The hotel also has a lounge area, pleasant restaurant and bar with a verandah, which is one of the best places in Pagan for a pre or post-sunset beer. If after a hard day's temple-seeing you have not got the energy to drag yourself to a temple top to catch the sunset, this is a very acceptable substitute. Since beer is only sold through government hotels (the cheapies have to buy their beer from here), this is one of the three cheapest places for beer in Pagan. The Thiripyitsaya also has the only money-exchange facilities in Pagan. It is about a 20-minute walk from the village centre.

Next down is the government-run *Irra Inn*, overlooking the Irrawaddy and much closer to the Pagan 'centre'. Rooms are K60/80; with bath they are K100/120. A larger, riverside 'Jr Suite' with refrigerator is available for K150. Although the inn is a little remote from the busy (well, busy by Burmese tourist standards) main strip, it's pretty good value for the money and most people who stay there reckon it's a good place. The clean rooms have high ceilings, and fans and towels are supplied. The outdoor bar is quite breezy, and service is good.

Places to Eat

The Thiripyitsaya has a restaurant and a bar, of course, but the *Co-Operative* is a particularly popular place although the basically Chinese-style food can be a bit 'western' according to some travellers. Still, the atmosphere is noisy and cheerful and in the evenings it's often crowded with locals and visitors. The *Co-Op* and the *Irra Inn* both have beer (cold too) at the cheaper government price, as well as Mandalay Rum.

If you feel like a splurge, the *Thiripyit-saya* does a good Burmese dinner for K34. You have to order it in advance and the food can be rather variable – a visitor reported having a superb fish curry one night – 'undoubtedly the best Burmese meal of the trip' – followed the next night by 'what I can only describe as chicken-bone curry'. You can also get sandwiches at the bar.

In the main part of the village the *Nation Restaurant* is very popular, the food is good and the lovely Mya Mya Aye is very popular with travellers and always interesting to talk with. Fried noodles and many other dishes are very good here. Other restaurants include the *Soe Soe*, the *Mya Ya Danar Restaurant* (particularly good for breakfast) and the *Burma Restaurant*, which is actually more of a Burmese tea shop.

The rather new *Marie Min Vegetarian* restaurant, just inside the old city gates across from Tourist Burma, is popular for its fresh guacamole and fruit drinks. It's run by a friendly Indian family, who serve a few vegetarian Indian dishes like dhal and chappati and vegetable curry as well as world-traveller favourites. Decor is rather simple, with dirt floors, but the place seems to be fairly clean. None of the places in Pagan are going to win any prizes for hygiene.

There are also several traditional Burmese tea shops along Pagan's main drag. The most popular one is across from the Pagan Guest House, and there is another next to where Thazi/Taunggyi trucks stop. Across from the Minchanmyei Guest House is a small Burmese grocery which sells staple foods; there's also a tea shop and a *mohinga* stall.

Off the road that leads to the Irra Inn is a restaurant that serves authentic Burmese dishes, the *Aye Yake Thar Nar* – look for the sign on the left just after you pass the Mahabodhi pagoda. Across the road from this intersection is the *Nay Pyi Daw Café*, which is a tea shop by day and a Burmese disco by night. The music is actually pretty interesting here – you might hear a Burmese rendition of *Surfin' USA*, for example.

Evening meals in Pagan tend to be a pleasant communal activity, as all the travellers sit around the table together and discuss their day's exploring. You can also eat in your guest house. Next to the old city gates is a sizeable morning market where you can get fresh fish, noodles and many other food items that might be worth bring back for your guest house kitchen prepare.

The Chinese restaurant beside the spot in Nyaung-Oo where the bus departs is friendly and cheap. They even open in the middle of the night (3 am) so you can get breakfast before departing.

Buying

There are lots of little craft shops in Pagan and this is a good place to bargain for souvenirs – prices can be quite low and most merchants love to barter for just about anything you have. For lacquerware, the *Oasis Lacquerware* next door to the Nation Restaurant is good, as is the newer *Sunshine Handicrafts & Trading Post* next door to the Moe Moe Guest House. Sunshine, the young proprietor, designs his own lacquerware and also has a good selection of tapestries. Check prices around town before investing a lot – most dealers will explain differences in manufacturing methods and quality, so that you'll soon become a mini-expert.

On the dirt road parallel to the main strip there are a number of lacquerware workshops where you can watch the stuff being made and buy direct. Near the Irra Inn is the State Lacquerware Training School, which welcomes visitors. Finally, if you're interested in highly collectible *shwe kyin doo* ('gold thread embroidery') tapestries, there is a warehouse a bit north of Moe Moe where you can find the largest selection in Pagan. Other items for sale in most of the shops include opium weights and scales, wooden marionettes, lacquer tables and Burmese clothing.

Traditional Massage
Several guest houses in Pagan now offer vigorous Burmese-style massage for around K30 per hour. But probably the best place in town to knead out the kinks is the *U Nyo Min* 'traditional special massage parlour' across the road from the Vegetarian Restaurant near Tourist Burma. U Nyo Min does the men and Daw Yi Yi the women; rates are K10 for a half hour, K20 for an hour, and K25 for 1½ hours.

Getting There
There are a number of ways of getting to and from Pagan – at least one of which I strongly advise should be avoided.

Air You can fly to Pagan from Rangoon or Mandalay – or from Inle Lake, although that flight normally operates via Mandalay. The Rangoon flight takes about 1½ hours, costs K445 and departs daily at 6.45 am. The Mandalay-Pagan flight departs at 3.40 pm, takes about half an hour and costs K152. If you sit on the right-hand side of the aircraft flying Mandalay-Pagan or the left-hand side flying Pagan-Mandalay, you can keep the Irrawaddy in view all the way and have a good view of Amarapura, Ava, the Ava Bridge and Sagaing while climbing out of or descending into Mandalay. You also get an excellent view of Pagan on the Pagan-Rangoon flights.

The Pagan airstrip is actually near Nyaung-Oo, the town a few km from Pagan itself. Tourist Burma provides transport for their foreign passengers. Flight bookings are made at the Tourist Burma office in Pagan, but you cannot find out whether you have a confirmed seat on the plane until it is too late to book the bus-train connection.

Rail There is no rail line all the way, so getting to or from Pagan by rail will also entail a sector by bus. It makes no sense at all to attempt to travel between Pagan and Mandalay by rail since you have to travel so far before getting a train – much easier to go by road all the way. Rangoon-Pagan or vice versa is a better possibility, although the first method is both very time-wasting and very uncomfortable.

Bus-Train 1 for the Pagan-Rangoon trip turned into one of the most miserable train rides I've ever had. Take a bus from Nyaung-Oo to Kyauk Padaung, the nearest railhead to Pagan. At something between 2 and 5 pm a train leaves for Rangoon. Officially the train should arrive in Rangoon around 8 am the following morning, but in practice it can take closer to 24 hours. The fare is about the same as Thazi-Rangoon. The train is a dirty, uncomfortable, unlit, slow, crowded, tedious, unpleasant cattle train. It is best avoided. The hardy can also make this trip up from Rangoon in a similar time, although you may have to change trains at Pyinmana, the junction on the Rangoon-Mandalay line where the line branches off for Kyauk Padaung.

Bus-Train 2 is a far better alternative. You first have to get to Thazi, which is something like half way from Pagan to Inle Lake. The old three-bus system by which you had to change vehicles in Kyauk Padaung and Meiktila has been replaced by a very efficient Tourist Burma pick-up that goes straight through to Thazi in plenty of time for the Mandalay-Rangoon express. The bus leaves the main strip in Pagan at 2 pm and gets to Thazi between 7 and 8 pm. The Pagan-Thazi road is very scenic, with a view of the Mt Popa volcanic dome in the distance near the start of the trip, villages, farms, lots of bullock carts, pedestrians bearing cargo on their heads, etc. The Japanese trucks used for the trip are relatively new and in good condition, though the ride is rather cramped with 18 official passengers in the back, two with the driver in front and three or four hangers-on. There are rest stops in Kyauk Padaung and Meiktila, the first a short intermission for fuel and the second a longer stop where you can refuel yourself with tea and *nam-bya* (Burmese roti). Fare is K55 per person.

When you arrive at the bus stop in Thazi, you can either walk to the railway station two blocks away, or else two of you can take a horsecart for K5. The 6.15 pm express from Mandalay will arrive in Thazi just after 9 pm and will leave a few minutes later. You can book your Thazi-Rangoon tickets in Mandalay (which is safer but will cost you K110/88 upper class/1st class, the full Mandalay-Rangoon fare) or try to buy tickets at Thazi for K99/72. A Tourist Burma official will be at the station to meet foreigners coming in from Pagan. See the Thazi section for things to do while you're waiting for the train.

Leaving Pagan at 2 pm means you have an extra half-day to enjoy Pagan. You can no longer charter a Tourist Burma truck in order to make the daytime express from Mandalay.

Bus-Train 3 is time-consuming and involves leaving from Nyaung-Oo instead of Pagan and changing buses in Kyauk Padaung and Meiktila. In view of the scheduled departures in Alternative 2, there is really no reason to go this route (unless you are avoiding Tourist Burma on principle), but it is feasible so long as you get to Thazi in time for the Mandalay-Rangoon express; otherwise you could end up on a slow train just as bad as the one from Kyauk Padaung.

See the Mandalay section for the complete train schedule.

Bus - Mandalay After flying, the fastest way to get to Pagan is the fairly regular bus from Mandalay to Nyaung-Oo. The Nyaung-Oo-Mann bus is supposed to operate every day, but you should check first before committing yourself. It departs Mandalay at 4 or 5 am, costs K22 and arrives Nyaung-Oo at around 2 pm. The schedule from Nyaung-Oo to Mandalay is exactly the same. Along the way you make a few tea stops – breakfast at Gume, lunch at Yewei. By Burmese standards this is not too uncomfortable a bus although the seats are wooden and there is very little legroom.

From Nyaung-Oo to Pagan count on around K5 to K10 for a horse and buggy with enough room for four people, or take a pick-up truck for K1 per person. The bus departs Mandalay from 84th St between 29th and 30th Rd. Faster but more expensive are the Tourist Burma pick-up trucks that leave Mandalay at 3 pm and arrive in Pagan about six hours later for K66.

Bus - Taunggyi You can bus, or rather pick-up truck, directly between Pagan and Taunggyi, for Inle Lake. This route makes it feasible for people to add Inle Lake to their itinerary even if they cannot afford to fly. The pick-up is the same Tourist Burma one which runs to Thazi (see Rangoon transport below) and continues on to Taunggyi if there are sufficient passengers. It's not the most comfortable ride since they pack 20 to 24 passengers into the small pick-up, quite apart from the hangers-on. Pagan departure is around 2 pm and you eventually arrive at Taunggyi around midnight or even later. The schedule in the opposite direction is the same. Fare is K77 per person.

The Tourist Burma bus generally won't operate unless they've got a full tourist load, but these days there are plenty of other similar Datsun or Toyota pick-ups about and you can generally organise your own transport if necessary, though this is not legal and is getting more difficult to do out of Pagan. The trip might cost around K700 to K1000 for the whole truck. Up over the hills east of Thazi the road is winding – beware if you suffer from motion sickness. This can be a long and gruelling trip.

Bus - Rangoon It is also possible to bus between Pagan and Rangoon, although the trip is long and wearing. I've travelled Rangoon-Pagan by pick-up truck and with a few brief meal and rest stops, a look around Prome and much fast travel, it still required a pre-dawn departure and an after-dark arrival.

Remember that although Pagan is an important tourist destination it's only really a small village. Long-distance buses in Burma are rather uncertain but there is said to be a twice-weekly bus direct from Nyaung-Oo to Rangoon for K50. More likely you will have to make the two-hour trip from Nyaung-Oo to Kyauk Padaung, about 50 km south-east. The cost is about K2 to K6, depending on the quality of the vehicle. The catch is that you have to be in Kyauk Padaung at 3 am to catch the Dagon-Popa bus line departure for Rangoon. It should get to Rangoon around 7 pm and costs about K50. Tickets can be booked a day ahead.

If you want to go to Prome you'll probably have to take a bus to Magwe and change there. There is a daily Nyaung-Oo-Magwe bus for K18. Given your time limitations, however, travelling between Pagan and Rangoon by bus really doesn't make much sense.

Boat The Prome ferry departs from Mandalay at 5 am every morning on its down-river cruise to Pagan – or at least it is supposed to depart at that time. The fare is K16 deck, K31 cabin class. The cabin (there's just one) should offer a little more comfort than the deck, but it gets mixed reports and apparently even if you book it there's no guarantee you won't find a band of monks haven't got it as well!

The cabin has four berths, a table and chairs. Even when overbooked, it still tends to be less crowded than on the deck. You can get on board the boat the night before departure and grab a piece of deck, thus saving the cost of a night's accommodation as well as staking your claim for deck space in the morning. The nights tend to be cold on the river so come prepared, and be ready to do battle with the mosquitoes too.

The ferry does not get to Nyaung-Oo until early the following morning (around 7 am if on schedule), so you've got a second night to spend on board. Usually the ferry stops for the night a little north of Pagan and on the opposite bank of the river at a town called Pakkoku, where there are several places to stay including the excellent *Myayatanar Inn* at 2288 Main Rd. It's about 250 metres down the main street from where you turn left out of the dock road. Rooms here are less than K10 a night and they'll pick you up from the boat. They have good food too. The next morning it's a further two hours down-river to Nyaung-Oo, but don't worry about over-sleeping in Pakkoku and missing the boat. Other boats pass by later on in the morning.

Although it's quite an experience to travel by boat on the mighty Irrawaddy, the river is wide and the banks flat with most of the villages set well back because of the risk of seasonal flooding, so you won't see too much off the river. There are plenty of stops, however, and people are always on hand to sell food and drinks. The ferries continue on down-river to Prome, where you could change boats and continue all the way to Rangoon. The first day takes you from Pagan to Magwe, the second day from there to Prome. You'd use up your entire visa on this trip, but it would be quite a ride. Travelling up-river from Pagan to Mandalay involves another night stop on the way, so unless you can spare at least two full days out of your meagre allotment, that is not worth considering either.

Think about it before leaping on the

ferry towards the end of the dry season – March or April. Getting stuck on sand bars can happen at any time of the year but as the river level falls you're more likely to get stuck and it's liable to take longer to get unstuck. People have wasted a day or more of their short stay sitting stationary in the middle of the Irrawaddy.

There is also a faster steamboat that leaves twice a week, usually Thursday and Sunday (but sometimes Wednesday and Saturday – check with Tourist Burma), leaving at 4.30 am and arriving in Nyaung-Oo at around 5.30 pm. Fare is K50 per person and food is an additional K50 if you want it. The ticket for this boat can only be purchased through Tourist Burma.

Getting Around

Although you can comfortably walk around the more central Pagan sites, if you want to get further afield you'll need transport. A major improvement in recent years is the availability of bicycles. Traffic around Pagan is so light that bike riding is a delight, although you should steer well clear when the occasional motor vehicle does chance by. There are a number of shops along the main road in Pagan which rent bikes. The usual cost is K20 or K30 per day or K15 for a half day. The K30 bikes are probably a bit better. Riding can be hard going down the dustier tracks and punctures are inevitable, but they're fixed or the bike replaced with alacrity.

You can take a bike for more than one day; your guest house will carefully lock it away at night. An early-morning or late-afternoon ride along the sealed road by the Ananda Temple to Nyaung-Oo is particularly pleasant. Check the bike over thoroughly before accepting one – make sure it steers, the brakes work and the tyres hold air. One traveller told of seeing a rider discover his machine's total lack of braking just at the bottom of the long slope to the Thiripyitsaya Hotel. The staff picked him up, carried him

inside and propped him up against the bar where a few beers restored his equilibrium. The same traveller was offered a bike with the suggestion that he pedal back to the shop every hour or so, 'to refill the tyres'. Riding out to some of the more remote temples can be hard going through the deep and dusty sand.

You can also hire horse carts from place to place or by the hour; count on an hourly rate around K10 to K15 an hour or K70 for the whole day. Some of the horse-cart jockeys are pretty knowledgeable too, and some travellers reckon carts are preferable to bikes. Technically speaking, jockeys are not supposed to act as guides – guides are required to have Tourist Burma licenses and charge a separate guide fee – but with an informed jockey, who needs a guide? One recommended jockey is Hla Maung, who drives cart No 40 and is usually parked in front of Sithu Guest House – he speaks good English, knows a lot, and has a good disposition. Another good driver is Ko Ye Myint, who was a Tourist Burma guide until he lost his permit. Jeeps cost around K30 an hour, less by the day. There is a bus service (pick-up trucks once again) between Nyaung-Oo and Pagan for K1; it departs about 200 metres from the bus stop in Nyaung-Oo.

Guides I'm not usually very keen on guides; too many in Asia seem to know less than the average thin tourist brochure, but some of the guides in Pagan are very knowledgeable and interesting people. Ask around to see who's in current favour; a woman named April continues to get good reviews. A guide costs K40 a day. Having a guide at Pagan has the important benefit that they should have the keys (or know where to get them) to many of the more remote temples that are kept locked up to protect their valuable contents.

MT POPA

If you look towards the range of hills that

rise, shimmering in the heat, behind Pagan you'll see a solitary peak behind them. That is Mt Popa, which has been described as the 'Olympus' of Burma. Rising to 1520 metres from the flat, surrounding plains, Mt Popa is said to be the core of an extinct volcano. The ground either side of the road is strewn with the remains of an ash-petrified forest.

Atop a rocky crag is a picturesque complex of monasteries, pagodas and shrines which you can climb to via a winding, covered walkway. It gets cooler as you get higher; the climb is steep, stiff and 20 minutes long. When you reach the top the views are fantastic. Mt Popa is the centre for the worship of *nats*; the shrine of the Mahagiri Nats, about half way up the mountain, is a major pilgrimage site. Down at the base of the hill there's a display of figures of the whole assembly of Burmese *nats*. During the month of Nayon (May/June) there's a Festival of the Spirits here, to which great numbers of people flock.

Places to Stay

There's a rather basic Forestry Guest House at the base of the mountain which may take visitors; or you could ask at the monastery, which is also located at the bottom.

Getting There

Mt Popa is about 50 km from Pagan or 10 km from the railhead at Kyauk Padaung. You can visit Mt Popa by day-tripping from Pagan or as a stop-off between Pagan and Thazi or Mandalay. Getting there by public transport would be very time-consuming (relative to a seven-day visa of course), but with pick-up truck charters becoming more readily available more travellers are managing to fit Mt Popa into their itinerary. A pick-up, with enough room for 12 to 14 people at a squeeze, would cost about K300 round trip from Pagan.

Inle Lake

Inle Lake is situated in the Shan States, and although the lake is naturally a major attraction there are a number of other places to visit. Since there is a fair amount of travelling to be done in the area, you'll find a visit much easier if you can get a group together in order to charter taxi-trucks, jeeps, or a boat when on the lake. The airport at Heho, the railhead at Shwenyaung, the main accommodation centre at Taunggyi, and the lake itself are all some distance apart.

Inle Warnings

There are several things to consider which can save you much time and trouble around Inle Lake. First of all there is no need to go to Taunggyi, the main town in the area and the location of the main Tourist Burma office. If you want to simply go to the lake you'll save a couple of hours' travel by skipping Taunggyi. If you're on a bus for Taunggyi just get off at the junction at Shwenyaung.

It used to be that if you needed to change money while at Inle Lake then Taunggyi was the only place with official money-changing facilities. Nowadays the Tourist Burma office at Yaunghwe at the lake handles money exchange as well as accommodation, some transport and lake tours. If you want Burma Airways tickets then you're supposed to go to the Taunggyi Tourist Burma office. Thazi-Rangoon railway tickets are also now available in Taunggyi, and you may even be able to book seats in Yaunghwe if you meet the right Tourist Burma person – apparently the Taunggyi and Yaunghwe TB offices are in close communication these days.

Another thing to remember is that transport between all the towns in this part of Burma is a bit less regular than around Mandalay and Pagan – mornings are generally the best time to find transport from one point to another. This is why travellers who want to see the Inle area often leave out either Mandalay or Pagan (usually the former). It's not uncommon to find people who only do the Kalaw-Pindaya-Yaunghwe-Taunggyi route during their whole eight days. Given the fascinations of Shan State travel this is quite understandable.

MEIKTILA

Only a short distance from Thazi, Meiktila is the town where the Pagan-Taunggyi and Rangoon-Mandalay roads intersect, just as Thazi is the place where the equivalent railway lines intersect. Just north of town, by the airfield, there's a WW II Spitfire on display in remarkably good-looking condition. In town the *Kanyeiktha* restaurant has an English menu and cold beer.

THAZI

The rail junction of Thazi is really nothing more than that, just a place where people embark or disembark from the train when they're travelling to or from Pagan or Inle Lake. At the station you may meet Yo Maung, a retired railway official who now works for Tourist Burma, dealing solely with foreigners who end up in Thazi. He's a very friendly chap and quite helpful, showing you where you can lie down and rest, giving advice on food in the restaurant, etc.

The Thazi bus stop is a couple of hundred metres from the railway station – just an empty building and a patch of dirt. Buses (Japanese pick-ups) to Kalaw and Taunggyi only leave here when they get 20 passengers or when some impatient foreigner pays the fare differential for any number less.

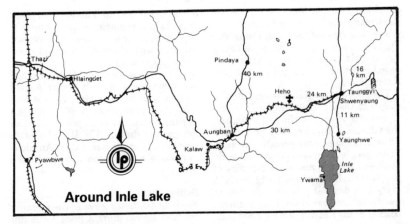

Around Inle Lake

Places to Stay & Eat

Close to the railway station, on the road through Thazi, there are a couple of places for food and lodging. A short distance on the Meiktila side of the railway crossing there is an extremely basic rest house with rooms at K10 for singles. The name is in Burmese but it's lit up with Christmas tree lights.

Nearby, the *Red Star* has very good Indian Muslim food. Try their chicken curry – the menu offers 'cooked rice & chicken curry & dhal soup – all together, one complete set' for K6! The proprietors will allow you to bathe and rest upstairs while waiting for a train departure. The nearby *Wonderful* has Chinese food and also has an English menu.

Around the bus stop there are several tea shops with endless free tea and cheap pastries. The best is diagonally across from the bus area – quite clean, with good pastries and service.

The restaurant in the railway station itself is pretty fair – soups are especially tasty. They serve no beverages other than soda water, not even coffee or tea. Take a stroll through the kitchen if you have time; it's dark and medieval, with huge woks over fierce wood fires, the air heavy with steam and cooking smoke.

KALAW

Situated 70 km west of Taunggyi, about half way to Thazi, Kalaw is on the western edge of the Shan Plateau. This was a popular hill station in the British days and it's still a peaceful and quiet place with a real atmosphere of the colonial era. At an altitude of 1320 metres (4330 feet) it's also pleasantly cool and a good place for hiking amid gnarly pines, bamboo groves and rugged mountain scenery. There's some good accommodation here (the hotels have that old hill-station flavour), and you can make interesting excursions outside Kalaw. The small population is a peculiar mix of Shans, Burmese and Indian Muslims, Burmans and Nepalis (Gurkhas retired from British military service), many of whom are missionary-educated. As recently as 10 years ago there were still American missionaries teaching in the local schools. Because of the colonial and missionary heritage, many people speak English.

There are three semi-interesting temples to see in town. Perched on the hill overlooking the Thazi-Taunggyi road is the Thein Tong Pagoda. In the 'downtown' area is a glittering pagoda covered in gold-coloured mosaics called Dama Yan Thi. Just across the street is the dilapidated Damar Yon chapel; it's not particularly interesting itself, but upstairs you get fair views of the town, Dama Yan Thi Pagoda and the ruins of the Su Taung Pye temple, now a field of crumbling pagodas behind the chapel towards the Kalaw Hotel.

The plateau near Kalaw is inhabited by people of the Palaung and Pa-O tribes. The women wear colourful costumes, and the villages of Ta Yaw, Pein Ne Pin and Shwe Min Phone are interesting to visit. Tribespeople often come into town to do business. You will also see a diversity of people at the Kalaw market, which is held every five days. If you want to trek to nearby villages, ask at the Tourist Burma counter at the Kalaw Hotel for directions.

Places to Stay & Eat

The only places to stay in Kalaw are the *Kalaw Hotel* and *Pineland Rest & Lodging*. The Kalaw Hotel, which looks like a cross between a Tudor mansion and a hunting lodge, offers rustic accommodation for US$7/9.50 (single/double) or lodging in the annexe for US$3.50/5. Set back well behind the town and reached by a foot path or jeep track, it's a very quiet and peaceful place to put up. The hot water works only sometimes, which is a concern during the cool season when Kalaw has very cold nights and mornings. The restaurant has your typical HTC menu but also serves a set Burmese meal for K35 that's not bad.

The Pineland, right in town near the cinema and jeep park (where you can hire jeeps to Pindaya, Yaunghwe or Taunggyi), has very basic rooms with brick walls and straw mattresses for K20 per person. You will be asked to pay for your room at the Tourist Burma counter in the Kalaw Hotel.

There are quite a few tea shops in Kalaw but nothing fancy. The Pineland is about the only true restaurant and serves Chinese food. Next door is the *Lin Sein Tea Shop*, which makes the best *nam-bya* (Burmese roti or chappati) we had during our latest Burma trip. This is a good place to get help in arranging a jeep for further explorations. Near the cinema is a Nepali tea shop with chappatis, tea and *raksi* (local moonshine).

It may also be possible to arrange accommodation through Father Angelo de Meiro, an Italian Catholic priest who has lived here since 1940 – despite Japanese suspicion of his possible British sympathies during WW II and British suspicion after the war. Father Angelo is very knowledgeable about local hill tribe villages.

Getting There

From Thazi, buses leave in the morning for K55 Tourist Burma price – the full Thazi-Taunggyi fare. If the Tourist Burma representative isn't around, it should cost K40. Travel time is 2½ to three hours. From Taunggyi to Kalaw it's the same story.

PINDAYA

About 50 km from Kalaw is the village of Pindaya, noted for its extensive limestone caves and picturesque lake. There is now a hotel here, so staying a night or two is feasible. The highly scenic road between it and Aungban, the turn-off for Pindaya from Kalaw, passes through the Pa-O and Danu villages of Bweh-La and Ji-Chanzi. Pindaya itself is a centre for the Burmese-speaking Taungyo people. There are fields of dry-cultivated mountain rice along the way.

The famous Pindaya Caves are in a limestone ridge overlooking the lake. It's a long walk from the lake up to the cave entrance; if you've chartered a jeep from Kalaw or Taunggyi, make sure you're driven all the way up to the entrance. Inside, there are literally thousands of Buddha images which have been put there over the centuries and arranged in such a way as to form a labyrinth throughout the various cave chambers – quite unlike Buddhist caves in neighbouring countries (where interiors are arranged much like ordinary temples). Some of the smaller side chambers are only accessible on hands and knees, and in these you may come across lay people practising meditation. From a temple complex built along the front of the ridge you can view the nearby lake and the ruins of Shwe Ohn Hmin Pagoda just below the ridge.

North-west of Pindaya, and near the village of Ye-ngan, is the most important prehistoric site in Burma, the Padah-Lin Caves. The interior of one of the caves is decorated with the remains of very old paintings (animal and human subjects) not unlike neolithic cave paintings in Europe. To get here you will have to charter a jeep – this can be added on to a Pindaya jeep trip from either Kalaw or Taunggyi for an extra K100 to K150 per vehicle.

Places to Stay & Eat

The *Pindaya Hotel* is a clean and comfortable place to stay and is located about half way between the town and the caves, just off the road to the caves and facing the lake. Singles/doubles/triples cost K61.50/84.70/110, not cheap if you have to pay in official kyats. A less expensive alternative, the *Diamond Eagle Guest House*, was under construction next to the lake in early '87 and was planned to be in the K25 to K50 range when opened later that year.

The Pindaya Hotel has a restaurant that is usually empty unless a tour group is passing through for lunch. Good food can be found in the market area in town – the best is at *U Aseik*, where you can get a four-course Burmese meal for around K10. At the cave temple as well as in the market you can buy delicious local avocadoes (called *dopati* in Burmese).

If for some reason you get stuck in Aungban (say your jeep loses a wheel nearby and there's no spare), you may be allowed to stay in the *Thazin Guest House* on the outskirts of town.

Getting There

From Kalaw it costs K12 to Aungban and another K12 to Pindaya by public transport. It can be difficult to find buses, especially between Aungban and Pindaya, so leave early in the morning and allow a whole day for the trip. You can also charter a jeep (a real Jeep, '40s vintage) and driver in Kalaw. If you don't want to stay in Pindaya, you could hire a jeep to take you from Kalaw to Pindaya, wait for a couple of hours while you take in the caves and have lunch in town, and then press on to Yaunghwe (Inle Lake). This should cost about US$25 or the unofficial kyat equivalent for the whole day – it's better to pay in dollars than kyats. One jeep can take four or five passengers with baggage. Actual road time is about two hours Kalaw-Pindaya (50 km) and three hours or more Pindaya-Yaunghwe (93 km). Add waiting time (which can be considerable) in Aungban and Shwenyaung if you go by public transport.

INLE LAKE

The Inle Lake is fairly long, fairly narrow and outrageously picturesque – flat calm, dotted with patches of floating vegetation and busy little fishing canoes. High hills rim the lake on both sides. It is famous for its leg-rowers, who propel their boats by standing at the stern on one leg and wrapping the other leg around the oar. This strange technique has arisen because of the floating vegetation found all over the lake – it's necessary to stand up to plot a path around the obstacles.

The lake is very shallow and crystal clear – a swim looks inviting and the Inlai Bo Te would be a good place to have one. Inlai means 'middle of', Bo is 'officer' or 'official' and Te is 'house', so the Inlai Bo Te is literally an official's house in the middle of the lake. It's no longer used as such, but makes a good place to stop for a mid-lake picnic or swim.

One of the best times of year to be here is during the Thadingyut festival in October (a bit later than the Inle Lake

Festival mentioned below), when the Inthas and Shans dress in new clothes and celebrate with fervour the end of Waso or Buddhist Lent. They are so religious that it's not unusual for families to spend all of their meagre savings during this one annual event.

During January-February nights and mornings around the lake area are cold, so you should bring socks and sweaters at the minimum. A warm sleeping bag would be a plus.

Yaunghwe (Nyaungshwe)

Yaunghwe is the small town at the

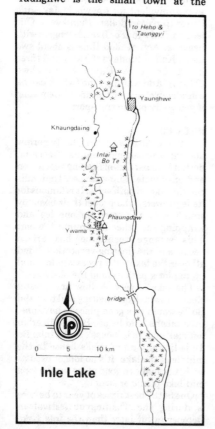

Inle Lake

northern end of the lake. Here there are a couple of places to stay and eat, and from here boats run out on to the lake. The Yatamamanaung Pagoda is worth a look around; look for the 'you will be old' and 'you will be sick' figures in glass cases. In the centre of the town near the Friendship Restaurant watch the women rolling cheroots. Ask to see the Yaunghwe Haw – residence of the local ruler. There are lots of interesting ruins around Yaunghwe, which is a peaceful and pleasant place for a short stay. There's a Tourist Burma office further round the channel.

Ywama

Regular boats run from Yaunghwe to the village of Ywama – known as the floating village since it has *chaungs* (canals) for streets, and since much of the day-to-day village activity, including marketing, is carried on from canoes. Wednesday is the big market day at Ywama and there is a very good floating market then not far from the main landing. As you approach Ywama you pass through floating fields. The *Inthas*, as the lake people are known, gather up patches of the floating weeds called *kyunpaw* and anchor them to make fields where they grow everything from vegetables to flowers. The fields make an unusual and picturesque sight. Unfortunately, you're not allowed to take the ordinary boat service to Ywama, but must book with a Tourist Burma boat.

The main landing at Ywama is the Phaungdaw Oo Pagoda, where you can see the five gold-leaf-covered images which each October during the Inle Lake Festival are taken out on the lake in beautiful ceremonial barges. Stalls around the pagoda sell brightly coloured cotton Shan shoulder bags and other local crafts. A shady *khamout*, conical straw hat, is another popular purchase here. Or a meal of *tophu kyaw* – fried bean curd.

On the west shore of Inle is the village of Khaungdine, which serves as a vacation site for 'Model Workers' and 'Outstanding Students'.

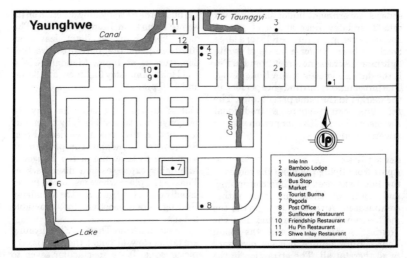

Yaunghwe

To Taunggyi

Canal

Canal

Lake

1 Inle Inn
2 Bamboo Lodge
3 Museum
4 Bus Stop
5 Market
6 Tourist Burma
7 Pagoda
8 Post Office
9 Sunflower Restaurant
10 Friendship Restaurant
11 Hu Pin Restaurant
12 Shwe Inlay Restaurant

Places to Stay & Eat

If you want to stay in Yaunghwe at the lake rather than in Taunggyi, the *Inle Inn* has singles/doubles at K25/45 and doubles/triples with softer beds and attached bath at K70/100. The more expensive rooms are in the solid-looking front building, and the large room in the front corner even has a fireplace. The cheaper rooms are in a long bamboo structure behind the front building. The Inn is a couple of hundred metres from the town centre. Between the Inn and the centre is the simpler *Bamboo Lodge*, which looks almost identical to the bamboo building behind the Inle Inn and charges the same rates – it's only supposed to handle the overflow from the Inn but you can request to stay there. The common bathing and toilet area at the Lodge is better kept than that at the Inle Inn; on the other hand, the Bamboo Lodge locks its gates a lot earlier. At both places there seems to be a shortage of blankets during the cool season, which happens to coincide with high tourist season – you may have to beg for even a second blanket for your bed.

Close to the water channel which leads

in from the lake to the centre of Yaunghwe is the *Friendship Restaurant*, a popular gathering place and 'business' centre. The food here is not as good as it used to be, and cleanliness has also taken a bit of a dive. The *Sunflower* next door has had better food of late and gets a more discerning Burmese clientele, most of whom wouldn't dream of eating at the Friendship. Sunflower has the best breakfast in town and also serves tea shop fare between mealtimes – pastries, Chinese rolls, etc.

Another good place for breakfast is the *Shwe Inlay* near the town entrance. The *Hu Pin*, around the corner from the Friendship near the canal, is known to be Yaunghwe's best Chinese restaurant and is also easily the cleanest place in town. The English menu is divided into three sections: chicken, fish and pork. The Hu Pin closes around 6 pm – which is not so unusual for a town that is almost completely shut down by 8.30 pm. The Hu Pin and the Shwe Inlay are the only restaurants in town that serve beer (K40 per bottle), also Mandalay Rum, though the Friendship sells *ayet piu* at K3 a shot, which mixes well with the lemon-lime soda. A government liquor shop in town sells Mandalay Beer and *ayet piu* at special government rates – K18 for a large bottle of beer, K8 for a bottle of 'white lightning'. Across the street from Hu Pin is the dark and not-so-clean *Kong Kong*. The impecunious can find cheaper food in the market in the same part of town. The *Inle Inn* can prepare a traditional Burmese meal for K30 per person if given advance notice.

Getting There

Apart from flying there, all the routes to the Inle Lake area are time consuming, and some of them are also rather complicated. Although Taunggyi is the main town in the area, and has the Tourist Burma hotel and the main Tourist Burma office, it is not necessary to go there at all. The attraction in the area is Inle Lake; if your time is short Taunggyi can safely be ignored and you'll save some travelling time.

Air If your time is limited then flying here will save a great deal of it. Getting to Inle Lake by land is definitely a lengthy business (though it might be worth it for stops in Kalaw and Pindaya). The Rangoon-Heho air fare is K357, Mandalay-Heho K152. To fly from Pagan to Heho costs K304, the sum of the Pagan-Mandalay and Mandalay-Heho fares. The flights through Heho are usually by F-27 or Twin Otter. Heho airfield is 30 km from Shwenyaung, from where it is a further 11 km to Yaunghwe or 20 km to Taunggyi. Burma Airways provides free transport between Taunggyi and the airport. Truck fare between Taunggyi and Yaunghwe is K9 and the trip takes 45 minutes to an hour. If you're coming from the Heho airport by Tourist Burma bus you can ask to be let off in Shwenyaung instead of going all the way to Taunggyi. From there you can get a bus for K5 that takes about 30 minutes to reach the market area in Yaunghwe.

Leaving by air, you can also pick up the TB bus at the Shwenyaung junction on its way to Heho from Taunggyi at 8 am. The daily Heho-Rangoon flight leaves at 10.20 am; in the opposite direction departure is at 1 pm. Mandalay-Heho and Heho-Mandalay flights are at 9.35 am and 2.40 pm.

Rail You can get all the way to Shwenyaung, the railhead, by train, but it's not really recommended. From Rangoon or Mandalay the programme would be to take one of the Rangoon-Mandalay expresses and disembark at Thazi – the place where visitors to Pagan usually catch the train. See the Mandalay Getting There section for timetable details.

The trains from Thazi to Shwenyaung are rather slow, although the route is very picturesque. It's a spectacular seven to nine-hour journey for K8 through the Shan mountains, partially on a zig-zag railway. Stations en route have masses of fruit, snacks and flowers for sale. The stationmaster at Shwenyaung will, with a little warning, ensure you have a reserved seat even in ordinary class.

From Shwenyaung the train leaves around 10 am. You can get a taxi-truck from the lake to Shwenyaung for around K5. Frankly, on a seven-day visa this is a trip for railway enthusiasts only. Take the train from Rangoon or Mandalay as far as Thazi by all means, but from Thazi onwards travel by road.

Road Travelling from Rangoon by road all the way to the lake is not straightforward, but you can travel to Inle Lake from Pagan, Thazi or Mandalay. In January the trip up over the mountains from the plains to Inle Lake can be very cold in an open truck – make sure you have some warm clothes.

The Pagan-Thazi Tourist Burma taxi-truck will continue on to Taunggyi if there are sufficient passengers. These days there will probably be other taxi-trucks around, and a group of people can probably charter one for around K600 or K700. Scheduled Tourist Burma trucks to Taunggyi are K55 per person. It's a long stretch of nearly 12 hours on Burmese roads, but with an early start you'll get there at a reasonable hour.

There are also regular taxi-trucks between Mandalay and the lake area. Fare is K77 per person. Departures are around 4.30 or 5 am and the trip takes about 10 to 12 hours. They leave from the market in Taunggyi or from 27th St in Mandalay; reserve your seat the day before. Bus lines on this route include Salween-Mann (the Salween is the major river through the Shan States), Cherry-Mann (because the Shan States are where the cherries come from in Burma) and Taunggyi-Mann. The old buses are cheaper, but also much more crowded, slower and far less reliable than the modern taxi-trucks.

Thazi-Taunggyi trucks are K55 (yes, the same as trucks that come all the way from Pagan), and fares are supposed to be paid to the Tourist Burma representative in Thazi. Trucks leave when there are 20 passengers or more, usually between 9 and 11 am. The trip takes about six hours.

Getting Around

There are fairly frequent taxi-trucks and jeeps between the lake-area towns (Yaunghwe to Shwenyaung, Heho or Taunggyi for example), although with a group it may be worth chartering a whole vehicle. You can even charter a taxi-truck to take you from the airport to the lake, wait while you go out on the lake, and then take you back to the airport, or elsewhere. The Inle Inn used to have horses available to ride but that seems to have stopped, due to fears that visitors might ride somewhere they shouldn't. Ordinary bus-truck fare Yaunghwe-Shwenyaung is K5; Yaunghwe-Taunggyi is K9.

On the Lake On the lake your only legal choice is to take a Tourist Burma boat from the Tourist Burma pier in Yaunghwe. Usually at least one boat goes out every morning around 8 am for K45 to K55 per person or K400 to K480 for a whole boat, including a guide, and you're supposed to purchase your ticket the night before – if there is room they will take morning arrivals. Exact price per person or per boat depends on the number of people – 12 is usually the max. The boat trip is not bad – you get to see the floating gardens, leg-rowers, fishermen, Paung Daw Oo Pagoda and whatever lake commerce is going on. Ywama market day is best, when there is a sizeable floating market with both shoppers and merchants in canoes. Tourist Burma may tell you that there is a floating market every day, but except on Ywama market day the only 'floating market' is a small fleet of souvenir boats. The lake itself is rich in wildlife, especially various waterfowl. The boat trip also includes a stop at a Tourist Burma souvenir shop near the pagoda. The selection is not bad, but prices are lower at the floating market or at the pagoda – at all three places you'll see Shan shoulder bags, Burmese clothing, tapestries and the other usual souvenirs.

A couple of people in town do shorter canoe trips on the canals branching off the lake and along the Yaunghwe shores of the lake for K20 per person for 1½ hours. It's not strictly legal, but the practice is tolerated and even recommended by Tourist Burma officials. The staff at the Inle Inn can help arrange such trips. You won't get to see the more magnificent lake sights, like the floating gardens and Ywama, but life along the canals is itself pretty fascinating.

One Tourist Burma guide in Yaunghwe who might be worth asking for is U Pyisson – he used to manage the Inle Inn and is very knowledgeable about things to see and do around the lake. He usually hangs out at either the Sunflower or Friendship restaurants at night.

TAUNGGYI

Situated at 1430 metres (4690 feet), the pine-clad hill station of Taunggyi provides a cool break from the heat of the plains. There are some pleasant walks if you are in the mood. Almost all the accommodation in the area is in Taunggyi, so for many people this is the base for visits to the lake or other local attractions. Taunggyi has an interesting market where you're likely to see colourful hill tribespeople – it comes to town every five days. From Taunggyi, the market moves to Kalaw, and from there in turn to Pindaya, Heho, Aungban and back to Taunggyi.

Taunggyi is the end of the line for westbound foreigners in Burma. Beyond lies a world of black marketeers, insurgent armies and opium warlords. The town was once a place of respite for perspiring Brits, though all that remains of the colonial era are an overgrown graveyard, a stone church, a line of cherry trees and a handful of timbered cottages, all on the fringes of town. The main street is strictly socialist realism, with signs done in raised concrete letters just like in Burma's sometime mentor China. But because of its function as a conduit for smuggled goods from Thailand, China and India, this is one of Burma's most prosperous and enterprising towns. Long-haired smugglers in army fatigues saunter down the street alongside turbaned hill people and sleek-suited Chinese businessmen. An abundance of black-market consumer goods are displayed in the Taunggyi market, which is located at the edge of a Chinese enclave whose residents include many illegal immigrants. The remainder of the population of 100,000 includes tribals, Shans, Burmans, Sikhs, Punjabis and retired Gurkhas who once fought for the British. Along Taunggyi's main streets you'll see Buddhist, Sikh and Hindu temples, mosques and churches.

The pagoda on the hill overlooking the plains and Inle Lake is nothing special, but the views of Taunggyi are good.

For those interested in Shan State cultures, the modest Shan State Museum and Shan Culture Department office near Taunggyi Hotel are worth a visit. Though only a relatively small number of items are labelled in English, you can get a look at local native costume, musical instruments, weapons, etc. If nothing else, you may begin sorting out hill tribe names (Kaw = Akha; Tai = Shan; Kachin = Jin-Phaw; Lahta & Yanglai are names for different Karen groups) and identifying kinds of dress with different ethnic groups. An inordinate amount of display space is devoted to an exhibit concerning the Panglong Agreement of 1947 in which Shan, Kachin and Chin leaders signed a document promising cooperation in the proposed Union of Burma.

Information

Find information on the street and at the Tourist Burma office in the Taunggyi Hotel, the only official place to change money in town.

Places to Stay

The *Taunggyi Hotel* is the HTC hotel and the most expensive in town. There are spacious singles/doubles at US$11.50/15, with attached bathrooms and all the mod-cons you could expect in Burma, including intermittent hot water. Rooms on the 1st floor are reduced to US$9.50/11.50 and 'superior' rooms are US$23. There's also a bar and restaurant with meals at the standard Tourist Burma prices.

The other places in Taunggyi are all quite central and pretty much alike – clean and well kept, but the rooms are bare little cubicles just big enough for two beds. They do have mosquito nets though. Only two places will take foreigners – the *San Pya Guest House*, on the main street toward the Taunggyi Hotel end of town near the post office and the museum; and the *May Kyu*, not far from the market and off the main street. Both charge K21/42 for singles/doubles.

Top: Cigar makers, Inle Lake (TW)
Left: Pink Buddha, Prome (TW)
Right: River commerce on Inle Lake (TW)

Top: Prome pagodas (TW)
Left: Yamaw village on Inle Lake (TW)
Right: Payagyi Pagoda near Prome (TW)

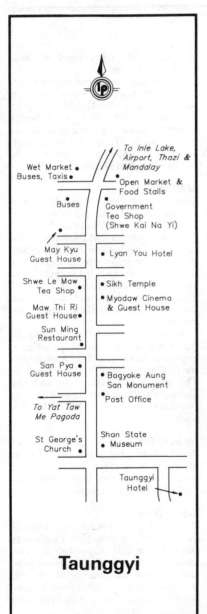

Taunggyi

The San Pya is the better kept and has a friendly staff. The May Kyu has an empty restaurant downstairs. Between these two on the main drag lie the *Maw Thi Ri* and *Myodaw* guest houses and the *Lyan You Hotel*, none of which admit foreigners at this writing.

Places to Eat

The *Lyan You Hotel* has excellent food – between a group you can dine on soup, rice, noodles, tasty fried vegetables and ginger pork, and have a great meal at reasonable cost. The *Tha Pye* used to be a good bet, but was recently closed. A small restaurant in the second row of food shops in the market, *Shan You Ma*, is well-known locally for its delicious Chinese and authentic Shan cooking. Very little English is spoken here, however, so your Burmese and/or point-to-order technique should be up to snuff.

There are a lot of good tea shops in Taunggyi. Best of the bunch is the government-run *Shwe Kai Na Yi* near the market, where prices are artificially low and the quality high. Besides tea, pastries and *nam-bya*, you can also order curries and *palata* ('paratha' or Indian-style fried bread) here. Another favourite with a more pleasant decor is *Shwe Le Maw*, across from the Sikh temple. They specialise in an extensive variety of pastries and tea snacks and also have a take-away window – Burmese fast food.

Getting There

Trucks to Taunggyi from Inle Lake are K9 and leave frequently from the Yaunghwe market area between 7 am and 3 pm. From Pagan a Tourist Burma truck costs K55 per person and takes most of the day; from Thazi you pay the same fare and arrive in about six hours. From Mandalay, Tourist Burma trucks are K77 per person. See the sections on Pagan, Thazi and Mandalay for more detail.

If you fly into Heho, Tourist Burma will provide free transportation to Taunggyi from the airport.

'Off-Limits'

You're limited in where you can go in Burma both by official ruling and by the limitations on your time. I suspect that one reason for the seven-day visa limit is that it dissuades people from getting any distance off the beaten track. Actually the Burmese are delightfully vague about just what is 'off-limits' and what is not. Read Paul Theroux's amusing account in *The Great Railway Bazaar* of his visit to forbidden Gokteik on the railway line to Lashio.

If you ask Tourist Burma if you can go to certain places, you won't be told 'no' so much as gently warned that it may be inconvenient. These places are really only very slightly off-limits and if you simply set out to get there you'll probably find few problems. Of course you may not be able to fly, since tickets for foreigners have to be bought through Tourist Burma. Even train tickets may pose some problems, although you can get a friendly Burmese to buy them for you or use similar ingenuity. If, however, you just set out by bus or taxi you're unlikely to have any difficulty.

In general, the more tenuous the government's hold is on a place the more likely it is to be off-limits. Areas where rebel activity is strongest are the most emphatically banned. These areas include north of Maymyo on the road to Lashio. Kengtung and the Golden Triangle area where Laos, Thailand and Burma meet, and where opium is the number one crop, are also firmly over the line. South of Taunggyi, in the roadless mountains that form the border between Thailand and Burma, is also off-limits. Insurgents here manage to operate on both sides of the border. Nor are things so happy on the Bay of Bengal coast towards Bangladesh. This is the Arakan coast; in 1978 thousands of Muslim Burmese fled Burma from this region and sought refuge in Bangladesh. Later most of them returned to Burma.

Despite these areas and places which are very definitely off-limits, there are others which, within the limits of your visa and the amount of effort you're willing to invest in getting to them, are quite possible. They include Bassein, Moulmein, Sandoway, Prome and the balancing pagoda of Kyaiktiyo.

BASSEIN

Situated in the Irrawaddy delta, about 190 km west of Rangoon, the port of Bassein is noted for its colourful hand-painted umbrellas and its pottery. The town is of some historic interest and was the scene for major clashes during the struggle for supremacy between the Mons and the Burmese. Today it is one of Burma's most important ports, even though it stands some distance back from the sea.

Bassein has a population of 140,000. In the centre of town the Shwemokhpaw Pagoda is the site of a major festival over the full moon period in May each year. The pagoda was built, along with the Tagaung Pagoda and the Thayaunggyaung Pagoda, by the three lovers of a Muslim princess.

Places to Stay

We've heard that *Kumudra Inn* on Merchant St is cheap and clean, with good toilet facilities and a pleasant, English-speaking manager.

Getting There

If you were allowed to fly there, it would be about half an hour from Rangoon to Bassein, but this is another of those places you are gently discouraged from visiting. Bassein is also accessible by rail, but since you have to travel some distance north towards Prome and then turn south, making a ferry crossing along the way, the train trip takes a lengthy 14 or more hours.

Most interesting would be the 18-hour ferry trip. A daily express steamer departs the Mawtin St Jetty in Rangoon at 4.30 pm and arrives in Bassein at 8 am the next morning. The fare is about K20 and the schedule is the same on the return trip. The boat travels along the Twante Canal and then winds its way through the delta waterways. You could leave Rangoon one afternoon, arrive in Bassein the next morning, spend the day there and return to Rangoon on another overnight trip.

MOULMEIN

Moulmein was once a major teak port, and much teak work still goes on although navigation difficulties have resulted in Bassein and Rangoon superseding it as Burma's most important ports. There is pleasant scenery around Moulmein, timber yards where you can see elephants at work (not too many these days), and some interesting pagodas. Moulmein is a very attractive tropical town with a ridge of hills on one side and the sea on the other. It was in Moulmein that Rudyard Kipling's poetic Burma girl was 'a-setting' in the opening lines of *Mandalay*:

By the old Moulmein Pagoda, lookin' lazy at the sea

It's probable that she was a-setting at the Kyaikthanlan Pagoda, as it offers fine views over the city and harbour from its hilltop location. Other beautiful pagodas include the Uzena Pagoda with figures representing an old man, a sick man, a dead man and a religious ascetic – the influences which sent the Gautama Buddha forth on his search for enlightenment. Near Moulmein the Hapayon Cave has many Buddha figures, while the Kawgaun Cave is also packed with Buddha images, hence its alternative name, the Cave of Ten Thousand Buddhas.

Thanbyuzayat, about 60 km south of Moulmein, has a cemetery for the many Allied prisoners of war who died in the construction of the infamous 'death railway' from Thailand during WW II. It was at Moulmein that the Japanese broke into Burma after marching over the rugged mountain range separating Burma from Tak in Thailand.

Amherst, about 45 km south of Moulmein, was a coastal resort during the British era and there is some talk of it being revived. Setse is the main beach here, but this is also an area of some rebel activity.

Places to Stay

Accommodation in Moulmein may be a minor problem, but there is a *Government Rest House* in Martaban, and the teaching college also has a guest house. *Diamond Guest House* on upper Main St is supposed to be cheap, clean and respectable.

Getting There

Moulmein is about 40 minutes by BAC from Rangoon, but once again you are unlikely to be allowed to fly there. Including the ferry crossings, it takes about six to eight hours by train. The service terminates at Martaban, on the north side of the Salween River while Moulmein lies on the south side. A ferry transports you across to the town. The daily express leaves Rangoon at 6 am and arrives in Martaban at 12.20 pm. The return express departs Martaban at 1.50 pm and arrives in Rangoon at 8.10 pm.

You can also travel to Moulmein by road – you could hire a taxi from Rangoon for several days – and on the way you could stop at Pegu and attempt the climb to the famed Kyaiktiyo Pagoda. Or you could travel to Pegu and take a bus from there for K25.

THATON

Long before the rise of Pagan, Thaton was the centre for a Mon kingdom in the south of Burma. It was known as Suvannabhumi, the 'Golden Land', when Ashoka, the great Indian Buddhist emperor, sent a mission there in the 3rd century BC. The thriving port carried on trade with the south of India and even as far afield as Ceylon. Shin Aran, a monk from Thaton, carried Theravada Buddhism north to the Burmese kingdom of Pagan, and in 1057 Thaton was conquered by King Anawrahta of Pagan.

Today little of ancient Thaton can be seen, as the modern town has been built over the old site. Thaton is on the main road and rail line from Pegu to Moulmein. Traces of the massive city walls can still be seen, and some interesting pagodas such as the Thagyapaya or Myatheindan and the Shwezayan.

There are a number of interesting sites in the vicinity of Thaton – the ruined fort walls of Taikkala, which is believed to be the actual city of Suvannabhumi, stand at the village of Ayetthema. There is also a very ancient pagoda here. The Tizaung Pagoda, another interesting old structure, can be found at Zokthok village, slightly south of Ayetthema. The sculptured wall known as Hsindat Myindat is here too.

KYAIKTIYO PAGODA

One of the most interesting 'off-limits' trips is to the incredible balancing pagoda of Kyaiktiyo. It's about 20 km from the town of Kyaikto, which in turn is about midway between Pegu and Thaton. The small pagoda, just 5½ metres (18 feet) high, is built atop the 'Gold Rock', a massive, gold-leafed boulder delicately balanced on the very edge of a cliff. Legends relate that the boulder maintains its precarious balance due to a precisely placed Buddha hair within the pagoda! The legend goes on to say that the rock was transported to its site from the bottom of the sea by King Tissa of the 11th century. He used a boat which then turned to stone and can be seen about 300 metres from the Kyaiktiyo – it's known as the Kyaukthanban or 'stone boat pagoda'.

The pagoda base camp, Kinpun, is 15 km from the town of Kyaikto, and from the camp you have a long and strenuous 10-km climb up to the pagoda itself. You certainly won't be alone though; a trip to the top accumulates considerable merit (even for those rich Burmese carried up in sedan chairs) and there are steady streams of pilgrims making the ascent. At full moons the number swells to the thousands.

The path ascends about 1000 metres in the climb to the top and it's impossible to miss – just follow the crowds. There are various rest halts along the way and shrines which relate the story of the temple's legendary creation. Kyaiktiyo is another of Burma's mildly off-limits places – if you ask about it, you may be told you're not allowed to go there, but if you just go nobody will stop you. Note, however, that it is only really possible to

Kyaiktiyo Pagoda

get to the top when the pilgrimage season commences, at the end of the rainy season in late October.

Since Karen rebel units have been known to be operating in the vicinity of the town of Kyaikto in recent years, the government has been increasingly touchy about the presence of foreigners in the area – best keep any travels to Kyaiktiyo as quiet as possible.

Getting There

The round trip from Rangoon to the Kyaiktiyo Pagoda takes two to three days. The easiest way to make the trip is to find a taxi or taxi-truck in Rangoon. Getting there on public transport is quite simple, although somewhat time-consuming. From Pegu special pilgrims' buses run directly to the camping/fair ground at the bottom of the mountain. It's wise to start from Pegu as early as possible and be prepared to overnight at the camp at the foot of the mountain or the one up top, near the pagoda. If you plan to do the latter, be prepared for the cold; you'll need a sleeping bag up there. Staying at the top does give you the sunset and sunrise over the pagoda.

MERGUI

In the extreme south of Burma, where Burma and Thailand share the narrow peninsula, is the Tenasserim coast with the beautiful islands of the Mergui Archipelago. This is a major smuggling route into Thailand and it's very much off-limits.

PROME

Two days south of Pagan by riverboat is the town of Prome, near which are the few remaining ruins of the ancient Pyu capital of Sri Kshetra. Very few visitors make their way to this remote site, although it has been the centre of the most intensive archaeological work in Burma almost all this century.

In the centre of the small town of Prome itself, the Shwesandaw Pagoda is the main point of interest. Looking across to the pagoda, which, like the Shwedagon in Rangoon, is perched on top of a hill, is an enormous seated Buddha figure. From the pagoda terrace you look across to the image eye-to-eye.

Sri Kshetra

Sri Kshetra is several km out of Prome to the north-east. If you take the Pagan and Paukkaung road you first come to the towering Payagyi Pagoda, an early, almost cylindrical pagoda, by the roadside. A few km further brings you to the junction where you turn off the Pagan road towards Paukkaung. The road runs

Payagyi Pagoda

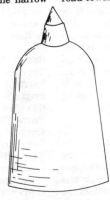

Bawbawgyi Pagoda

Bebe Pagoda

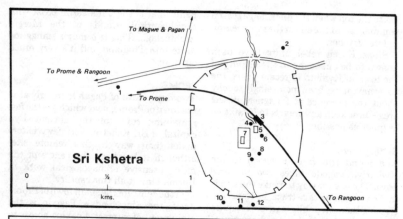

7 Palace Site	1 Payagyi Pagoda
8 East Zegu Pagoda	2 Payama Pagoda
9 West Zegu Pagoda	3 Hmawa Railway Station
10 Bawbawgyi Pagoda	4 Hsinchitaing Pagoda
11 Bebe Pagoda	5 Museum
12 Laymyetnah Pagoda	6 Payataung Pagoda

alongside the extensive city walls of Sri Kshetra, and ahead you can see the Payama Pagoda, similar in form to the Payagyi, to the north of the road.

At a bridge you turn into the city and pass the small Hmwaza railway station. The railway line to Prome was built straight through the middle of Sri Kshetra. By the old palace site there's a small museum with some artefacts from the excavations and a map of the area. It's six km from the Payagyi Pagoda to the museum. South of the museum, outside the city walls, are the cylindrical Bawbawgyi Pagoda and the cube-shaped Bebe Pagoda. Archaeological enthusiasts could easily spend some time here, investigating these rarely visited ancient sites.

Around Prome

There are other places to visit south of Prome, like Gautama Hill, flanking the Irrawaddy, with countless Buddha images in niches. The Shwenattaung Pagoda is further south again; both are well off the road.

Places to Stay

There are a number of places to stay in Prome, including the rather basic *People's Hotel*, although the local authorities may not approve of you staying here. A traveller wrote of the difficulties he got into after taking a room at the *Saw Pya Hotel* on Bogyoke St opposite the railway station. After he paid K24 for a room the local authorities came round and told him to be on his way to Rangoon, pronto.

Getting There

You can travel to Prome by riverboat from Pagan; it's a further two days' trip with an overnight stop at Magwe. The railway line north from Rangoon terminates at Prome. You can also get there by road since Prome is on the alternative Rangoon-Pagan route. A bus from Rangoon will cost K20 to K25. Coming south from Nyaung-Oo or Kyauk Padaung, you will probably have to change your bus at Magwe. Even with your own transport, however, Rangoon-Pagan via Prome is a long day's drive with time for only a brief look around Prome.

SANDOWAY

Burma's beach resort, a favourite of the nation's elite when on holiday, is not off-limits, but is closed for the entire monsoon season – when this stretch of the Arakan coast gets something like 500 cm of rain. It re-opens in November. Situated on the Bay of Bengal, if offers several beaches and bays, including Ngapali, which is said to have been named by a homesick Italian who thought the area looked rather like Naples. There's a three-km-long stretch of appropriately silvery sand, and the water is said to be good for snorkelling. Other beaches are Lintha and Andrew. With your stay limited to seven days, there's no overpowering reason for you to go to Sandoway when there are a lot of beaches elsewhere in the world.

Places to Stay

The *Ngapali Beach Hotel*, also known as the Ngapali Strand, costs US$9.50/11.50 for singles/doubles, but is 'best described as unsophisticated'. The lights go off at 7.30 or 8 pm and the bar also closes then, although even when it's open the beer is warm. Plus the food is limited and poor. Over the Christmas period (20 December to 5 January) and during Thingyan (11 to 19 April) accommodation is heavily booked here and you have to plan well ahead.

There are also many beach houses and hotels like the *Sea Breeze Beach Hotel*; or there is the *Burma Railway Corporation Hotel*.

Getting There

Tourist Burma no longer offer tours to Sandoway. Scheduled BAC flights from Rangoon are also no longer in operation at this writing, and Tourist Burma gave no reason for the interrupted service. If BAC begins flying again, flights only take about a half-hour, but when you come to

leave be ready to rush. The flights were often overbooked and it's first on, first flies; next day's flight may well be delayed or cancelled. And the flight the day after.

Sandoway is still a favourite resort area for party officials and foreign diplomats stationed in Rangoon, who must charter flights to get there.

MYOHAUNG

In Arakan, close to the Bangladesh border, Myohaung is reached by riverboat from Akyab – it's well off the beaten track. Until the first Anglo-Burmese war it was known as Mrauk-U, but the occupying British commander shifted his garrison to Akyab so Mrauk-U became known as Myohaung, 'old city'.

Strategically situated in hill country, Myohaung is heavily fortified due to the many enemies the Arakanese had to contend with. Amongst the most important buildings are the Shitthaung or '80,000' Pagoda, built in 897 AD and so named because of the 80,000 Buddha images found here. There is also the even earlier Dukkan Thein ordination hall and many other pagodas. Myohaung has fallen prey to the encroaching jungle, but is particularly interesting for its Arakanese art and architecture.

HILL TRIBES

Although you may occasionally see colourful hill tribe people in Mandalay or even Rangoon, and quite often around the Inle Lake area, you would have to get much further off the beaten track to really arrive in their area. Kengtung would be a very interesting palace to see the hill tribes – here you might find the Kaw tribespeople, their women wearing hats decorated with pieces of locally mined silver.

The 70,000 or so members of the Padaung tribe in eastern Burma are probably the most unusual of the myriad hill tribe members. At around five years of age young girls have a coil of brass worked around their necks. As the girls grow, more and more rings of brass are added until they become the 'giraffe women'. Actually, as a *National Geographic* article indicated, the women don't really develop extremely long necks at all. It's their shoulders and ribs which are pushed down rather than their necks being stretched up. Eventually the polished brass coils, hung with ornaments, may weigh up to 10 kg and that much weight again may be worn in more brass coils on their legs.

OTHER

Traces of Pyu cities can be found at several places in Burma; the Pyus were a forerunner of the Burmese people and their cities were in their prime several centuries before Pagan. Pyu cities can be seen at Halin, near Shwebo north-west of Mandalay; at Beikthano in Magwe district, south of Pagan; and most particularly at Sri Kshetra (also known as Thayekhittaya) close to modern Prome.

Tagaung, almost directly north of Mandalay, is believed to be a northern outpost of the kingdom of Pagan and was known as Upper Pagan. There are many other historical or interesting sites scattered all over Burma. Not a great distance north of Mandalay, but also 'off-limits', is Mogok, where a high percentage of Burma's precious stones, including the famous rubies, are mined.

Of course people have been getting around Burmese travel restrictions for many years. Vic Esbensen from Toronto, Canada, sent us this account of a highly unofficial trip through Burma in the early '60s.

With a German friend I tried to get around the restriction in 1963 by paddling a canoe across the saltwater bay between Teknaf in East Pakistan (Bangladesh) and Maungdaw in Burma. But it didn't work. The immigration office in Maungdaw made us paddle back to Teknaf. We protested that we came across salt water and not by land. But our argument was useless. The immigration officers were,

however, friendly and helpful. They suggested we take the plane from Chittagong to Akyab and then come back to Maungdaw to continue the land journey. That's exactly what we did. Back in Maungdaw, the legal way, the immigration officers gave us a little party. How anyone could get to central Burma overland from Arakan was beyond their understanding. But they wished us luck and sent us on our way.

Being foolish idiots we decided to walk to Myohaung and from there across the mountains to the Mon River, which flows into the Irrawaddy. The trip to Myohaung was easy. About half by bus and river boat and half by walking through settled farmlands. But it was insurgent country. The government collected taxes by day and the Communists by night. Government officials didn't dare to leave the towns without military escorts. However, there was little open fighting and as foreigners we were neutral. Everyone said there were no mines or booby traps on the road and that the insurgents only killed government officials, soldiers and 'traitors'. Therefore we were reasonably safe.

Myohaung is an absolutely fascinating place. Today there is a small town and military fort inside the ancient 30-foot-thick palace walls; it was once a large city. All around the palace walls are ancient ruins and pagodas that are totally untouched by archaeologists and tourists. The monks still maintain the most important pagodas, some said to be over 1500 years old. The oldest ones have labyrinths of 'secret' tunnels on the inside. The monks took us on torch-lit tours of these tunnels (real torches, not flashlights). The tunnels were moss grown and damp. The walls were covered with deteriorating paintings. Carvings and surprises emerged around every corner. At the monks' monastery there were ancient Portuguese coins from the first European visitors back in the 1500s, ancient documents, the usual Buddha bones and relics, etc. I am sure no foreigner has seen those things since we were there, and the last foreigners before us were in the 1930s. I would like to go back again to take photographs and record things as they are in an untouched archaeological treasure trove.

In Myohaung the military was, naturally, curious to know what we were doing. But they were also friendly and helpful. They allowed us to copy their topographic maps of the mountains (pre-WW II British maps) and did not object to our plan to walk across to central Burma. Later we learned that they believed it was impossible to walk across the mountains. Therefore they thought we were crazy idiots who were really not going to try to do it. And therefore, with true Burmese politeness, they did not try to stop us! Once the army learned that there really were two crazy foreigners walking across the mountains they warned all the troops on the other side to look out for us and bring us in for questioning when we were found. But they had no control over the mountains and therefore could do nothing except wait for us to reappear.

Thus one fine day we started walking upriver from Myohaung. During the afternoon of the first day we were suddenly surrounded by armed men. They proceeded to poke us and pull the hair on our arms, wondering what strange creatures we were. Then back to their camp. It was the Arakan headquarters for the White Flag Communist Party! We had walked within 100 feet of it without knowing the place was there. The Communists had, of course, seen us go by and they were absolutely astonished. The Communist school teacher spoke good English. There were about four hours of intensive interrogation. Finally they believed we were innocent travellers. So, let's have a party! They threw a big banquet for us with serious talk about America and communism, and lots of Burmese songs and music. The next day we were given two soldiers for guides and a pass to travel through Communist areas, and we set off upstream towards the mountains.

After that the routine was quite simple. There were villages along the river every four to eight hours of walking and well-developed trails. Thus a good morning walk brought us to a village, then an afternoon siesta, dinner with the headman, evening around a fire trying to explain to the village who and what we were by sign language (my Burmese word book was useless), sleep on the verandah of the headman's house, and off again the next morning. After four days the Communist guides vanished and no more guns were seen in the villages. Presumably we were beyond both government and Communist control.

One day we saw huge tracks in the sand by the river. I pointed to the tracks and acted like a tiger. The locals who were accompanying us agreed. Yes, it was a tiger. A few hours later there it was right in front of us. The locals

jumped up and down with their spears and shouted at the tiger. But it didn't care. It just calmly stopped to look at us and then wandered off across the river.

There was only one section of the trip where there were no villages. That was a three-day walk across the height of the land. From the top we looked back to see our route for the previous two weeks. For that trip we carried rice and water on our backs in bamboo tubes and our guide picked wild vegetables.

At the last village towards the Mon River the headman broke into a fit of laughter and ridicule when he saw our Communist passes. The reason became obvious the next day when we met the first soldier for several weeks. He asked for identification and became very angry at the Communist pass. He was a government soldier! But how could we know? They all looked the same to us! So off we went with him. At the Mon River he turned upstream. We protested. No, no, we want to go downstream! But one doesn't protest too long against a gun.

Upstream on the Mon River we came to Kyindwe (directly south of Mt Victoria). There was a large village on the banks of the river and a fantastic wild west fort on top of a hill a thousand feet above the river. That's the only way to describe it. I have seen such things in movies, but never in life. The jungle was cleared off the hill. There were trenches all around with sharp bamboo spikes pointing out in all directions. At the top of the hill was a bamboo stockade with a moat around it and numerous slits for guns to point out. Inside were bamboo buildings built half into the ground. This was the government hide-out fortress in the mountains. There are no roads or helicopters to this place. It is a two-week march up the Mon River. It was fabulously photogenic - but alas, we could not carry cameras on such a trip (couldn't afford to buy film anyway).

At the fort we were guests of the commanding officer for three days waiting for we didn't know what. We wandered all around inside and out the fort and down to the village. This village was full of rice wine. On the porch of every house there was a big earthen pot of fermenting rice with a straw sticking out of it. One simply drank from the straw and poured in water from a dipper to fill up the amount drunk. When the villagers saw strange white creatures every head of a household waved us up to his porch for a drink. The headman had six pots with different flavours of wine from very dry to very sweet. It was impossible to walk through the village without becoming drunk. There were pots of wine in most villages, but the military must have made this place worse than usual.

One morning the reason for the delay became clear. There was a gigantic, dug-out freighter canoe down by the river. There were four crew men and room for about eight passengers and several hundred pounds of freight. So off we went down the river. This was a wild, white mountain river. Never have I had a canoe ride like that. The crew was superb. Often the bowman would hop onto a rock, hold the canoe off as it rushed by, and hop into the stern, all in a couple of seconds. The canoe ride lasted for a week and we all slept on the bank of the river at night.

Finally, the river calmed down, the canoe was going no further, and the trip became more peaceful, with walks along the river, rides on bullock carts and peaceful village evenings until we reached the army camp at Pwinbyu.

At Pwinbyu we had to pay for our sins. Our visas had expired a month earlier and the army asked a thousand questions – how many Communists did we meet, how many guns did they have, where was the Communist headquarters? But again the Burmese hospitality came through. We stayed in the officers' quarters and ate at the officers' mess. After a couple of days the army was satisfied. But they could do nothing about our visas. The army simply advised us to proceed to Rangoon on our own and then report to the immigration.

There was no hurry. So we took our sweet time hitch-hiking to Rangoon, stopping here and there. Three weeks later we reported at the immigration office in Rangoon. There was a court hearing, a K1000 fine, a rather angry immigration minister and, amazingly, a one-week visa extension.

A couple of months later I heard that all tourism to Burma was stopped. Nevertheless I spent some weeks in Rangoon in 1966 and 1969 as a sailor.

You said that many areas of Burma are today off-limits. But I bet they don't do much if you actually manage to reach some forbidden place. And what if you disappear somewhere and fail to get back to Rangoon within seven days? All they could do is give you a fine and maybe deport you so that you will have difficulty coming back again. Indeed there are insurgents. But most of them are friendly. The army told us that only the Red Flag Communists were likely to deliberately harm foreigners. These Red Flag people were said to be vicious killers. Various insurgent groups actually operate border control posts and collect taxes. They are said to have no objections to foreigners passing through. The problem is trying to get into a Rangoon government area from an insurgent area. It's not physically dangerous, but the government troops will arrest you. Also, I would think the Golden Triangle would be dangerous because of the opium.

Walking overland from central Burma to India or Bangladesh should be possible even today if one can get away from the government lowlands. Once into the mountains the government cannot stop you. One simply has to adopt the mountain way of travelling from village to village along the main trails. Never under any circumstances wander away from the trails. Such a trip costs nothing. The mountain people do not use Burmese money. However, their women have large necklaces of silver coins (some very ancient – a fantastic place for coin collectors). Give a few coins to the little girls for their necklaces and the whole village will be happy and surprised. For guides on a trip that takes a few days give a knife or some useful item.

I have rarely been as healthy as after I came out from the mountains. The food was plentiful, exercise fantastic, and the air crystal clear. The main danger is one's total isolation from the outside world, so that a small accident can cause death. I saw people painfully dying of horrible infections from small wounds. And one absolutely must take malaria pills. My friend was one of those people who refused to take pills. He got malaria and the last two weeks were pure hell for him. An injection of quinine cured him instantly – but there is no such thing as medicine in the mountains.

Glossary

Achaeik htameins – open skirts woven with intricate patterns and worn on ceremonial occasions.
Aingyi – traditional Burmese shirt and dress.
Apyodaw – dancer responsible for placating the appropriate deities at the start of a pwe.
Avatars – previous incarnations of a deity.
Ayet piu – 'white liquor', a strong alcoholic beverage distilled from rice or palm sap.

Bedin-sayas – astrologers, very important people in Burma, where everything must be done on an auspicious day.
Beikmoke – Burmese cake.
Betel – the nut of the areca palm which is chewed as a mild intoxicant throughout Asia.
Bo gyi – literally 'big leader'.
Bo tree – the sacred Banyan tree under which the Buddha gained enlightenment.
Buddha-pads – Buddha footprints, distinguished by 108 identifying marks.

Cantonment – the part of a colonial town occupied by the military – a carry-over from the British days.
Cedi – see pagoda.
Chaung – stream, often only seasonally flooded.
Cheroots – truncated cigars. In Burma they range from huge to massive, but are actually very mild since they contain only a small amount of tobacco.
Chindits – the 'behind enemy lines' Allied forces who harried the Japanese during WW II.
Chinlone – an extremely popular Burmese sport in which a circle of up to six players attempts to keep a cane wickerwork ball in the air with any part of the body except the arms and hands.
Chinthe – half lion/half dragon mythical beast that guards pagoda entrances.

Dah – slashing knife.
Devas – spirit beings.
Dhamma – Pali word for the Buddhist teachings.
Dharma – dhamma in Sanskrit.
Dobat – rural musical instrument – small two-faced drum worn around the neck.

Flat – covered pontoon used to carry cargo on the river, often up to 30 metres long.
Furlong – obsolete British unit of distance still used in Burma; one-eighth of a mile.

Gaung baung – formal male hat made of silk over a wicker framework.

Highway trip – journey up-country (away from Rangoon) by road.
Hintha – mythical, swan-like bird.
Hne – part of the Burmese orchestra, a wind instrument like an oboe.
Htanthimoke – Burmese cake.
HTC – Hotel Tourist Corporation, the state corporation that runs all Burma's more expensive hotels.
Hti – umbrella or decorated top of a pagoda.
Htwa – traditional Burmese measure – half a taung.
Hundy – a bill of exchange in local currency; you must declare any hundies you happen to be carrying on arrival in Burma.

Ingyi – traditional woman's blouse.

Jataka – traditional scenes from the Buddha's life, generally referred to as the 550 Jatakas although there are actually only 547.
Karaweik – the royal bird-mount of Vishnu (Sanskrit = Garuda); also the royal barge on Inle Lake.
Kauk hnyin boung – Burmese sweet made from glutinous rice and coconut.
Kamma – Pali word for the law of cause and effect.
Karma – Sanskrit word for kamma.
Khaukswe – another national dish, noodles with vegetables and meat.
Kutho – merit, what you acquire through doing good.
Kyaung – Burmese Buddhist monastery, pronounced 'chiong'.
Kye waing – circle of gongs used in a Burmese orchestra.

Lin gwin – cymbals in a Burmese orchestra.
Lokapalas – guardian spirits of the world.
Longyi – the Burmese unisex sarong-style lower garment – unlike men in most other South-East Asian countries, few Burmese men have

taken to western trousers. Very sensible in a tropical climate.

Manuthiha – half-lion, half-human, twin-bodied mythical creature; see some around the Shwedagon Pagoda.

Ma ya nga – 'lesser wife', a man's second wife.

Mohinga – traditional and very popular Burmese dish found at many street stalls; it consists of noodles, fish and eggs.

Myit – river.

Myo – city, hence Maymyo (after Colonel May), Allanmyo (Major Allen), or even Bernardmyo.

Naga – snake, often seen sheltering or protecting the Buddha.

Nam-bya – flatbread cooked in a clay oven.

Nats – guardian spirit beings; Burma's Buddhist beliefs also embrace a wide variety of good and bad nats.

Nat pwe – spirit festival.

Nga pi – fermented fish or shrimp paste, an all-purpose Burmese flavouring.

Oozie – elephant rider.

Ozi – a big, goblet-shaped one-faced drum used for accompanying folk music in the country.

Pagoda – traditional Burmese religious structure, a solid hemispherical or gently tapering cylindrical building.

Pali – language in which original Buddhist texts were written; the 'Latin' of Theravada Buddhism.

Pa tala – bamboo xylophone used in the Burmese orchestra.

Patma – Burmese bass drum.

Phongyi – Buddhist monk.

Phongyiban – important cremation ceremony for a sayadaw.

Phongyikyaung – monastery.

Pi say – traditional tattooing, once believed to make the wearer invulnerable to sword or gun.

Pwe – Burmese festival, often all-night (and all-day) affairs.

Pyatthat – wooden multi-roofed pavilion, usually turret-like on palace walls, as at Mandalay Palace.

Pyithu Hlutaw – Peoples' Congress.

Sayadaw – the usually venerable chief abbot of a monastery.

Saing waing – circle of drums used in a Burmese orchestra.

Sanskrit – very ancient Indian language.

Saung gauk – musical instrument; 13-stringed, boat-shaped harp.

Shawtaing – popular event at country fairs in which participants attempt to climb a greased bamboo pole to collect prize money from the top.

Shinpyu – ceremonies when young boys from seven years old upwards enter a monastery for the period every young Buddhist male must spend there. Girls have their ears pierced in a similar ceremony.

Shwe le maw – orange brandy distilled in the Shan State.

Sikhara – Indian-style corncob-like temple finial, found on many temples at Pagan.

Sima – ordination hall.

Sinbyudaw – royal white elephant.

Singoung – head elephant man, above an oozie.

Soon – alms offered to monks.

Stupa – see pagoda.

Taung – traditional Burmese measure, 46 cm or 18 inches.

Tazaung – shrine building, usually found around pagodas.

TB – Tourist Burma, the state tourist organisation responsible for all visitors to Burma.

Thabeik – monk's food bowl; also a traditional element of temple architecture.

Thanaka – yellow sandalwood paste, worn by many Burmese women as a beauty mark on their faces.

The Thirty – the '30 comrades' of Bogyoke Aung San who joined the Japanese during WW II and eventually led Burma to independence.

Tonga – horse-drawn, two-wheeled cart – popular transport in many towns.

Tripitaka – the 'three baskets', one of the classic Buddhist scriptures.

Up-country – out of Rangoon.

Vihara – Sanskrit word for sanctuary or chapel for Buddha images.

Viss – traditional Burmese weight, 1.6 kg or 3.6 lb.

Votive Tablet – inscribed offering tablet, usually with images of the Buddha.

Wah let-khoke – bamboo clapper, part of the Burmese orchestra.

Yagwin – Burmese cymbals.

Zat Pwe – Burmese classical dancing.

Zawgyi – alchemists.
Zayats – rest houses around a pagoda.
Zedi – see pagoda.

Index

174

Temperature

To convert °C to °F multipy by 1.8 and add 32

To convert °F to °C subtract 32 and multipy by 5/9

Length, Distance & Area

	multipy by
inches to centimetres	2.54
centimetres to inches	0.39
feet to metres	0.30
metres to feet	3.28
yards to metres	0.91
metres to yards	1.09
miles to kilometres	1.61
kilometres to miles	0.62
acres to hectares	0.40
hectares to acres	2.47

Weight

	multipy by
ounces to grams	28.35
grams to ounces	0.035
pounds to kilograms	0.45
kilograms to pounds	2.21
British tons to kilograms	1016
US tons to kilograms	907

A British ton is 2240 lbs, a US ton is 2000 lbs

Volume

	multipy by
Iiperial gallons to litres	4.55
litres to imperial gallons	0.22
US gallons to litres	3.79
litres to US gallons	0.26

5 imperial gallons equals 6 US gallons
a litre is slightly more than a US quart, slightly less
than a British one

°C / °F thermometer scale:

°C	°F
50	122
45	113
40	104
35	95
30	86
25	75
20	68
15	59
10	50
5	41
0	32

Lonely Planet

Lonely Planet published its first book in 1973. Tony and Maureen Wheeler had made a lengthy overland trip from England to Australia and, in response to numerous 'how do you do it?' questions, Tony wrote and they published *Across Asia on the Cheap*. It became an instant local best-seller and inspired thoughts of a second travel guide. A year and a half in South-East Asia resulted in their second book, *South-East Asia on a Shoestring*, which they put together in a backstreet Chinese hotel in Singapore in 1975. The 'yellow book', as it quickly became known, soon became *the* guide to the region and has now gone through five editions, always with its familiar yellow cover.

Soon other writers started to come to them with ideas for similar books – books that went off the beaten track and took an adventurous approach to travel, books that 'assumed you knew how to get your luggage off the carousel,' as one reviewer described them. Lonely Planet soon grew from a kitchen table operation to a spare room and then to its own office. It also started to develop an international reputation as the Lonely Planet logo began to appear in more and more countries. Always the emphasis has been on travel for travellers and Tony and Maureen still manage to fit in a number of trips each year and play a very active part in the writing and updating of Lonely Planet's guides.

Today over 20 people work at the Lonely Planet office in Melbourne, Australia and there are another half dozen at the company's US office in Oakland, California. Keeping guidebooks up to date is a constant battle and although the basic element in that struggle is still an ear to the ground and lots of walking, modern technology also plays its part. All Lonely Planet guidebooks are now stored and updated on computer. In some cases authors take lap-top computers into the field with them. Lonely Planet is also using computers to draw maps and eventually many of the maps will also be stored on disk.

At first Lonely Planet specialised extensively in the Asia region but these days it is also developing major ranges of guidebooks to the Pacific region, to South America and to Africa. The list of walking guides is also growing and Lonely Planet is producing a unique series of phrasebooks to 'unusual' languages. In 1982 the company's *India – a travel survival kit* won the Thomas Cook Guidebook of the Year award, the major international award for travel guidebooks and the company's business achievements have been recognised by twice winning Australian Export Achievement Awards, in 1982 and 1986.

The people at Lonely Planet strongly feel that travellers can make a positive contribution to the countries they visit both by better appreciation of cultures and by the money they spend. In addition the company tries to make a direct contribution to the countries and regions it covers. Since 1986 a percentage of the income from each book has gone to aid groups and associations. This has included donations to famine relief in Africa, to aid projects in India, to agricultural projects in Nicaragua and other Central American countries and to Greenpeace's efforts to halt French nuclear testing in the Pacific. In 1987 $30,000 was donated by Lonely Planet to these projects.

Lonely Planet Newsletter

We collect an enormous amount of information here at Lonely Planet. Apart from our research there's a steady stream of letters from people out on the road. To make the most of all this info we produce a quarterly Newsletter (approx Feb, May, Aug, and Nov).

The Newsletter is packed with down-to-earth information from the pens of hundreds of travellers who write from first-hand experience. Whether you want the latest facts, travel stories, or simply to reminisce, the Newsletter will keep you in touch with what is going on.

Where else could you find out:

- about boat trips on the Yalu River?
- where to stay if you want to live in a typical Thai village?
- how long it takes to get a Nepalese trekking permit?
- that Israeli youth hostel stamps will get you deported from Syria?

One year's subscription is $10.00 (that's US$ in the USA or A$ in Australia), payable by cheque, money order, Amex, Visa, Bankcard or MasterCard.

Order Form
Please send me four issues of the Lonely Planet Newsletter. (Subscription starts with next issue. 1987 price – subject to change.)

Name and address (print) ....

....

....

Tick one
☐ Cheque enclosed (payable to Lonely Planet Publications)
☐ Money Order enclosed (payable to Lonely Planet Publications)
Charge my ☐ Amex, ☐ Visa, ☐ Bankcard, ☐ MasterCard for the amount of $......................

Card No ....   Expiry Date ....

Cardholder's Name (print) ....

Signature ....   Date ....

Return this form to:

Lonely Planet Publications   *or*   Lonely Planet Publications
PO Box 2001A   PO Box 88
Berkeley   South Yarra
CA 94702   Victoria 3141
USA   Australia

Lonely Planet guides to South-East Asia

Thailand – a travel survival kit
Beyond the Buddhist temples and Bangkok bars there is much to see in fascinating Thailand. This extensively researched guide presents an inside look at Thailand's culture, people and language.

Malaysia, Singapore and Brunei – a travel survival kit
These three nations offer amazing geographic and cultural variety – from hill stations to beaches, from Dyak long-houses to futuristic cities – this is Asia at its most accessible.

Indonesia – a travel survival kit
This comprehensive guidebook covers the entire Indonesian archipelago. Some of the most remarkable sights and sounds in South-East Asia can be found amongst these countless islands and this book has all the facts.

Bali & Lombok – a travel survival kit
This book gives detailed information on the Indonesian islands of Bali and Lombok. Bali is a picturesque tropical island with a fascinating culture. Lombok is less touched by outside influences and has a special atmosphere of its own.

The Philippines – a travel survival kit
The 7000 islands of the Philippines are a paradise for the adventurous traveller. The friendly Filipinos, colourful festivals, superb natural scenery, and frequent travel connections make island hopping addictive.

South-East Asia on a shoestring
For over 10 years this has been known as the 'yellow bible' to travellers in South-East Asia. The fifth edition has updated information on Brunei, Burma, Hong Kong, Indonesia, Macau, Malaysia, Papua New Guinea, the Philippines, Singapore, and Thailand.

Also available:

Indonesia Phrasebook and Thailand Phrasebook

Guides to the Indian sub-continent

Kathmandu & the Kingdom of Nepal – a travel survival kit
Few travellers can resist the lure of magical Kathmandu and its surrounding mountains. This guidebook takes you round the temples, to the foothills of the Himalaya, and to the Terai.

Trekking in the Nepal Himalaya
Complete trekking information for Nepal, including day-by-day route descriptions and detailed maps – this book has a wealth of advice for both independent and group trekkers.

India – a travel survival kit
An award-winning guidebook that is recognised as the outstanding contemporary guide to the subcontinent. Looking for a houseboat in Kashmir? Trying to post a parcel? This definitive guidebook has all the facts.

Kashmir, Ladakh & Zanskar – a travel survival kit
This book contains detailed information on three contrasting Himalayan regions in the Indian state of Jammu and Kashmir – the narrow valley of Zanskar, reclusive Ladakh, and the beautiful Vale of Kashmir.

Trekking in the Indian Himalaya
The Indian Himalaya offers some of the world's most exciting treks. This book has advice on planning and equipping a trek, plus detailed route descriptions.

Pakistan – a travel survival kit
Pakistan has been called 'the unknown land of the Indus' and many people don't realise the great variety of experiences it offers – from bustling Karachi, to ancient cities and tranquil mountain valleys.

Bangladesh – a travel survival kit
The adventurous traveller in Bangladesh can explore tropical forests and beaches, superb hill country, and ancient Buddhist ruins. This guide covers all these alternatives – and many more.

Sri Lanka – a travel survival kit
This guide takes a complete look at the island Marco Polo described as 'the finest in the world'. In one handy package you'll find ancient cities, superb countryside, and beautiful beaches.

Lonely Planet travel guides

Africa on a Shoestring
Alaska – a travel survival kit
Australia – a travel survival kit
Bali & Lombok – a travel survival kit
Bangladesh – a travel survival kit
Burma – a travel survival kit
Bushwalking in Papua New Guinea
Canada – a travel survival kit
China – a travel survival kit
Chile & Easter Island – a travel survival kit
East Africa – a travel survival kit
Ecuador & the Galapagos Islands
Egypt & the Sudan – a travel survival kit
Fiji – a travel survival kit
Hong Kong, Macau & Canton – a travel survival kit
India – a travel survival kit
Indonesia – a travel survival kit
Japan – a travel survival kit
Jordan & Syria – a travel survival kit
Kashmir, Ladakh & Zanskar – a travel survival kit
Kathmandu & the Kingdom of Nepal
Malaysia, Singapore & Brunei
Mexico – a travel survival kit
New Zealand – a travel survival kit
North-East Asia on a Shoestring
Pakistan – a travel survival kit
Papua New Guinea – a travel survival kit
Peru – a travel survival kit
Philippines – a travel survival kit
Raratonga & the Cook Islands – a travel survival kit
South America on a Shoestring
Sri Lanka – a travel survival kit
Tahiti – a travel survival kit
Thailand – a travel survival kit
Tibet – a travel survival kit
Tramping in New Zealand
Travel with Children
Travellers Tales
Trekking in the Indian Himalaya
Trekking in the Nepal Himalaya
Turkey – a travel survival kit
West Asia on a Shoestring

Lonely Planet phrasebooks

Indonesia Phrasebook
China Phrasebook
Nepal Phrasebook
Papua New Guinea Phrasebook
Sri Lanka Phrasebook
Thailand Phrasebook
Tibet Phrasebook

Lonely Planet Distribution

Lonely Planet travel guides are available round the world. If you can't find them, ask your bookshop to order them from one of the distributors listed below. For countries not listed, or if you would like a free copy of our latest booklist, write to Lonely Planet in Australia.

Lonely Planet Distributors
Australia
   Lonely Planet Publications, PO Box 88,
   South Yarra, Victoria 3141.
Canada
   Raincoast Books, 112 East 3rd Avenue,
   Vancouver, British Columbia V5T 1C8.
Denmark, France & Norway
   Scanvil Books aps, Store Kongensgade 59 A,
   DK-1264 Copenhagen K.
Hong Kong
   The Book Society, GPO Box 7804.
India & Nepal
   UBS Distributors, 5 Ansari Rd,
   New Delhi – 110002
Israel
   Geographical Tours Ltd, 8 Tverya St,
   Tel Aviv 63144.
Japan
   Intercontinental Marketing Corp,
   IPO Box 5056, Tokyo 100-31.
Netherlands
   Nilsson & Lamm bv, Postbus 195,
   Pampuslaan 212, 1380 AD Weesp.
New Zealand
   Roulston Greene Publishing Associates Ltd,
   Private Bag, Takapuna, Auckland 9.
Papua New Guinea see Australia
Singapore & Malaysia
   MPH Distributors, 601 Sims Drive,
   £03-21, Singapore 1438.
Spain
   Altair, Balmes 69, 08007 Barcelona.
Sweden
   Esselte Kartcentrum AB, Vasagatan 16, S-111
   20 Stockholm.
Thailand
   Chalermnit, 108 Sukhumvit 53,
   Bangkok 10110.
UK
   Roger Lascelles, 47 York Rd, Brentford,
   Middlesex, TW8 0QP
USA
   Lonely Planet Publications, PO Box 2001A,
   Berkeley, CA 94702.
West Germany
   Buchvertrieb Gerda Schettler, Postfach 64,
   D3415 Hattorf a H.